DIARY OF A
STAGE
MOTHER'S
DAUGHTER

DIARY OF A
STAGE
MOTHER'S
DAUGHTER

Melissa Francis

WEINSTEIN
BOOKS

ISBN-10: 1-6028-6172-2
ISBN-13: 978-1-6028-6172-5

First Edition
10 9 8 7 6 5 4 3 2 1

To Wray, who makes the sun rise and set every day

DIARY OF A STAGE MOTHER'S DAUGHTER

INTRODUCTION

She pulled to the side of the road and told me to get out. "Find your own way home. And another place to live while you're at it."

With a deep breath, I pushed the release button on my seatbelt and slowly tumbled out. This had been coming for years. I almost welcomed it. I was relieved that it had finally happened, and I wouldn't have to wonder when anymore. I'd watched my mom throw my older sister out of the car countless times. Tiffany would walk sadly, pathetically, along the sidewalk until my mom finally circled the car around and picked her up, waiting longer and driving farther each time, to intensify the humiliation.

Now it was my turn. I was eight years old.

I watched the car disappear into the distance and then around the corner. I had mouthed off. Even as I did it, I knew I was baiting the shark.

The moment the brown station wagon was out of sight, I ran up onto the golf course that bordered the suburban street and lay down behind a bush. This was my turf, where my sister and I had stolen golf balls in play and then hidden while their owners searched furiously for them. The same spot where we'd sold watered-down, bitter lemonade to initially charmed, then disappointed players. I knew every blade of grass.

Mom took her time, but, eventually, she circled back looking for me. No, I was not slowly walking along the sidewalk, sulking the way Tiffany did.

My face slowly flushed as I saw Mom drive by a second time, looking increasingly frantic. She circled the block a third time as I lay there, paralyzed. I wanted to run out from my hiding place, but I knew she would be so furious, there would be no happy ending. What did I want? An apology from her for throwing me out of the car? Maybe just an end to the domination. It didn't matter. I was hiding in the grass of the Porter Ranch Golf Course, and I couldn't picture how the deadlock would end.

The station wagon stopped circling. I looked at the empty street with a rush of victory. I didn't know what to do next, but then again, neither did she. I drifted off to sleep, then awoke with a start, and the bizarre reality of what had happened flooded back. Without a watch, I had no idea how much time had passed since I'd left the car, but it was growing dark and I was starving.

The long walk home stretched out in front of me, with an uncertain reception at its end. I turned homeward anyway. I had no money. I didn't have a jacket. I hadn't planned to run away from home.

Pausing at the mouth of our quiet cul-de-sac, I racked my brain for other options. There were none.

As quietly as I could, I turned the painted gold knob on our large, brown oak Spanish-style front doors. If you held the doorknob and pushed at the same time, the door swung open silently. I wasn't ready to announce my return. I heard both my parents talking in the kitchen. I decided to show myself and get it over with. Whatever "it" was.

Casually I strode through the narrow doorway into the kitchen, my father to my right, in his usual spot, drinking a glass of wine and talking. Mom was straight in front of me, facing him with her back to the sink. Dad didn't really look in my direction as my sneakers squeaked across the tile floor, but kept talking as if he didn't notice the sudden electric charge in the air, as if he didn't know that his younger daughter had been missing somewhere in the California suburbs for the better part of four hours. Clearly, he hadn't been informed.

I walked to the fridge, as casually as I could, my pounding heart muffling Dad's words in my ears. Mom locked eyes with me. A look passed over her face, a mixture of relief, anger, and what I chose to interpret as a shred of respect.

"What are you doing?" she asked in a voice laced with so many other questions. Who was going to tell on whom?

"I'm hungry. I'm going to take a sandwich to the TV room." Drunk with fear and triumph, I felt my fingers tremble as I smeared peanut butter on an English muffin. I hated the prospect of cold bread, but I didn't have the stomach to wait fifty years for the toaster to work. I slapped a lid on my sandwich and walked out of the room before my legs crumbled beneath me.

No. I was not Tiffany. I was not the same.

This was half my life. When we were at home, my sister and I lived in a state of constant wariness, always reading Mom's mood and bracing for impact when that mood turned ominous. She was mercurial, domineering, but also devoted. She took her job of molding us into outstanding examples of young American girlhood very seriously, and she brooked no nonsense when we resisted her efforts. We were treated to riding lessons, skating lessons, the best schools my parents could afford. But her vigilance was also a leash, one she could pull tight enough to strangle.

In the other half of my life, Mom and I were allies. She had established for both Tiffany and me thriving careers as child actors, and in that context her ambition for us—her unrelenting desire to see us succeed, and release our family from the banality of middle-class life—felt more like a warm rush of motherly support.

When Mom and I worked together, we were an unbeatable team. "The other kids wasted their gas" was the rallying cry I invented for auditions. The routine was the same. Mom would pick me up from school, OshKosh overalls hanging in the right rear car window paired with a white blouse with a Peter Pan collar. Add red bows to the ends of my long braids, and that was the uniform that had landed dozens of roles already.

When I saw the outfit swinging in the window, I knew I had no choice—it was time to shine. But I also knew I would be treated like a princess to make sure I was prepped and happy to perform.

The routine had given birth to a natural competitive spirit. I wanted to win. The pushing, the priming, had taken hold. I loved to succeed, in school, at auditions, anywhere Mom wound me up and set me loose.

On one unremarkable afternoon just weeks after I'd been thrown out of the car, the day's audition was for a part in a successful television show set in Midwest in the 1800s. We went through the usual motions: show up, sign in, wait with a dozen other eight-year-olds to be called in and asked to read a few lines of script. But this time, as Mom sat beside me, she seemed unusually alert and expectant.

When I came out of the audition she was particularly solicitous, which perversely made me hold back. "Was Michael Landon in the room?" Her eyes were wide with hope.

I had no idea who that was. Clearly the right answer was "yes," but why not make her work a little? "Who is that?" I asked.

"You know! Brown curly hair, handsome . . ."

This meant nothing to me.

"He's Pa!" she exclaimed.

I honestly didn't know whom she was referring to. I was still trying to figure out why the people in the audition room had made me speak the way they did. Who says "reckin"?

The day I won that part may have been the highlight of Mom's life. Our two years on *Little House on the Prairie* were without question her happiest. There was no reason for me to talk back, or for her to take a scissor to my favorite shirt in front of me in response. I cried on cue, the adoration on the set enveloped me. Rebukes from Mom were short-lived, lest I show up for work uncooperative. But in truth, we were both so happy there was nothing to struggle over. She woke me at 5 AM to make an early call and we worked well into the evening, but I loved the sense of purpose an acting job gave me, as well as the sense of accomplishment, and, of course, feeling so very special.

Still, as I look back at those long days when the two of us lived one gilded life, I know that not everyone in our family basked in my limelight. My sister fell deeper and deeper into shadows. I had no idea how she got to and from school during that time. We never saw her.

CHAPTER ONE

When I was growing up, people often asked me, "How did you get into show business?" They came up with all kinds of theories and assumptions that were all wrong, like my parents must have been actors, or worked on a production set, or one of them was a talent agent. But Mom loved to tell the real story.

She had been standing in line at a carnival in West Hollywood with my sister, Tiffany, who was three years old at the time, when a man approached her and gave her his card. He claimed he was a big children's agent, and said he thought Tiffany was so beautiful she should be on TV. Mom didn't believe him, she always said, but the offer got her thinking. The following week she set out to discover who represented Rodney Allen Rippy, the most famous child actor of the time. Rodney was making a mint hawking Jack in the Box burgers, and Mom convinced his agent to take on Tiffany.

When Tiffany had about half a dozen commercials under her belt, Mom took me with them to a shoot. I was less than a year old. I don't remember the day I earned my Screen Actors Guild membership card. But Mom always described how she bounced me gently to keep me quiet, though I hadn't made a noise. I was too mesmerized by what was happening to my sister. Tiffany was twenty feet away, soaking in a tub, surrounded by lights, practically drowning in bubbles.

Tiffany's long, brown, shiny hair was piled on top of her head, wet strands curling around the base of her neck. She was adorable, but hardly the cheerful toddler the directors were anticipating. Her eyes were wide and timid.

"Me!" I shouted. Mom flushed as the crew turned and looked at us, and she wished she had left me at home. The director walked in our direction. Now I was going to ruin Tiffany's first national commercial, she thought. Johnson & Johnson's No More Tears baby shampoo. Only Gerber had launched more careers.

"Is this her sister?" the director asked.

I smiled, flaunting my two new teeth.

"Yes, I'm sorry," Mom said. "My sitter fell through. I can take her in another room . . ."

"How do you feel about putting her in the tub with the other one? Does she sit up well?"

Mom lit up. "Oh, yes! She'd just love it. They usually bathe together, that's why Tiffany isn't smiling." That and the thirty-five fully clothed strangers watching her.

Mom said that before she could finish her sentence, six hands had stripped me down and plopped me in the warm sudsy water. I let out a big laugh and slapped the surface of the water, catapulting a perfectly formed bubble to the tip of Tiffany's round nose. She giggled.

"Please tell me you were rolling," the director said to the cameraman.

Mom always describes it as the moment she knew I would

be a star, though I can't swear to any of it, since I was too young to remember. My earliest actual memory is of my first best friend, Brian. Like most three-year-old friends, we didn't choose each other. We had older siblings the same age who went to the same schools. We were thrown into the same carpools and played on the floors at the same ladies' casserole potluck luncheons. I still remember how Brian's mom's brown loafers looked standing next to my mom's tan wedges.

Brian was a great playmate. He let me have whatever I wanted. He was a keeper. He had soft blond hair that fell in his eyes as we spent countless hours together playing house. Even when he wasn't there, I pretended he was. He didn't say much, either in person or in my imagination, making him the perfect match for a bossy, precocious girl like me.

Brian and I went to a little Presbyterian preschool in Granada Hills, California, that we called Turtle School because of the large turtle that lived on the grass-covered playground. We ran into the yard every morning and force-fed the poor beast dandelions until she escaped in slow motion or just recoiled inside her shell to wait out the storm of toddlers.

Brian and I were blissfully joined at the hip until the day his mom decided she was a lesbian and ran off with her girlfriend. The whole family moved away from our neighborhood in Northridge to Chicago or maybe the moon. Wherever they went, it was tough forgetting Brian, even though he was virtually mute and his mom had a girlfriend (the latter hardly seemed like a distinction, though Mom kept mentioning it). He silently hugged me goodbye, and I cried like crazy.

Brian left on the first day of my second year in Turtle School when I was four years old, and I was unusually blue when I got home. I played lethargically in my room in our tract home in the San Fernando Valley. My room was sandwiched between my parents' bedroom and my sister's on the second floor of the house. The carpet in our home was a bright Kelly green, which Mom said made it look as if the perky lawn outside extended inside our home. I liked to trim the indoor "grass" with scissors.

But having recently lost my scissors as a result of some indoor gardening, I wandered down the hall into Tiffany's room, where she was conducting a kindergarten class with her dolls. I had arrived just in time for reading.

The green carpet stretched to the far wall of her room, which Mom had covered with pink and green fabric printed with a repeating pattern of bunnies and farm scenes. She'd made two pillows out of the same fabric to throw on Tiffany's bed. The room was perpetually frozen in a cheerful spring day.

Tiffany raised her eyes to mine. "Why are you pouting? Beth is gone too, you know." Beth was Brian's older sister. I couldn't consistently count on Tiffany for sympathy.

"Here, let's work on my homework." Tiffany was in first grade now and extremely advanced. She went to San Jose School for the Highly Gifted, which apparently meant she was the smartest person in the universe. I thought that made me brilliant by association. I noticed she tensed her shoulders when Mom sang the name of the school to other adults, emphasizing the words *highly gifted* as if you wouldn't notice them otherwise.

"Sit here," she said to me. "Here are the words in the sentence. Unscramble them." I looked at the words on the page. I knew most of them on sight.

"Here's a trick," she continued with the authority of a flight attendant who knows the location of the only emergency exit. "The one with the capital letter goes first." She pointed at the only word that started with a big letter. Neat trick.

"The one with the period next to it, that dot, goes last. The rest you have to figure out on your own. No more shortcuts."

I looked at the page; there were only two words left! This was so exciting I forgot to grieve over the loss of Brian for a moment.

"Finish your homework and you can play with my toy," Tiffany said.

I glanced at the red Mattel box on the shelf with the picture of Tiffany playing with a car on a ramp on the side. I loved that she was featured on a toy box. This particular piece of packaging was so very special that Mom told us we were not allowed to actually play with it or its contents. But she left the alluring red box on the high shelf in Tiffany's room, so we'd climb up there and get it as a special treat.

You could always hear Mom coming down the long hallway. Even though the hall was covered with carpet, the floor creaked in predictable spots. She'd thundered down it so many times to stop us from wrestling over a toy or making a racket that when we heard the first footfall, we knew exactly how much time we had before she reached the bedroom to murder us both.

This time we were just looking at the toy when the footsteps started. We jumped even though we weren't technically guilty yet.

"What are you two doing?" Mom asked.

"Missy's doing her homework," Tiffany said. Mom looked over at me, sitting on the floor with a workbook open in front of me.

"What's the assignment?" she asked, as though a four-year-old really could have homework.

"Unscrabble the words," I started.

"Un-scramble . . ." Mom corrected.

"Yes." I looked at the page. *I* was easy and was already a

big letter so I knew it went first. *Book* had a dot after it, so I knew it was last. *See* was there. That was an easy one too. Jackpot!

"I see the book!" I said proudly. Perhaps I was also highly gifted. Tiffany looked pleased at having orchestrated this show.

"Very nice," Mom said. "Tomorrow, though, no one is going to school. McDonald's has booked both of you for a national commercial."

My sister and I were often booked together because we showed a family resemblance without appearing too much alike. Tiffany was always referred to as "the pretty one." With her thick brunette hair and heavy brows, she reminded casting directors of a young Brooke Shields, which at the time was a major selling point. By contrast I was always "the cute one," with my distinctive yellow eyes, a ready smile, and round cheeks. Between us, we had appeared in dozens of commercials already.

We shot the commercial at a fake McDonald's on Highland Avenue. Even though the building sat on a major street in Hollywood, the public couldn't see the production because of a two-story fence that surrounded the lot.

From the outside, the fake McDonald's looked like any other McDonald's, except that it appeared brand-new. Inside, an elaborate maze of greenrooms and production storage bins were set up in the basement to accommodate the constant flood of commercials shot on-site.

When we arrived on set, they let Tiffany and me play behind the counter, using the register and running around the kitchen, even touching the stove. No one moved a muscle to stop us. There was something thrillingly wrong about being let loose in what seemed to be a real McDonald's. I felt like an indulged criminal.

They shot one scene of us ordering at the counter, then one of us sitting with our fake mom in the main restaurant. The latter was much more challenging than I had anticipated. Not only was I supposed to eat a cheeseburger, which I didn't normally like, but the burger was ice cold and doctored with food coloring to look perfect. It wasn't exactly toxic, but it wasn't completely edible either. A grip held a bucket off camera so we could spit out the painted rubbery food after each take. They had stand-by burgers for the rehearsals, and a more realistic "hero" burger for the actual filming

The first time I lifted a hero to my mouth, I grimaced.

"Cut." The director looked nonplussed. Mom called me over.

"You have to smile and look like you can't wait to eat the cheeseburger," Mom said.

"But I don't want to eat it. I hate cheeseburgers." Tiffany stepped up to my side, as if she couldn't wait to see how I was going to get out of this.

"That's why it's called *acting*," Mom said. I didn't care that much about acting.

"You have to eat it," she said forcefully, with an edge of panic in her voice. The crew and even the wardrobe girl took turns nervously glancing in our direction.

Then she softened and whispered, "Eat it with a big smile and I will take you to Creative Playthings on the way home and buy you anything you want. Anything."

SOLD.

A long tradition of barter was born that day. An extended series of negotiations during which, at exactly the right moment, Mom would promise something irresistible in exchange for my doing something that, ironically, I would usually be willing to do otherwise. But now that I knew there was a potential payment floating nearby, I would extract it. My childish blackmail started with toys and ended with a pony. Naturally. Though by the end, I couldn't help feeling bought and sold myself.

CHAPTER TWO

B y the time I got to kindergarten, I was an old soul. That's not to say I was joyless; far from it. I had just been around the block many more times than my peers. I was barely five years old, but I was comfortable working with adults and had the self-assurance of a child twice my age. When a director says, "Action!" and you're the only one allowed to move or make noise, you get a heightened sense of your own importance. Even Mom wasn't allowed to make a peep while I did my thing for the camera. And if you did your bit right, the seas parted when you walked off the set.

I was the last person to arrive at my fifth birthday party that year. Kentucky Fried Chicken, it turned out, was more important. I knew my party was taking place that afternoon, so I was suspicious when Mom announced that we were going to squeeze in a quick callback after school. As Tiffany and I settled ourselves in the back of the brown station wagon, I began to wonder how this would work. I had a sense that interviews, as a rule, were really far away, and generally involved a car trip long enough to make me nauseous.

This happened to be a callback for a national commercial, so it had the potential to run like crazy. Mom was particularly excited because they only called back the kids they were serious about hiring. Tiffany and I stood next to her as we all waited for the casting director to call my name. Mom talked into the receiver of a payphone, whispering orders to my aunt Marilyn, her sister. Marilyn didn't have children of her own, and spent most of her time with us.

"Just let everyone in. We will be there in fifteen minutes. Get them started."

Tiffany sighed and rolled her eyes. She knew we were getting hosed somehow, as were the party guests. But I was more optimistic. Today was my birthday, and birthdays were full of surprises, so this interview had to be part of the plan. Maybe they were giving me the commercial for my birthday! Maybe we would get special chicken to bring to the party. I did know we could not possibly get home in fifteen minutes.

When we finally arrived home, my party guests, including my friends' parents, were huddled on our porch. Piles of children slumped in their parents' laps, jammed together on the stoop. Marilyn frantically explained that she hadn't been able to find the keys. Everyone was very quiet. No one said "happy birthday."

One of the moms broke the silence. "Abby and some of the others left after an hour. Marilyn kept saying you were five minutes away . . ."

I'd never seen party guests so angry with the birthday girl. Luckily, goodwill can be bought with a halfway decent party favor and none of the kids appeared to hold a grudge. I can't imagine the same could be said of the parents.

By the next day, my friends and I were back to playing my

favorite schoolyard game, Star Wars. The main appeal of Star Wars was that there was only one female character. As a result, I could play with all the boys at once, and none of the girls, which was ideal.

If I thought it felt like a Star Wars kind of morning, Mom made two braids on either side of my head and coiled them up into round balls so I would look like Princess Leia. What the hairdo lacked in beauty and style, it made up for in its sheer declarative spirit. When I stepped out of my family's station wagon and walked onto the playground, the "Leia Do" served as a beacon announcing to my classmates which game we'd be playing at recess.

I jumped and climbed and flew around the jungle gym while Thomas and Mike and Scott sliced the air with imaginary light sabers and shielded me from impending doom. It was glorious. Gloria Steinem would not have approved, but she wasn't there and I didn't care.

While I basked in the glow of my favorite Jedi knights, most of the girls made mud pies in the sandbox, an activity that held zero appeal for me. As far as I could tell, sand was hideous. Make it into as many pies as you like, you still can't eat it, and you still can't get every grain out of your shoes or out from underneath your fingernails after you play with it. Who was going to buy all these inedible pies? Why put so much time into patting them down tightly into their dish, if no one wanted the finished product? It made no sense to me.

The one girl I respected was Abby. She was as fast and tough as any boy I ran with, and she had a perfect head of shiny blonde hair that looked like her mom had put a salad bowl over her head and snipped around the edge. Except for being shorter than me, she could have been Brian. And if I pushed or shoved her a little, or had to have my way, she held her own like a boy instead of crying like a girl.

My only other female friend was Christy. She was my spy inside the girly world. She loved to bake pies and organize elaborate games that involved dolls. And even though I'd sooner die than join in, we could usually find common ground around the edge somewhere. She didn't mind my allergy to dolls. Hers was the first phone number I memorized after my own.

Of course, the one girl I really relied on early in life was my sister. Because Tiffany was three and a half years older, she was more often cast in the role of caretaker and protector. That summer, I'd refused to learn to swim at camp. I was five now but still terrified of the water. Once I reached the point where my toes couldn't feel the smooth concrete bottom of the pool, my breath would become jagged and panicked. I couldn't regain my composure long enough to even float.

Mom had paid extra for swimming lessons, and one diligent swim counselor after another would try to coax me into deeper water day after day, even though I'd cry and refuse. Eventually I would cry so hard and loud, the ill-equipped teen counselors would have to go find Tiffany in her group all the way across camp, and bring her to the pool to calm me down.

Day after hot summer day, Tiffany was forced to leave her friends and whatever craft or archery lesson she was involved in, and come quiet my hysteria. The poor counselors never did teach me to swim that summer, and Tiffany never stopped dropping whatever activity she was enjoying to come save me. Exhausted from the battle, I'd lie in her lap and fall asleep the whole way home on the bus. She'd roll her eyes at my theatrics, but she never let me drown.

Despite my hatred of dolls, I was cast in a Barbie commercial around that time. This was a bit of a chore since Barbie made about as much sense to me as mud pies. Her body was hard and oddly deformed. When you stripped her down, which I always did whenever I encountered a Barbie, she had pointy mounds on her chest and weird joints where her disproportionately long legs connected with the trunk of her body. You couldn't hug her, but I did like to style her hair, since that was the only part of Barbie that was malleable.

This commercial was a big event for me since Tiffany was generally the Team Barbie favorite. They liked beautiful girls to do the Barbie commercials. Tiffany had started to do more print, though, which meant they took still photos of her and another girl playing, and the photos later showed up in catalogs or the newspaper. It was thrilling to have the newspaper come to the front door with a black-and-white photo of one of us inside.

There was something about commercials that Tiffany didn't like, even at an early age. When the director said "Action," she shrank into her shell like the turtle on my school playground. Mom initially tried to coax her into being more playful, but as Tiffany grimaced and recoiled, Mom got increasingly annoyed and angry. I couldn't understand why my sister didn't embrace the attention. One thing was clear: the more Mom tried to tug some enthusiasm out of her, the more she resisted.

Commercials turned out to be my specialty, and the Barbie formula always dictated that one brunette girl and one blonde girl, both the same age, sit and play with the latest version of the doll. This time I was paired with another girl who was also about five years old. Her name was Lisa and she had whitish blonde hair that hung all the way to her waist.

"Can you sit on your hair?" I asked.

"Only if I put my face up to the sky, like this." She tilted her head back and sat on the very end of her blond mane.

Lisa's mom wore one of those red knit sweaters with a Christmas scene on the front, even though Christmas was still months away. It had ornaments on it that jingled when she walked. I thought the sweater was delightful, but Mom said it was beyond tacky. I had seen Lisa at a bunch of auditions, and her mom never let the time of year stop her from celebrating the holidays.

The on-set stylists took forever to do our hair and makeup, and when they finally finished, we looked like child Barbies, minus the plastic mounds in front. A pitiless woman with strong hands had even filed my nails and cut my cuticles with a terrifyingly sharp clipper. I cried, and then got scolded by Mom for making my eyes red. I felt like a dog after a particularly grueling trip to the groomers.

Next, Lisa and I sat together on a fake living room set to play. But even that turned out to be torture. We had to hold the dolls a certain way, so the camera could see their best parts, and move them exactly as we'd rehearsed. There was no grabbing, no spontaneous play, and definitely no undressing of Barbie.

For any five-year-old, this would be tedious. Lisa was nervous and a little too loud. Her voice had a nasal quality to it, and she'd come back from a series of talks with her mom looking slightly paler and more frightened than when she'd left. Acting was going to be too stressful for this kid, I thought.

"Action!" the director said.

It was my turn first. "I love new Disco Party Barbie!"

I held my breath. It was Lisa's turn, and she'd blown her line half a dozen times already.

"Look at her skates!" she shouted in a singsong voice.

"Cut." The crew let out a collective sigh.

Lisa's mom rushed in from the sidelines. "Look at her ROLLER skates, sweetie!" Her mom's voice was shrill as she gripped Lisa's wrist. Lisa winced. "Roller skates. Don't forget ROLLER."

Eventually, the director gave both lines to me, and just had Lisa say "Yeah!" She was clearly relieved, but her Christmas Loving Mom was devastated. I wondered if she'd send Lisa to bed without dinner later. I wanted to warn Lisa to eat what she could before she got in the car to go home.

Still, the atmosphere during commercial work was every man for himself, and I'd done well. It wasn't my fault that Lisa wasn't very bright. I'd tried to help her by eyeing Barbie's roller skates during my lines, but she was hopeless.

We changed back into the clothes we'd arrived in and got ready to go home. Usually this was when they gave me the toy I'd been playing with as a present to take home. I was ready to look thrilled and surprised.

The director smiled broadly as she ushered Lisa and me toward the door. "Honey, you did such a great job! Both of you." Lisa smiled dimly. "I wish we could give each of you a Disco Barbie, but we don't want anyone seeing her and copying her before she hits the shelves. You understand. I'm sure your moms will take you to the store when she comes out and get you your very own."

What a rip-off.

On the way home in the car, I felt exhausted but happy. "You did a nice job today. Much better than poor Lisa. She was horrible, poor girl," Mom said.

I beamed. I loved it when my mom was proud of me. I knew I'd been the better child that day.

"You're my special girl. I love you so much. You're such a star." She held my hand and all at once, I was so tired and proud, I wanted to cry. A tear fell down my cheek and I wiped it quickly before she saw it, because I couldn't really explain why I was crying. I leaned across the front seat of the station wagon and rested my head on her arm.

"We'll be home soon. I'll make you macaroni and cheese for dinner, your favorite."

CHAPTER THREE

"**Y**ou think you're SO perfect!" Maryjane screamed. "But you look like a bug with those huge weird eyes!"

I hadn't said I was perfect. I didn't even think it. Far from it. So it was impossible to understand why pint-sized yet deceptively strong Maryjane was yelling that at me, her fists flying in my direction.

Mom had brought me to school that morning and announced loudly in front of the first-grade class that I'd be shooting another commercial the next day, so I needed my assignments for school on the set.

"I'm sure she can make up whatever she'll miss. But her agent told us to get used to her missing school because there's a ton of demand out there for Missy now that she's six and can work more hours."

She jingled the big clump of keys she always carried in her right hand, a signal to the teacher that time was money. I hung next to the leg of her jeans and looked down at the red toenails that peeked out of her tan espadrilles.

"That's wonderful, Mrs. Francis," my teacher, Mrs. Jones, said. "But since she's here now, she can just take her seat and we'll keep going. I will put her assignments in her backpack at the end of the day."

I noticed then that I was the only student standing at the front of the class with Mrs. Jones and Mom. All the other kids were sitting at their desks, doodling or watching us.

A group of girls at the back of the classroom whispered to each other. Christy smiled and waved at me. She was always a friendly face in the crowd. Then my view shifted to Maryjane, whose narrow dark eyes shot darts from the fourth row. She and I had an ongoing grudge match to prove who was smarter, since we were both the best readers in the class. Plus she liked Mike Reed, who was really my boyfriend. That bundle of facts made us sworn enemies.

At recess on the playground, the grudge match got physical. Maryjane's red braids bounced in the air as she tried to pummel me. I searched her pale freckled face between swings to figure out why she was unleashing such fury on me that particular morning.

"Stop it!" I shoved her as hard as I could and she flew backward, landing in a heap next to the swings. The skirt of her frilly white dress flew up, exposing her bony legs and ruffled pink underwear.

"I can see your underwear, Maryjane," Mike said, laughing from the sidelines.

The mockery reignited her fire. Now a white patent-leather shoe came flying in my direction. I dodged the kick and took hold of the bib of her dress and tossed her as if she were a rag doll. She flew through the air like Raggedy Ann and landed in the dirt.

"Girls!" Mrs. Jones shouted.

Maryjane scrambled to her feet and charged again. Mrs.

Jones grabbed her shoulders just as the heel of her shoe made contact with my leg. "What's going on?"

"Missy thinks she so perfect! She's not! She has huge weird bug eyes!"

"Her eyes do look like a big bug or a frog or something," her friend Jennifer chimed in helpfully from the sidelines.

"Enough. Maryjane! March right up to Mrs. Nan's office! *Now*. Missy, would you like to go with her?" she scolded.

"No, ma'am."

"I want you to go sit on the wall right there and wait for me," Mrs. Jones instructed.

I walked over to the small concrete block wall that separated the grass playground from the walkway. I sat down and dusted myself off while she trailed Maryjane to the office, I assumed to await her execution. The scrapes on my knees bled. Christy walked over and took a seat next to me.

"Boy. She does not like you!" Another master of the obvious. Christy's blonde curls were cut short and framed her whole head like a lion's mane.

"Why? What did I ever do to her?" I asked.

"Well, you and your mom kinda seem like you think you are better than everyone else because you're on TV." She kicked the dirt and looked at the tiny cloud of dust that rose and settled at our feet.

"That's not true. I don't think I'm better than everyone else," I said.

"Oh, I know that. I always say that," Christy responded.

"And she said I think I'm so perfect? I do not," I added.

"I know! I said that. When you came in, we were sitting at our desks. Maryjane said you think you're so perfect, and I said, 'No. You're not perfect! You wear those same pants all the time!'"

I looked down at my favorite blue corduroy pants. I had thrown them on at the last minute when Mom yelled for me to come downstairs to breakfast. I had also grabbed my favorite blue sweatshirt, which similarly got too much wear. Underneath I'd thrown on a brown T-shirt that didn't match, but had been at the top of the pile in my drawer. I figured the T-shirt didn't matter because it wouldn't see the light of day under my sweatshirt. Now it was hot, and I couldn't take off my sweatshirt because everyone would see I was wearing a T-shirt that didn't match.

The heat rose under my clothes, and the perspiration stung my cuts. I tried not to cry, but a few tears leaked down my cheek.

"Don't cry." Christy put her hand on top of my hand.

"My mom says other kids are jealous," I said, floating a test balloon.

"Oh, yeah. I am. I'd like to be on TV and do commercials and sing and dance!" Christy seemed ready to burst into song all the time, and she often did.

"Do my eyes really look like a frog's?" I asked.

"Yes." She smiled.

By the next week, the Incident was nearly forgotten. Maryjane wanted a piece of Mike, so she didn't stray far from him. As much as I tried to remind Christy and Mike of Maryjane's attack, no one could focus long enough to stay mad at Maryjane. I thought it was important to remember who your enemies were, but I got the idea that Christy wanted to play both sides of the fence.

One day while we sat at our desks, Mrs. Jones walked around the room handing back our music projects. The assignment had been for us to use materials around the house to make our favorite musical instrument. I had forgotten about the project until the night before it was due, when I scrounged around the house for scraps to make something that made noise. There wasn't much to choose from, but I came up with a white plastic plate and some glitter and glue. Then I cut little bells off an old

Christmas stocking I'd found in the garage and attached them to the plate with pipe cleaners, and voila! I had a sad little tambourine. It wasn't the greatest instrument, but I'd ginned it up myself and it made noise. I thought it wasn't bad.

Mrs. Jones didn't agree. She returned my tambourine to me with an *S–* scrawled on the plastic plate, which meant my effort was below satisfactory. My heart sank.

I looked over at Eric, who beamed as Mrs. Jones handed back his papier mâché tuba. His appallingly realistic instrument dwarfed his desk. The paint even shined like solid brass. This thing could have led a New Orleans funeral parade.

Eric smiled at me. "I got an E+! For exemplary!" He left out the *l*, so it sounded like "exempary," but his minor speech impediment didn't diminish his joy. I leaned closer to Eric's masterpiece and wondered how he'd gotten the keys to look so real. He read my mind and said, "It took forever!"

A week later, Mom brought the tambourine home from Parents' Night.

"This isn't good. Did you actually turn this in?"

I didn't say anything, since the answer seemed obvious.

"You can't turn in crap like this. This is truly horrible. Why didn't you tell me you had a project to do? What else are you too lazy to do properly?"

It seemed like a good time to be honest about my next assignment.

"I have to make a mission. I picked the Santa Barbara Mission," I said hopefully.

"When were you planning on telling me about that?"

I shrugged.

"Where's the assignment?"

I pulled a paper out of my backpack and handed it over.

"This . . ." She held up the tambourine as if it were excrement. "This is awful. Do not turn in anything like this again. Ever. I was embarrassed for you, and you should be too."

She dropped the tambourine in the middle of the floor and one of the bells came loose.

When she left, I jammed the sorry piece of plastic and glitter in the back of my closet, behind the gray sneakers that I never wore because they gave me blisters.

The following Tuesday, I walked into the kitchen after school and found my spectacular mission.

My jaw dropped.

The model filled a third of our kitchen table, and consisted of three shoe boxes superglued to a cardboard foundation. The walls of the mission were covered in white cake frosting, perfectly feathered and fanned to mimic traditional Mexican stucco. Elbow macaroni lined up like infantry soldiers along pitched pieces of cardboard to create a tile roof. Diced pieces of kitchen sponge had been stapled in the middle, glued to the base, and painted Kelly green and oak to resemble shrubs. The pièce de resistance was a tiny cross, made of carved Popsicle sticks, that hung over the door, underneath which a Play-Do friar waited to greet pioneers migrating west, his arms stretched out to welcome them.

This was no humble homework assignment; it was an architectural wonder. There was even a color picture attached of the real mission to prove it was a perfect replica. Very few adults had enough artistic talent to produce such a work, much less a first grader.

Mom stood behind the model. "What do you think?" There was a hesitation in her voice.

I loved it and was ashamed of it.

"You can't tell anyone I helped you with this." *Helped?* She looked me in the eye. "Do you honestly think Eric made that tuba?"

It hadn't occurred to me that my tambourine and I had been so thoroughly outclassed by Eric's *mother*.

The next day, Mom carried my mission into class. It was far too heavy for me to lift. She set her elaborate handiwork on the counter next to all the others and smiled proudly.

"Didn't she do a nice job?" Mom said. Mrs. Jones just smiled.

I scanned the crowd of miniature buildings with new eyes. For the first time, I could pick out exactly which ones kids had assembled, and which ones parents had built.

I still didn't feel right about cheating, but clearly I wasn't the only one working with backup. Though I felt a little dirty, I was grateful that Mom had figured out the game and won. I decided that if Mrs. Jones handed out grades based on the final product without regard for how it was produced, we had no other option. It was the grade that counted.

And Mom got an E+.

Saturday mornings meant getting up early to ice skate at the Topanga Plaza Mall. Tiffany had asked for lessons, and as with everything else, I went along for the ride at first and then joined in after a few weeks.

This Saturday, we arrived at the rink in our thick tan tights and baby blue skate dresses, with white rabbit fur coats on top. The air was cold in the ice rink, but once we started skating, we always got too hot to keep the coats on. Mom had bought Tiffany her own beautiful white skates, but I still skated in worn tan rentals that I stood in line to pick up once we arrived at the rink.

We stepped onto the ice and skated off to opposite ends of the rink to start the lesson with our own age groups. I was six now, so I skated with the six- and seven-year-old group, Tiffany with the nines and tens. Today, every time I looked over at her, Tiffany had fallen. Mom sat in the front row of the bleachers looking annoyed.

I did a small jump, skating forward on my left skate, then leaping and turning backward in the air, and landing on my right foot with my left leg extended. The teacher was trying to teach the group a waltz jump. Tiffany had shown me this trick at home and I'd practiced a million times on dry land. Just as she had taught me to read, Tiffany had taught me the jump before I arrived at this class, so I could outshine my classmates from the get-go.

I landed it gracefully, and looked over to see if Mom was watching. I thought she'd be proud. But every time I looked, she was staring hard at Tiffany, who was sitting on the ice.

The lesson ended and I skated to the side with my group. Mom's arms and legs were crossed tightly, her eyes still locked on Tiffany, who sulked as she skated to the side, looking down at the ice in front of her, shoulders slumped in defeat. I could tell the drive home would be a painful one.

After the lessons, we ate lunch in the mall's food court, as usual. Tiffany ordered a hamburger. I had chicken fingers and french fries. We sat on the bright red molded plastic seats without speaking; the only noise was the crinkling of paper and the conversation of passing shoppers. I could feel Mom's frustration in the air like a pressure change before a thunderstorm.

"You don't have to eat so fast; no one is taking your food away from you," Mom said, slapping my hand as I grabbed for another fry. Then before I could eat any more, she said, "That's enough," and dumped our trays.

Tiffany and I hurried to our brown station wagon in the

mall parking lot, and as the car came into view, we both bolted for the backseat. Neither of us wanted to sit in the hot seat next to Mom when she was in a bad mood. I beat Tiffany to the back door and smiled. She ruefully climbed up front.

As we drove north on Topanga Canyon Boulevard, Mom started in.

"What was wrong with you today, Tiffany?"

Tiffany was silent.

"You were round shouldered and pigeon-toed the whole lesson. Why am I wasting my money if you aren't going to try? Every time I looked at you, you were tripping over your own skates. Maybe you're too lazy to skate, or maybe you just don't appreciate the time and money I am pouring into you."

Silence.

"Sometimes I think you have no dignity and self-respect. You don't seem to care about anything."

Silence.

"What do you have to say for yourself?" Mom demanded, seething.

"I have no dignity and self-respect." She said it quietly but it sliced through the air like a boomerang.

"*What?*" Mom screeched, filling the car with her voice.

"I have no dignity and self-respect." I watched the volley from the backseat and knew exactly what would come in return. *Smack.*

Mom raised her right arm and slapped Tiffany with an open hand on the left side of her face without slowing down the car.

"You have anything else to say?" Mom said, her voice as strong as iron.

"I hate you."

I ducked low in my seat. Mom screeched to the side of the road and slammed on the brakes.

"Get out," she said to Tiffany, who didn't budge. "You heard

what I said! Get out of the car! I mean it. I'm done with you. Get
out! I don't ever want to see you again for as long as I live!"

Tiffany still didn't budge, so Mom jammed her finger into
the seat-belt release button, reached across Tiffany to grab the
door handle, and forced the door open. With that she shoved
Tiffany out of the car as hard as she could with both hands.
Tiffany couldn't get her hands out in front of her fast enough
and tumbled on the sidewalk face-first. She lay there for a few
seconds before scrambling to her feet still in shock.

As Tiffany took a step back to steady herself I could see the
tears starting. But before Tiffany could say a word, Mom leaned
over again, grabbed the door handle from the inside, slammed
it, and drove away.

I whipped around in my seat to watch Tiffany as we left her
on the side of the road. I saw her crumple a little and cry. Tears
rolled down my cheeks as I turned back toward the front and
accidentally caught Mom's eyes in the rearview mirror.

"You want to go with her?" she asked.

I didn't say a word. I tried to suck in the air around me and
cry as silently as I could.

"I am so sick of both of you. I do everything I can to help
you. I've devoted my entire life to you. My mom never cared
about me like this. All she cared about was my brother, her precious son! My sisters were the only ones who took care of me,
ironing my clothes and making sure I got to school. They made
sure I did my homework, not her. She didn't care. If only I'd had
someone who cared about me the way I care about the two of you
I could have achieved anything. But no! It kills me that neither
of you appreciate everything I am always doing for both of you!"

Her cheeks flushed bright red with anger and she slammed
her hand on the steering wheel as she yelled. I wanted to be anywhere but in that car. I appreciated what she did, even if Tiffany
didn't seem to. Mom was right about everything, but I still

thought kicking Tiffany out of the car was extreme. I looked for
landmarks on the road so I could tell Dad later where we'd left
Tiffany and maybe he could go back for her.

After a mile or two she sighed heavily. "I guess I have to go
back for her. I'm very tempted not to."

We circled back and pulled up next to Tiffany, who was
standing on the sidewalk sobbing right where we'd left her.
Tiffany got back in the car. I saw her face for an instant before
she climbed back into her seat. Tears covered her cheeks, her
eyes were red, and the sides of her mouth were slack with fear
and humiliation. She was a shadow of the girl who charged
across summer camp to save me from the swim counselors.

I didn't know why she mouthed off like she did. I would
never have said those things to Mom. Her acts of resistance
always made things worse. I felt sorry for her but I was angry
with her at the same time for causing all this drama. We both
knew exactly what to say to mollify Mom, or to bait her. Tiffany
almost always, illogically, chose to bait her.

CHAPTER FOUR

"Come on, Missy. It's time to go. Dad's in the car."

I finished brushing my teeth, wiped my face, and looked in the middle drawer of the bathroom vanity for a thin ribbon that would match my shirt. I'd taken more care with my wardrobe in the months that had passed since the fight with Maryjane. I'd switched to wearing only polo shirts or blouses; no more miscellaneous T-shirts now that I was almost seven years old. I brushed my hair long and straight, and tied a ribbon around my head like a headband to hold my hair away from my face.

If I had time, I also liked to find matching argyle socks. Mom didn't do the laundry that often, so this new part of my morning ritual could be a challenge.

I found my backpack and bounded down the stairs. I usually made myself a peanut butter sandwich without jelly for lunch and took it in a bag with a fruit roll, but there was no bread in the kitchen, so we had nothing to hold the peanut butter. And we were out of fruit rolls.

Mom stood next to the door in a housedress, waiting for me to leave.

"There's nothing for lunch," I reported.

"Oh, fine. I will go to McDonald's and bring a Happy Meal to the parking lot at noon. Does that meet with your approval?"

"Yes, but . . ."

"I know! Chicken nuggets. No hamburgers. God." She rolled her eyes.

"Thanks, Mom!" I kissed her and ran out. From nothing to hand-delivered McDonald's, that was quite an upgrade.

Dad sat in the car with the engine idling. For all the fuss to hurry, he now lounged casually in the front seat smoking a cigarette, letting the car warm up. He wore blue jeans and a crisp blue and white button-down shirt under a navy sweater. His thick salt-and-pepper hair had been blown dry smooth and shiny. He was forty-two years old and still had a full head of hair. When I rode on his shoulders, I liked to grab clumps of his mane in my fists to steer him. Then I'd tease him that I could see a bald spot that he didn't know he had. He'd laugh at the very idea.

His sleek, relaxed demeanor hid a serious mind and a sensibility shaped by his childhood on the rough South Side of Chicago. He loved to say his parents were so poor he had holes in his shoes growing up. The button-down shirts and loafers he wore now were all chosen by Mom. It didn't matter to him what he wore.

He was an engineer who ran his own business designing and installing screening rooms and commercial theaters. He'd started the company mostly because he bridled when anyone gave him an order.

With his thick hair and his Marlboro Man swagger, he was the type of dad who was noticed by all the ladies. I'd heard one of the moms at drop-off ask, "Who's that?" while throwing her shoulders back with a big smile. I'd shot back, "That's my *dad*."

Our house sat at the highest point on a hill overlooking a golf course in a little suburb of Los Angeles called Porter Ranch. My parents had lived downtown when my sister was born, and they'd crammed her into their small apartment. Before long they realized they needed more space, and perhaps some distance from Mom's parents and sisters, who lived two blocks away.

All of the homes near them in neighborhoods Mom liked, like Hancock Park, were far out of their newlywed price range. So they'd hunted deeper and deeper into the Valley until they found a four-bedroom house they could afford. Dad loved to tell the story about how, by the time they got all the way out to Porter Ranch, there were only two houses still for sale in our division of tract homes: the pretty little model home at the bottom of the hill that was small but smartly trimmed, and the big expensive one at the very top of the mountain.

The developer wanted forty thousand dollars for the model, but Dad got him to fork over the crown jewel for just four thousand more. It had already more than doubled in value since we'd lived there, and we weren't selling anytime soon, no matter how many open houses Mom dragged Tiffany and me to on the weekend. The white stucco façade, Spanish tile entry, and brown shingle roof suited Dad and us girls just fine, even if Mom was permanently aspirational.

When my parents had recovered from the down payment, they put in a rolling green front lawn to meet the long black tar driveway, creating arguably the nicest home for blocks around. The house itself sat back on the lot for privacy, and the sweeping backyard offered a one-hundred-and-eighty-degree view of all the unsettled territory to the north and east of our development. The hills just beyond our community rolled on for miles, unspoiled by other homes or any sign of life. We seemed to live on the very edge of Los Angeles, and I imagined that somewhere way off in the distance lay Nevada, or maybe China.

The cliff our house sat on dropped straight down to the twelfth fairway directly below, and Mom lived in fear that the wind would blow one of us off the edge, tumbling hundreds of feet down the hill. But it never happened. Tiffany and I often made plans to scale the brush down the cliff rather than driving or walking all the way around on the road, but it was impossible if you weren't a mountain goat. Coyotes lived in the undeveloped area to the north and ventured into the brush on our cliff after sunset, eating more than one of our cats for dinner over the years. Anytime a cat didn't show up for a few days, we'd know he'd turned into a meal.

Dad put the silver-blue Pontiac into reverse and backed down the driveway, then coasted out of the cul-de-sac. It was only a ten-minute drive to school, but at this rate, the trip would take three days. My father never hurried for anybody.

"How long does it take you to get to the office after you drop me off?" I asked. I had been to his workplace before and played with the Xerox machine in the office area where a dozen or so people worked at desks. The office part, where they designed and sold sound and projection equipment, connected to a huge warehouse filled with inventory. The complex seemed very far away from our home. I figured that if he drove the whole way at this pace, he would just get to work every day and have to turn around.

"Oh, it takes like an hour or so for me to get there, really depends on the traffic. It's all the way in West Hollywood."

"Where I go for interviews?"

"Yes, basically the same area." He took a final drag of his

cigarette and then flicked the stub out the window. I wondered if anyone's grass would catch fire. "Are you excited to start work tomorrow?"

I'd been cast in my first role as a series regular, which meant I had my first steady job, according to Mom. I'd done a few Movies of the Week for ABC, and even one real feature film that we saw in a movie theater, but this was really the big time, Mom said. I had a job that could go on and on, like Dad's. She'd lavished me with toys and praise and love and attention since I'd been cast, so it had to be huge. I had a whole new team of stuffed animals in my room as evidence.

NBC bought eleven episodes of the show and named it "Joe's World." The story centered on a midwestern working class family with five kids. The producers cast Christopher Knight, who had played Peter Brady on *The Brady Bunch*, as the oldest brother. I played the youngest kid.

"I gather it's a sitcom. Like that show with Gary Coleman. What's it called? Mom says you're the comic relief. You just walk in the room and deliver punch lines," Dad said.

He took a left on Rinaldi Street and picked up a little speed as the golf course disappeared behind us.

"You and I are going to be heading to work together instead of school for a while. Did Mom tell you that? I'm going to take you to the lot at Metromedia, and your grandmother is going to stay with you on the set so Mom can take care of Tiffany."

He laughed to himself. "And I'm betting that arrangement will last about a day."

"Why?" I asked.

"Because your mom is addicted to showbiz."

He was right. Grandma sat on the set for the first few days of table reads, and then, sure enough, she and Mom swapped positions. I was happier with this new arrangement. Grandma loved to talk and talk to everyone on the set, mostly just bragging about Tiffany and me. But she wasn't as good at helping me as Mom. With her tight gray curls and ample build, she was a big soft pillow to run to during breaks in the action, but she knew very little about the mechanics of working, like when I was supposed to deliver a line.

Herbert, the director, helped quite a bit and smiled and cued me, but I felt better when Mom was there, making sure I was doing my job properly. I hated to mess up a line or hold up the other actors, especially because they were all older and had been working even longer than I had. I didn't want to be the worst or the least professional in the group, even if I was the baby. I had a standard to uphold.

And when it came to work, so did Mom. When we weren't working, she made running out of gas or crashing into the occasional fire hydrant seem like typical, unavoidable occurrences. But when we were working, she was careful and precise. We always arrived on set at least thirty minutes before my call time. And I checked in well rested and scrubbed clean, with my hair smelling like soap, my skin soft and sweet with baby powder.

At home, the laundry might pile up for days. The cupboard stood bare for weeks before she broke down and hit the grocery store. But when it came to working, she was a machine. She made sure I knew every line, hit every mark. She'd nag, cajole, mentor, bribe, threaten. Whatever it took. I realized when Grandma stood in that I very much preferred the more intense support Mom provided.

When we arrived home from work, Grandma generally sat yapping at my annoyed father, while Tiffany did her homework at the kitchen table. Tiffany seemed undercut by all the attention Mom lavished on me, but she was still the boss when we were alone.

"Don't touch," Tiffany said when I entered her room after dinner in search of the new miniature horses she'd gotten as her consolation prize when Mom decided to switch jobs with Grandma.

I ignored her warning and took the dapple gray with the English saddle.

Tiffany grabbed my wrist and seized the horse, prying it loose from my fingers.

"That's mine!" she said through gritted teeth.

"That doesn't mean I can't play with it," I said.

"Yes, that's precisely what it means. You're in my room and I make the rules here," she said.

Now that Tiffany was ten and nearly grown up, Mom had let her take down the childish fabric that had covered her walls for years. All that remained now was the stark white paint that had hidden underneath and few pictures of horses she'd put up with Scotch tape.

"You can play with this one," she offered, handing me a horse she'd had for a while and no longer played with. It was a small bay with a tall white sock and a chipped tail.

"I will name this one Princess," I said.

"That's a stupid name for a horse. And you already have a cat named Princess. Don't be a moron." She went back to reading a magazine at her desk, but she shifted in her chair so she could keep an eye on me.

I put the horse in a stall in her play barn and went back for the gray.

"Don't be a pest!" she said as she smacked my hand away from her horse. "I don't care what they give you on the set. In my room, these are my toys. Now get out!"

"Why are you being such a jerk?" I asked, confused.

Tiffany turned her back on me and said nothing. Then she faced me again. "Why don't you just take all the horses and get out! They're for babies anyway." She put a tape in her tape deck and blasted the music before I could say anything.

On the set of the new sitcom, I may have been the baby, but I felt like a real professional. We rehearsed for a few weeks to work out the kinks, and then taped the pilot. The network brought in a real audience off the street to sit in metal bleachers and watch us perform the show while three large cameras maneuvered around the studio floor recording the scenes.

We'd do the whole show all the way through twice for two different audiences in one night, and then the producers sliced and diced the two versions together to make the final episode that would air a few weeks later. They called the genre "three camera live" because we performed for a live audience, but the show was actually taped.

The applause and laughter and feedback overwhelmed and thrilled my senses. The warm-up comedian would call out the cast members one by one before the show started to introduce us to the audience. He saved me for last, and the crowd would laugh and cheer when I came out. So small in comparison to the six actors who had preceded me, I was like a tiny dot of punctuation at the end of the list of cast members.

Nerves fluttered through my limbs before he shouted my name, but the crowd yelled and clapped so loud each time I got out there, I looked forward to it after the first try.

I loved being part of a team with a goal to accomplish. We played our parts and put on our show, and soared on a cloud when the final scene ended. Mom wasn't the only one addicted to showbiz.

* * *

We finished the pilot near the end of December, just after my seventh birthday, and the network invited the whole cast to the NBC Christmas party. The celebration took place at a sprawling studio on the Metromedia lot in Hollywood that they'd turned into a winter wonderland. All the stars from all the NBC shows—early '80s hits like *Diff'rent Strokes* and *The Facts of Life*—promised to show up. The network even sent a limo to our house to get us there and back in style.

Mom dressed Tiffany and me in brand-new holiday dresses from Saks for the occasion. They were both hunter green velvet, though mine was shapeless and short with a round collar, and Tiffany's was nipped at the waist and more grown-up. Mom had washed and curled our long locks and even put a little blush on our fair cheeks and mascara on our lashes.

When Mom finished curling the last tendril of my hair, I looked in the mirror to admire the finished product, and saw two different-sized versions of the same doll looking back at me.

"You look so cute," Tiffany said, putting her arm around my shoulders and smiling at my image in the mirror. When her eyes shifted to her own appearance, her shoulders tensed and she grimaced a bit, even though I thought she looked perfect.

"You look beautiful. I love your dress more," I said wistfully.

"Do I?" she asked.

"You do," I said, utterly convinced. She smiled.

Mom and Dad pulled out all the stops too. Mom shimmered in a long black dress that glittered and danced when she walked, and Dad put on his most handsome navy suit with a red tie. They looked as perfect and happy as I'd ever seen them, like the newlyweds I imagined they'd been before we arrived.

When we pulled up to the party, security and staff ushered us down a red carpet. Mindy Cohen and two other girls from *The Facts of Life* buzzed around a chocolate fountain inside and squeezed my cheeks and arms as they greeted me. They all worked on the set next to ours, and would allow me to come play with them during lunch, as if I were their mascot.

Mom floated joyfully around the party with the three of us in tow. She stopped to talk to the other moms, and drifted toward the bubbling fountain of melted chocolate. Her eyes lit up when she saw the show's writers; she was eager to pick their brains and see if the show had any hope of being picked up for another season. Tiffany hung a step behind me and eventually stopped making the rounds with us. She and Dad gravitated to a table, where they sat and talked and eventually looked bored. They'd both been excited to dress up and come to the party, but the glitz wore thin once they'd visited all the food stations and danced a few numbers.

At the end of the night, we slowly coasted back out to the North Valley in our limo. Tiffany and I chose the novelty of riding backward, trying hard to fight off sleep.

I opened the robin's-egg-blue box with the red ribbon they'd handed me on the way out. The colorful packaging fell away to reveal a shiny silver box lined with red velvet. It was as heavy as lead. On the bottom, the box was stamped TIFFANY & CO. On the top, the inscription read NBC with a tiny peacock next to it. I ran the tip of my finger back and forth over the engraving and thought about what treasures I'd hide inside.

That Christmas, Santa brought every toy I'd ever imagined, and a few I hadn't thought to wish for. Tiffany and I awoke before dawn and crept to the top of the stairs, where we sat on the first step waiting for Mom and Marilyn to say it was time to go down and tear open the cornucopia of presents that spilled out around the base of our enormous white flocked tree. Marilyn always spent Christmas Eve at our house so she could see our faces in the morning when we greeted our haul.

"Whoa," I said to Tiffany as we stretched to see everything that waited below. The lights on the tree danced and bounced off the wrapping paper and walls, making the living room look more like a disco.

"I know. They outdid themselves. They must have been up all night!" Tiffany said.

"They?" I asked, suspicious but still wanting to believe in the red-suited god who delivered pure joy once a year.

"The elves. That help Santa," Tiffany reassured me with a smile.

Mom and Marilyn strode out of the kitchen, bleary-eyed, hair disheveled. They were already sipping coffee in holiday mugs.

"I thought I heard you two," Mom said with a smile.

"Should I wake Dad, or can we start?" I asked with a jolt of excitement.

"Don't wake him. Just come down and get started. But you have to open one at a time so Marilyn and I can see your faces. It will be hours before Dad stirs, but you still won't be done. Look at everything Santa left!" she squealed.

As we came down the stairs, I could see that the presents stretched all the way to the far walls of the sitting room. We weren't normally allowed to play in the sitting room, with its white couches and chairs, too perfect for dirty little hands. But once a year, the room was transformed.

This time there had to be nearly a hundred wrapped presents in every shape and size. Each one had a tag with an "M" or a "T" to tell us to whom the mystery delight belonged. Two new bikes with enormous bows sat in the middle of the room, a large blue ten-speed with white-walled tires for Tiffany, and a smaller, light blue two-wheeler for me.

By the time Dad woke up, the sitting room looked like a wrapping paper bomb had exploded, spraying red and green shrapnel everywhere. I sat in the middle of the debris, exploring a Fisher Price doctor's kit I'd been praying for.

"Jesus," Dad said in Mom's general direction. "Think you overdid it?"

"Santa, darling. Not me," she smiled back.

"Most of this was from Santa, Dad. It didn't cost you anything," I reassured him. "Although this was from Mom!" I said giving Tiffany a pretend shot in the arm with my toy needle. Next I planned to jump-start her heart.

"I'm too tired to keep opening," Tiffany said. She brushed me off and laid back on the ground in her holiday pj's, admiring a new white leather purse she'd just unwrapped.

"I'll take everything that hasn't been opened, in that case," I said, eyeing the loot. Dad groaned and wandered into the kitchen for some coffee.

CHAPTER FIVE

Mom placed her hand on my shoulder to wake me up. I jumped.

"It's okay. You just need to get up. It's a special day. We need to go to school to get your assignments. Then we're going on a plane to Sonora. Come on, sweetie," she said.

I'd landed what Mom called the role of a lifetime on *Little House on the Prairie*, a show that was already a hit. Being cast on a huge show that was already up and running was like being born on home plate with the crowd cheering. You'd done nothing to help the team win, but that didn't mean you couldn't bask in the glory. The victory was especially sweet for Mom since my last show, *Joe's World*, hadn't lasted more than a season.

I plodded slowly down the hall to the bathroom I shared with my sister. She brushed her teeth at the far sink, which right now was hers. We each liked to claim ownership of one of the two sinks, but anytime we agreed on the division of territory, I got the sense I'd been had. I was eight years old, and she was nearly twelve. That was a lot more time to gather the skills of negotiation.

"How long are you going for?" Tiffany asked with tooth-paste foaming out of her mouth.

"I don't know. We're shooting the first episode on location and then coming back for the rest of the season I think."

"Mom told me you're going on an airplane that doesn't have regular people on it," she added, wiping her mouth.

Who would be on it then? Aliens? I wanted to ask but she shut off the tap and left.

An hour later Mom and I walked down the outdoor pathway to my second-grade classroom. My black and white saddle shoes scuffed the cement walkway as we hurried along, the leaves of late fall occasionally drifting into our path and crunching under our feet. The swings in the middle of the playground right next to the classes hung silent and motionless. All the other kids were in class.

My mom opened the door to my classroom and I saw Mrs. Sandberg standing at the front by the chalk board, holding a piece of chalk. Her skirt flowed down to her ankles and her glasses were perched on the tip of her nose.

All eyes, which had been fixed on her, moved quickly to me. I shifted uncomfortably. I was wearing the uniform Mom dressed me in for every single audition: OshKosh overalls rolled at the knee, paired with a white blouse that had short puffed sleeves and a Peter Pan collar, white socks with eyelet trim folded over at the ankle, and saddle shoes. I wore the outfit so often that I hated every thread of it.

Mrs. Sandberg put her fingers in her short, curly, blondish-gray hair and smiled as she looked me over.

She liked me, and seemed to think highly of me, thanks

to yet another tip on how to be first in the class, this time from Mom. At the beginning of the school year, Mom told me that when Mrs. Sandberg asked a question about something we read, I needed to repeat the question at the beginning of my answer. So if she asked, "Why did Mary buy an apple?" I was supposed to write, "Mary bought an apple because she was hungry." Oddly enough, this tidbit came in handy on the first day of school during Reading Comprehension. I'd never heard of Reading Comprehension, but I was the first to raise my hand when Mrs. Sandberg asked, "Why did Billy bring his jacket?"

I responded, "Billy brought his jacket because it was cold outside."

My answer dazzled Mrs. Sandberg, and just like that, I had started another year as the smart kid. That I had just learned this skill the day before was pure coincidence, but I'd take it. As a bonus, I knew that just across the room, Maryjane was fuming.

Now Mrs. Sandberg walked over to her desk and picked up a folder. "I have Missy's assignments right here." She addressed Mom as if the other kids weren't there.

"Don't you look adorable?" she said to me with a smile.

Mrs. Sandberg had never commented on my clothes before, or anyone else's. I didn't know what to say. Mom squeezed my hand hard.

"Thank you," I piped up.

"This should get her through the next two weeks. After that, you'll have to come back for more. I'm sure keeping up won't be a problem, but we'll miss her." She tugged the bottom of my braid gently.

So I'd be gone for more than two weeks. That was news. I looked at my friends Mike and Christy and wondered when I'd see them again.

* * *

An hour later, we pulled up to the Van Nuys airport and got out of the long black limousine they'd sent for us.

"Just stay with me and be good, okay?" Mom said, her voice sounding strained. I'd never seen her this nervous.

The driver got out and ushered us through the airport and onto the tarmac, where a small jet waited with an even smaller staircase leading up to its door. I'd flown on planes a few times before, but they had been big and we'd had to wait with a bunch of people before getting on them.

Now just Mom and I mounted the stairs, and when we ducked inside, I saw a boy sitting there with his father.

"I'm Jason. Jason Bateman, your new brother," he said officially. He had shiny reddish brown hair that fell to his collar, with a curtain of bangs, bright blue eyes, and freckles that covered his cheeks and nose.

He had a playful spark, which I welcomed, since it seemed clear we'd be the only two kids for a while. He was older than me, which would normally mean he'd ignore me, but I knew since it was me or nothing, I had a shot.

Just then a booming voice filled the plane. "Hey, kids! What do you think? Not bad, right?"

This was the man I'd seen at the audition. He ran his fingers through his long wavy hair and tugged on the front of his blue chambray button-down shirt. His tight jeans gave way to weathered tan cowboy boots. He laughed a big, bellowing laugh that made his eyes glint. It was impossible not to love him immediately.

Even though he stood a few inches shorter than the pilot behind him, he was larger than life. He had the magnetism of God and Santa Claus rolled into one. I looked over at Mom, who had been struck silent. He seemed to get a kick out of that.

"I'm Michael Landon," he said, his lips curled up into a smile.

For once, Mom had nothing to say. She seemed to just melt.

I had no idea that this man was the creator and director of *Little House on the Prairie*, which was by then one of the most successful family dramas on television. Much of Middle America, especially in the Bible Belt, loved watching the tear-jerker about a pioneering family carving out a tough but wholesome life a century earlier.

The premise was popular, but it was wearing thin after seven seasons. Jason and I had been brought in to add fresh energy. The original Ingalls children were grown-ups now, and they needed younger actors to fill the void.

I looked over at Mom, who still appeared oddly paralyzed.

"Hey, Mr. Landon!" Jason piped up, immediately taking advantage of our stunned silence. "This is awesome! Can I fly the plane?"

Michael let out another thunderous laugh and slid into the seat next to Jason. Mom recovered long enough to look disappointed that he didn't sit next to her.

"It's Michael. Call me Michael. Are you both ready?" He swiveled his head to the pilots in front. "Warren? You ready to get this old heap of bolts into the air?"

We looked around at the fine leather seats and even finer flight attendant waiting with small, filled glasses.

"Champagne?" she offered. "Orange juice?"

The plane lifted into the air gracefully like a bird taking flight in the morning. I felt weightless. My stomach dropped, but I couldn't tell if it was the plane or the whole situation. This airplane ride seemed very special, but then again, it represented about a third of my flying experience to date, so maybe it was normal.

Michael chatted with Jason and his dad, and for the first

time, I noticed the blonde woman who had come on board with him. She looked like the Barbie dolls I'd sold in commercials.

We were at least halfway into the flight when Michael started to laugh devilishly. "I have something really fun for you. Warren? You know, like last time?"

The pilot looked back from the cockpit and nodded.

"Here, take this. You won't believe it!" With that, Michael handed me a glass of orange juice, even though I didn't like juice and hadn't joined in the first round of drinks. Mom nodded at me enthusiastically as if he'd given me a gold bar.

"Okay, here we go! Hold the drink and watch it, sweetheart." Michael pointed to the glass in my hand.

And with that the plane began to roll like a log, righting itself before a drop of juice spilled from my glass.

The tiny, yippy dog the blonde had brought on board screeched in terror and leaped into Michael's lap. He laughed as the blonde tried to pull the panicked dog back into her lap.

Mom squeezed my arm so tightly, her fingernails dug into my skin and I wanted to cry. For so many reasons.

"See? The G force kept all the juice in your cup. Not a drop spilled. Not a drop! That's your astrophysics lesson for the day, kids. Stick with me. I will teach you everything you need to know, better than you'd learn in any boring old schoolroom!" Michael said.

I looked at my mom as I tried to swallow my rising hysteria. But the hard look in her eyes told me to pretend we were having fun, even though what was happening flew in the face of everything she'd ever taught me about protecting my personal safety.

When we finally landed in Sonora, another car met us and took us to the motel we'd be camping out in for the next two weeks. The Super 8 was modest compared to the Learjet we'd flown in on. Still, it was probably the best accommodations the dusty gold miners' town had to offer. In the last century, glittering nuggets had lured prospectors seeking their fortunes. But it seemed as if they'd taken every fleck of prosperity with them when they'd left. Now the town limped along with farmers, a few tourists, and, this week, a huge television crew from L.A.

Our room was located across the parking lot from Jason's. I wanted to go see what he was up to, but I was still rattled from the death-defying journey, and Mom said I had a really early call the next morning.

"Don't worry. You'll be spending every minute with him. He's your brother," she said.

The clerk directed us to a coffee shop for dinner. We headed down the street on foot, stopping at a drugstore on the way to buy an alarm clock. I picked a white digital radio alarm clock that Mom said I could keep and take home. I loved it. I hadn't had anything but a watch until now, and this clock had an AM/FM radio too. It was very adult.

As promised, the next morning the clock blasted local chatter at 5:30 AM. A man rattled off the weather for the next few days. He warned that the temperature wouldn't reach into the fifties until after lunch, which was much cooler than I was used to in Los Angeles. I fell back to sleep thinking about the pink jacket I'd brought with me. I hoped they'd let me wear it when we were shooting.

Turns out the clothes they put on me were nothing like the clothes I brought.

"Look, the honey wagons are right there," Mom said, pointing to the row of trailers that held small changing rooms with the actors' names on the doors. She rushed me along, even though I was still half asleep.

The wardrobe lady was right on our heels. She carried a lavender dress with tiny bouquets of flowers printed on the fabric and had another sleeveless dress with her, made of decidedly drab sackcloth. Around the neck hung a blue unstructured bonnet.

"Hi, sweetie. Are you Missy? Our new Cassandra?" she asked following us up the stairs of the trailer and right into the room with MISSY FRANCIS on the door.

Her fluffy brown hair was parted on the side and feathered over her ears. Big round red glasses attached to a gold chain that hung around her neck. She wasn't much taller than me, and probably weighed about a loaf of bread more than I did. Clothespins were clipped to the cuffs of her plaid blouse, and half a dozen safety pins were fastened to the hem. Her red Keds matched her glasses.

"Put this on first," she said, handing me the sackcloth dress and closing the door behind her. Now the three of us were jammed into the tiny room. "This is the petticoat. Put the dress over it."

I couldn't believe I would wear both dresses at the same time. I guess it was even colder than I thought outside.

"You can leave your underwear on underneath but nothing else. If you are too cold, I can give you a long john to wear under the whole thing. Then pull on these stockings, and slide these bands on the top and then roll them down with the fabric to hold up the stockings."

I looked at the weird itchy socks and the giant bands.

"Ha! You have no idea what I'm talking about. This is the prairie! They didn't have elastic in those days." She gestured toward the mysterious bands. "There's no other way to make your hose stay up and look authentic. Don't worry, put on the dress and I'll do your socks. Oh! I left your boots outside. I'll be right back."

She disappeared and returned with scuffed brown boots that laced halfway up and then had hooks at the top like ice skates. There were so many layers to put on and fasten, I could barely walk when I was done. And everything itched.

She smoothed my skirt over the petticoat, admiring the fit, while Mom watched from the sidelines. "There! Now let me tie the bonnet around your neck and we'll get you to hair and makeup."

I carefully climbed down the stairs of my trailer, worried I'd slip in my boots, which didn't bend at the ankle. They had a thin sole, but the thick hose added some padding. Unfortunately, the bands holding up the hose stopped the flow of blood to my feet.

We walked a few paces and then climbed up another set of stairs at the end of the next honey wagon. The sign on the door said HAIR/MAKEUP.

When I pulled open the heavy metal door, a flamboyant man with white hair and an odd white hat turned and looked me over from head to toe. He wore jeans and a crisp white shirt with the collar flipped up. The button holding the shirt closed over his paunch belly strained when he talked.

"Oh, boy. Another one. Come on in! I'm Larry. I'll be braiding your hair for the next decade. If you're lucky." I sat in his chair and looked in the mirror at my unusual costume, while he scraped my scalp with a punishing brush. I winced but it had no impact on his technique.

"Her hair actually parts on the left. And I usually hold the bangs back on the right with a small barrette," Mom offered.

He rolled his eyes. "Mom, they don't have barrettes on the prairie. Everyone else wears the part in the middle. Sorry."

This time, she wasn't staying silent.

She smiled and clucked. "Oh, I know *you* know best. You

must deal with horrible stage moms everyday! Aren't we the worst? Bunch of hens!" She poked his belly with her French painted acrylic nail. "Come on. Just a little bit to the side? What do you think?"

She smiled in a way I'd seen her look at the Christmas tree salesman when she wanted him to deliver the tree to our house for free. She had always told me I looked terrible with my hair parted down the middle. But Larry seemed used to being the boss of his domain. I couldn't wait to see if she could pull this off.

"Just a little." She smiled and winked at him in the mirror.

He rolled his eyes again, but smiled and sighed deeply.

"Fine. Just a little." He hummed to himself as he moved my part two inches to the left of center. He then proceeded to pull my braids so tight, I could hardly open my eyes. He wrapped thin ropes of fake hair around the ends of the braids to hide the rubber bands, rather than finishing with red bows like Mom usually did.

I stood up, feeling as if every hair on my head might be ripped from my scalp at any second. Next it was time for makeup. An older woman whose heavy lids made her look half asleep painted my face with a creamy orange foundation and then caked powder on top of it. I looked like one of Willy Wonka's Oompa Loompas.

I climbed down the stairs of the Hair/Makeup wagon in a daze, having just been run through a paint and body shop. Jason stood nearby talking to a grip. His face was the same disturbing brownish-orange color as mine.

"Not a drop spilled out of my glass! We must have rolled ten times!" Jason was telling the assistant director the story of our harrowing flight. And, apparently, the trip wasn't terrifying enough for him, so he was taking artistic license in retelling it.

His eyes danced when he talked about our near-death experience. His voice had the slightest accent or maybe a lisp, I couldn't tell which, but he had my attention. He was three or four years older than my current flame, Mike, and he had the second grader completely outgunned.

Michael clanked down the steps of another trailer. He still had on high boots, but his skintight jeans were replaced by similarly tight brown woven pants with suspenders, and a soft white cotton button down open to the middle of his chest. White tissue sprouted from the neck of his shirt to protect his wardrobe from the orange makeup every one of us was wearing.

In his right hand he held a Styrofoam cup filled with steaming hot coffee. In his left hand he held a broad-rimmed hat. He looked like he had just roared in on a covered wagon from another century for a cup of joe.

"Hey, Jason, Missy . . . you guys ready to work?" His eyes settled on my hair. He frowned. Then he barked at the first assistant director, or "AD," "Her hair is supposed to be down. She doesn't wear braids until we get back to Walnut Grove and Caroline gets her hands on her and then she's transformed into one of the Ingalls and looks just like a little Laura. Take her back to Larry and tell them to *hurry*. Now we're going to be behind because they didn't read my goddamn notes carefully."

Back to Larry!

It wasn't even 8 AM and I wanted to go back to the Super 8 and hide in bed.

During my second scalping, Larry broke down and used a barrette from Mom to hold back the front of my hair, since I had no bangs. I looked in the mirror and admired the final look, even as my scalp pulsated from the abuse.

This time when I emerged from the Hair/Makeup wagon, an AD rushed me to the set where Jason was already waiting, sitting in a chair by the craft services table with his dad.

Michael sat thirty feet away behind the camera, perched on a stool, coiled like a cheetah gaming his prey. He stared intently into the lens with one eye closed. Then he sprang down from the dolly that held the camera and marched to the center of the action, where two stand-ins crouched in the back of a covered wagon in clothes vaguely resembling mine.

Michael turned to the cinematographer, "Okay. I want you to start wide so we can see the whole mining camp. Those guys over there walk to the stream with their pans.

"You!" He pointed at an extra in gritty miner's gear. "You, cross from that campfire and land right here."

He indicated a spot in front of the wagon. "Here, we shift focus from him to the kids. And then . . . boom. I will come out from the driver's side of the wagon and land here, we do the dialogue . . . I leave to talk to Uncle Jed. You go close on the kids in a two shot and cut. Got it? Let's do it."

I didn't have it. But I had focused in on what the girl stand-in was doing. And she was sitting in the back of the wagon. I could definitely do that.

I also knew I didn't have any dialogue in this scene, which was comforting for a first round with this crew. Mom had read the scene the night before, and explained helpfully that my pretend mom and dad would soon be crushed and killed in a harrowing wagon accident. I wondered about the logistics. How do you die in a wagon borrowed from a Western Pioneers coloring book? I had horses. They could kick you, or bite you, but death seemed far-fetched.

But in this shot, Mom had explained, I would be happily arriving with my still-alive dead parents and meeting Michael.

Jason and I walked over to the wagon to take our marks. He climbed in first, and the AD lifted me in next. Jason took my hand and helped me settle in. He smiled, showing his perfect white teeth. I scootched a little closer. Alone at last.

"Don't worry. Sit here with me. I have a line but you don't have to do anything."

Michael yelled, "Action!" and the scene flew by in one take, no rehearsal necessary. This group didn't mess around.

That night, Mom wiped the orange sludge off my face. "You did a great job today. Don't let Jason muscle you out of the way though. Make sure you keep your face toward the camera."

"But don't look at the camera, right?" This was rule number one. The camera wasn't there. Never ever make eye contact with it.

"No. You can be aware of it without looking at it." She took the rubber bands out of the ends of my braids and started to undo the plaits. My shoulders sank and I felt tired to my bones. My calves ached, unused to my retro footgear. My back hurt from riding in a hard wooden wagon with no suspension and my scalp just burned.

"Let's look at the script for tomorrow," Mom said.

Seriously? I couldn't keep my eyes open. I followed her to the bed, where she had laid out the script as if it were a bedtime story. "This is the only time we can learn your lines for tomorrow. Even if you don't say anything you have to know what's going on around you. Acting isn't just what you say, it's what you do and how your eyes react to what's going on."

She kept talking, but the last thing I heard her say was something about a big train. Then I was asleep.

The enormous black steam engine roared toward us, smoke filling the sky and blotting out the sun. I had never seen anything so enormous move. It was magnificent.

In the morning we had filmed a scene where Michael loaded us on the train and said goodbye forever. The covered wagon had gone out of control, fallen down a ridge, and crushed our parents to bits, but Michael's character, Charles Ingalls, couldn't afford to adopt us, so instead he shipped us off to an orphanage.

Then as the train left, he felt guilty and changed his mind.

Now the train thundered down the track, with more smoke billowing from it than I'd ever seen come from something that wasn't on fire. With similar dramatic flair, Michael rode his wagon onto the track in front of the speeding train and pulled the horses to a wrenching stop

The conductor would either stop or crush Michael, his fictional son, Albert, who was along for the ride, and two perfectly good horses, to smithereens.

Both in the story and in real life, it looked like Michael was taking a huge risk.

I was sure the train would stop.

Pretty sure.

The horses were more confident than I was. All day, the wranglers kept swapping out two sets of big burly chestnuts to serve as the horses in Michael's team. I could tell the difference between all four horses because I'd been riding for as long as I could remember. Still, I was amazed that they assumed the viewers of the show were so gullible or nearsighted that they wouldn't notice.

All four horses seemed accustomed to Michael's brand of high drama, and didn't flinch as a hundred tons of steaming steel barreled toward them. They stood bravely on the track and waited for the engine to grind to a halt.

As the train roared closer, Michael pulled the reins tight and rapped them snuggly around the brake handle. Then he leaped down from the wagon seat and strutted to the middle of the tracks, where he stood boldly watching the train screech and scrape, finally slowing and stopping, leaving only the smallest cushion of air between them.

"I've put two children on board. I'm here to take them

back!" Michael shouted the line to the conductor who hung his head out of the window. He then ran to the side of the train and boarded.

He did the take once and yelled, "Print!"

Michael was the king of the one-take scene. I was learning quickly that he worked efficiently and wasted nothing. For a man who flew around in his own Learjet, he was tight with a penny, as the modest honey wagons and Super 8 attested. Even I noticed the downgrade a few hours after we'd landed.

Now it was my and Jason's turn. The camera and lighting team set up inside a passenger car, making the focal point a row of seats in the middle. Extras in similar costumes sat in the other seats.

We rehearsed once. I had no lines. Supposedly, I was still in a state of shock after seeing my parents pulverized.

Jason and I held hands at the doorway of the train car. The assistant director yelled the standard questions that set every scene in motion: "Rolling? Speed? Speed! Marker!"

The next line fell always to Michael: "Action!"

The conductor ushered us down the center aisle and pointed to the seat. We sat down and Jason started his dialogue: "It's going to be okay, Cassandra. We'll find a way. I can take care of both us without Ma and Pa. . . ."

After a few more sentences, tears started rolling down my cheeks. I didn't know why I was crying. The writers hadn't put that in the script. But everything Jason said made our lives sound so hopeless. Plus I just felt stressed and tired. I was supposed to be mute, but I couldn't help it. And once the tears started flowing, they turned into a flood.

Fortunately, Jason kept going, even though he had to be wondering why I was crying. Halfway through Jason's speech, Michael shoved his way past the conductor to our row.

"Listen, how would you two like to come with me?" he said.

"Yes! Oh, yes!" Jason said. I hoped Michael didn't see my tears, but by now I was sobbing, so there was no way he could miss them. He didn't seem mad.

"It's not forever. Just until we find you a more permanent home. You can do chores and help out."

"What if you don't find us a home?" Jason asked.

"Well, then you'll have to go on to the orphanage, but at least it's hope. It's something," Michael said, near tears now himself.

He swept me up into his arms like a western superhero and carried me off the train with Jason on our heels. We got outside the train and he yelled, "Cut! And print!"

Then he laughed loudly and kissed my cheek while squeezing me so tight I thought my head might pop off.

"That was great!" Michael said. "Who told you to do that?"

I didn't answer but just buried my head in his shoulder, thrilled I wasn't in trouble.

Mom took me back to the honey wagon so I could change out of my clothes. She was wearing a purple plaid Ralph Lauren dress with a flowing skirt that made her look like a modern version of the other women on the train. She had curled and teased her short dark hair, but it wilted a bit during the long workday. Her makeup, which had initially been flawless, smeared around her eyes a little after hours of wear.

She sat me on the stiff bench that was supposed to be a couch, and started unlacing my boots. I looked in the mirror and noticed that my yellow eyes matched hers.

"You were perfect today. Did you really cry during the train scene? I couldn't hear what was going on from outside." She gripped my calf as she struggled to free my foot from the pitiless boot.

"Yes."

"Why?" she asked.

"I don't know. Everything Jason said made me sad. I couldn't help it."

"He did all the heavy lifting, and you stole the scene," she said with a smile.

"Jason's nice. I like him."

"Well that's fine. Just be careful. Don't let him upstage you."

I didn't know what she meant and I was too tired to care.

When we got back to L.A., we filmed the indoor scenes on Stage 15 of the MGM Studios lot in Culver City, and the exterior scenes on the permanent outdoor set where the fictional town of Walnut Grove had been thriving for the past seven years. In both locations, the cast and crew fell back into their well-worn groove, and I realized that Michael was in fact the center of the universe. He called all the shots, got all the attention, and drove all the action. He was the energy that made the earth rotate.

We pulled up to a chain link fence that seemed to guard absolutely nothing.

"The whole town of Walnut Grove is supposed to be here somewhere. But I don't see a thing," Mom said, looking off into the distance.

We had followed a sheet of directions into the low rolling hills of Simi Valley. The crew in Sonora had described the location of the permanent outdoor set as "the middle of nowhere." It turned out "nowhere" was roughly twenty minutes from our house.

An AD stood at the opening of the fence holding a clipboard in one hand and a walkie-talkie in the other. He leaned into the open car window and addressed my mom, who wore a frilly western shirt and dark blue jeans. She was really getting into the frontier theme.

"Who do we have here?" he asked with a smile.

I smiled back. "I'm Missy!"

"You're the third Missy then actually."

I had heard this in Sonora. Apparently, almost all the brunette actresses playing Ingalls children were named Melissa, or Missy for short. What an odd coincidence. There was Melissa Gilbert and Melissa Sue Anderson. Melissa Gilbert was the star. She played Laura Ingalls Wilder, the real-life pioneer who had written the *Little House* books, on which the show was based.

I hadn't read the books, and I'd only seen the show once, after I'd already landed the role. Mom let me stay up late to watch it so I'd understand why we wore bizarre clothes and spoke strangely. *Little House* came on at 8 PM when I usually went to bed, so I was thrilled to stay up late, curled up in one of our family-room chairs with my white Persian cat in my lap.

The show itself was really boring, at least to me, an eight-year-old more used to sitcoms and cartoons. All the characters ran around, literally, in the dirt, and rode in the backs of wagons with dramatic music playing loudly in the background. They endured a lot of heartache over stuff that didn't seem like a big deal to me. Mom said the story was basically a nightime soap opera, whatever that meant. She showed me a section of the *Los Angeles Times* that reported television ratings, and claimed that more Americans watched *Little House on the Prairie* than almost any other show. I just couldn't figure out why. But it was starting to sink in that my role was a big deal.

The two other Melissas were both super old. Melissa Gilbert still starred on the show every week as the married schoolteacher, Laura. But in real life, Mom said she was dating someone named Rob Lowe, who was supposedly gorgeous because he had, among other things, pink cheeks. This made absolutely no sense to me.

I wondered if he was overheated a lot. She and my aunt buzzed about how handsome he was, and how handsome Michael was, which made even less sense. Whatever.

Melissa Sue Anderson played Mary, the oldest sister in the Ingalls family. Like me she was called Missy. She was very pretty with shiny blonde hair and big blue eyes. Mom explained that Missy "didn't know what a good thing she had" and quit right before I arrived. From what I'd seen so far, I agreed with Mom. There were so many great places to play on the set and most of the crew were willing to entertain you. Being part of the regular cast was hard work for sure, but the food was good and there was loads of praise when you did a good job. I couldn't figure out why anyone would quit.

The man with the clipboard opened the gate and directed us to a small group of parked cars. We parked and got out of the white Porsche with the red and blue racing strip that Mom had just bought from Dick Clark. Another person everyone but me seemed to know. All the moms at school had been startled when Mom traded in the brown station wagon for a slightly used Porsche that she had bought from a glorified game show host. But Mom figured we were celebrities now too, so we needed a ride that reflected our shift in status.

A white van idled nearby. We climbed inside and it took us up a path carved into the side of the hill. We drove for about five minutes before we saw a small wooden house on the left with a barn and a corral next to it. With its asymmetrical roof, the house looked more like a big outhouse than a place where people would live. The barn dwarfed the house, but it still looked as if it could be blown down by a good strong wind.

We kept driving past the buildings, and after another five minutes we arrived at a ghost town. An old mill with a big spinning water-wheel was attached to a small bridge that led to the town. All the buildings there were clustered in a circle as if they were huddling together for warmth. At the far end of the circle sat a church or a schoolhouse, I couldn't tell which. To the right was a long red hotel, and across the circle from that was a big white storefront. There wasn't a human being in sight.

The van passed through the town and rolled up another small hill, where we found a team of honey wagons and prop trucks. That's where all the people were hiding. The driver let us out and Mom took my hand, gripping it so hard I thought the bones might crack.

The AD jumped out in front of us. The walkie-talkie peeked out of the pocket of his already dusty jeans as he ran his right hand through his shaggy brown hair. He pointed to a honey wagon on the left. "Missy's dressing room is right up there. She can get something to eat, and get dressed and report to makeup. She needs to be on the set by eight. We're doing the wagon roll scene first."

Everything was shot out of sequence. So in today's shot, Mom had explained, I would be watching my still-alive pretend parents meet their disastrous fate.

I looked around at all the people in jeans holding coffee cups or smoking, as we climbed the metal stairs to the dressing room marked MISSY FRANCIS." Inside, the same purple dress and limp blue bonnet that I'd worn on the set in Sonora were waiting for me. Even worse, the sackcloth petticoat had made the trip too, along with the awful boots. Just looking at them made me cringe. The blisters on my ankles had yet to heal.

Mom helped me put on the getup, including the rubber band socks. Then we wandered over to the craft services truck and hopped on the long line for food.

"Let the little girl cut to the front," a rough-looking guy on the crew said. He winked at me as he sipped his coffee. I stepped up to the window where the short-order cook listened to our hopes and dreams about breakfast. The crackle of frying bacon made my stomach growl.

"She'll have an egg and bacon burrito. Scramble the egg and add a little bit of American cheese. I will just have a hard-boiled egg." Once again, Mom had joined the latest diet craze, which usually lasted a few weeks. She'd shed weight, and was simultaneously thrilled and viciously cranky until she went back to Baskin-Robbins chocolate fudge ice cream and traded the hunger-induced mood swings for defeated depression. The crash dieting tended to coincide with important events. Apparently, my new job qualified as one.

Always hungry at breakfast, I wolfed down my burrito in record time. I had never seen eggs and bacon wrapped together in a burrito. Genius! It seemed like a dish that had been invented so the crew could eat standing up without utensils.

"Does she go to school?" an extra's mom asked my mom while we were eating.

"Yes. And even though she works all the time, she's first in her class, bless her heart." I'd heard this speech before. She'd go on to say how I got a 99 on some standardized test and now I was in a special reading group. It seemed like a good opportunity to slip away and get seconds.

I slid down from my chair and went over to a picnic table that smelled like heaven. A huge box of doughnuts was nestled between baskets of muffins and a rainbow of fresh fruit. I swiped a glazed doughnut and tried to eat most of it before I turned back to Mom. She'd be furious that I was eating more.

I scarfed it down and then skipped back to the table in time to hear Mom delivering the wrap-up to one of her half-dozen or so talking points that she regularly used with new mothers.

"So that's when the teacher told me just how gifted Missy is. She already reads at a sixth-grade level. Her teacher actually said that her being out of school will give the other kids time to catch up! Can you imagine? I was so upset. I've got to find her another school, I guess, if the rest of the class is holding her back like that." She smiled at the extra's mom, who was nodding politely. "We're thinking about Lycee International. It's French immersion. Jodie Foster goes there, but it's just so far, I can't imagine dragging her through the traffic every day."

Well, that didn't make any sense, I thought. We sat in mountains of traffic every day when we went for interviews. But I had made the mistake of speaking up during one of Mom's stories before and learned that no one but Mom was allowed to talk. Afterward, when we'd gotten in the car, she'd pinched my arm ferociously and said, "You are never to contradict me in front of another adult ever again. Do you understand me?" The pain shooting through my arm confirmed how serious she was.

This time I stood quietly while she finished. I didn't care much about the accuracy of these stories.

"So let's go get you into hair and makeup, sweetie," Mom announced, ushering me back toward the honey wagon.

"I have to go to the bathroom," I said. We walked back up to my dressing room and I went in alone. By now I was too full, and felt like I needed to throw up. All the breakfast food I'd devoured was sitting heavily in my stomach.

I emerged from the bathroom to find Mom waiting outside at the base of the trailer steps.

"Are you okay?" she asked.

"My stomach hurts."

"That's because you stuffed yourself full of so much junk. Why did you do that?" She shook her head sadly. "I saw you eat that doughnut, by the way. You better be careful. You're getting a real tummy. Do you remember what the doctor said? You need to watch it. You are right on the verge of being fat. Do you want to fight this terrible battle your whole life like every woman in our family? We're genetically predisposed to fat bodies. We come from fat stock. Do you want to follow in those footsteps? Look at your sister. She's packed on so much weight. I think it's too late for her."

I was taken aback by Mom's criticism of Tiffany. My sister looked fine to me. After all, she was the pretty one. Her hair was lighter and longer than mine, and Mom let her have bangs, which made her look grown-up. We had the same big round eyes, but Tiffany didn't smile as much as I did, which made her look more soulful.

As for Mom, I thought she was the most beautiful woman in the world. Her dark hair set off her light eyes, and she had a big smile that showed off her perfect teeth. Although she was always on a diet, she never seemed fat to me.

Now I looked down at my protruding belly and tried to suck it in. It didn't work. I wished I had a sweater to hide the bulge.

The AD rushed over and saved me. "We need Missy in hair and makeup like ten minutes ago."

When I got to the set, Michael stood on a grassy landing. He gestured with his arms, explaining to the cinematographer where the action would lead.

"So Cassandra, James, Albert stand here." He pointed to wooden crosses lying on the ground as marks. "I'm here. . . . Then when the wagon picks up speed, I'll go to my second mark here. Then we'll push close on the kids as the wagon rolls off the hill and cracks up into a million pieces. We can do the tight on James and Cassandra as a cutaway if they don't get to the emotion and it doesn't work as one shot."

The AD turned to Mom. "Is she ready?"

"Yes."

She kneeled down next to me and my fat belly. "You need to watch the wagon fall off the side of the hill and go from scared to really crying, imagining that your parents are inside it. Can you do that? This is really critical. This is the scene that got you this part. You need to really look scared and then produce real tears while you're watching. You can do it, sweetie."

She paused for a second.

"You absolutely have to do it now."

No pressure.

It was true, I had produced real tears on demand at the audition. We'd learned I was the only eight-year-old who had done it right that day. Now they wanted to see if I could deliver again. I got the feeling that they'd give me a car if I succeeded.

What Mom didn't know was that crying on demand wasn't a new trick for me. I'd discovered that talent years earlier when Tiffany and I were playing Atari upstairs at home. We each had a hard black plastic joystick that we used to play Pong. We sat in front of the TV, glued to the game, which had evolved into a death match.

Tiffany scored on me one last time and celebrated with a whoop. In a fit of rage, I raised the joystick high over my head and decided I would use the square base to crush her skull.

I brought the joystick down as hard as I could, and then both of us staggered back in surprise. Neither of us could believe I'd done it. She began to wail in pain, and within seconds, her screams brought the pounding footsteps of Mom rushing to see who had been maimed.

I knew I was dead. I had to think fast.

So I burst into tears, just like Tiffany.

I gambled that when Mom got there, she wouldn't be able to tell what had happened if we were both hysterical. Throwing a distraction into the mix was my only shot at avoiding an instant death sentence.

Mom walked in and saw us both screaming and crying and couldn't make sense of what had happened, much as I had bet.

So she picked up Tiffany by the arm and smacked her as hard as she could on her bottom and dragged her into her room, slamming the door with nearly as much force as I'd used in hitting Tiffany over the head with the joystick. Poor girl.

She then returned and repeated the process on me.

So I didn't escape punishment, and poor Tiffany got hit twice. But, more importantly, I learned I could produce tears on demand.

In acting, it didn't count if you scrunched up your face and made crying noises but no water actually came out of your eyes. Directors hated that. They could always stop the cameras and dribble Visine down your cheeks, but that didn't win you any points.

Now I stood on my mark waiting to watch my imaginary parents get crushed to death. The pressure was on, and I knew it. So I thought about what it would be like to watch my real parents speed down the hill and I started to freak myself out. Then I pictured my cat in the wagon with them, and I was on the verge of a breakdown before they even got rolling.

Michael yelled, "Action!"

An AD motioned with his arms behind the camera to show us the imaginary wagon picking up speed. We looked scared. Then he mimed diving as if the wagon were diving off the side of the hill. For most kids, a mime routine would not provide sufficient motivation to show fear and panic, and shed real tears, but we were pros.

Jason yelled, "Oh, no!" and I let loose. Tears flooded my cheeks. I wailed and cried, as if I'd just been cracked over the head with a joystick.

"Cut and print!"

From then on Michael called me the One Take Kid.

CHAPTER SIX

Butterflies fluttered in my stomach at the thought of walking back into the classroom. We had shot the two episodes of *Little House* that introduced Jason and me to the show and had gone on hiatus for the season. I returned to second grade, having missed about a month of school. Usually I enjoyed a bounce in popularity when I returned from an acting job because of the novelty of being an actress, but I never knew for sure what I'd encounter. My friends could all have new friends. Luckily, my first week back at school flew by without incident, friendships still intact.

Then, as my premiere on the show approached, Mom buzzed around like a six-year-old who had downed a bag of sugar. Much to my horror, she told every person we encountered to watch me on the show. She was a one-woman *TV Guide*. Even at the cleaners: "Make sure you watch Missy tonight at eight PM! She's the new star of *Little House on the Prairie*!" And also at the pharmacy: "She's in every scene! She cries. I don't want to spoil the end, but Michael Landon adopts her!"

I shrank inside the collar of my polo shirt. Her promotional efforts were mortifying.

Mom got her hair and nails done and invited the extended family over to watch, which included her parents, her sister, Marilyn, who was her closest friend, and her other, more bizarre sister, Gloria, whom we saw much less often because she tended to clash with Mom at every turn. Gloria was even louder and more opinionated than the rest of Mom's family, which was really saying a lot. Plus, I never knew what color her hair was going to be when she walked in. This time, she didn't fail to surprise me, showing up with hair the exact color and style of Ronald McDonald's.

The whole family crowded into the living room. Tiffany and I squeezed ourselves into one armchair, pushing each other for space. Mom was on the phone gathering viewers until the minute the show started. I could have been landing a space shuttle on Mars.

The opening credits began to roll. The whole room cheered when my name appeared on the television screen. They screamed again the first time I was on camera.

"There she is! What a doll," Grandma clucked.

In the second scene, Jason and I were sitting at a dining table with Michael and our about-to-be-dead TV parents, all having breakfast.

"Look at her wolfing down the food. Didn't they feed you? No wonder you can't fit through the front door anymore," Tiffany said with a laugh. I gave her a sharp elbow to the ribs.

When we got to the scene where the wagon rolls down the hill, tears welled up in Marilyn's eyes as she watched me wail. Slightly taller than Mom, Marilyn always quipped about being the naturally blonde sister. Her red T-shirt said, "Blondes have more fun," in cursive writing, but it didn't seem to be the case. She was a quieter, more rigid and reserved version of Mom. She always insisted we call her "Auntie M." I didn't understand the reference.

Tiffany turned toward me and said in a low voice, "You look like a frog when you cry. Why didn't anyone stop you from making that face?"

I looked at the image of myself on the screen and realized she was right. I hopped down from the chair and left the room. No one noticed.

I wandered into the kitchen and opened the fridge. It was empty as usual, except for a few leftovers and some expired milk. Mom liked to go to the grocery store once a month at best, and buy more than we could possibly eat before it all went bad. Then we'd scrape and scrounge and stop for takeout until she broke down and went food shopping again. Anytime I went to a food store I tried to stock up on emergency peanut butter and English muffins. They were like gold by week three.

Tiffany followed me into the kitchen and took a seat at the counter near the fridge. I didn't look at her.

"I'm sorry," she said. "You did a good job. It's just that you look funny when you cry. And you did eat a lot in that scene."

"No danger of that now," I said with my head still in the fridge.

"I know." She sat down at the kitchen table. "When you and Mom were in Sonora, dad and I made hamburgers every night or went out to dinner. It was pretty cool. Or I ate at Tiffany's house."

Tiffany's best friend in her fifth-grade class was named Tiffany Peacock. She was petite and Hawaiian, with long dark hair and dark eyes and tan skin year-round. Mom said she had a promising future as a topless dancer, between her name and her early run at puberty.

It occurred to me then that I had no idea how my sister got to and from school when I was working. Mom was with me from dawn until after dark when we limped home from the set exhausted.

"What did you do after school while I was working?" I asked her. She was wearing Op short-shorts like the ones the other Tiffany liked to wear with white tank tops. I wondered when she got them.

Her right hand brushed her long, dark hair behind her shoulder and she shrugged. "I hung out at Tiffany's house until Dad picked me up. Or Auntie M came and got me."

"It's like you don't have a mom when I'm working," I said sadly.

"Exactly." She smiled.

I didn't really buy it. "I wish you could come with us."

"Nah." She slid off her chair and left the kitchen.

The show ended and Mom got back on the phone in the kitchen so she could be congratulated by everyone she knew, while Dad tucked me into my bed. He sat down next to me and paused, as if he were rehearsing his words in his head.

"I want you to remember something."

"What?"

"It's a wonderful thing you are doing. Very special. And I'm so proud of you. Millions of people watched tonight. You did a great job. You should be very proud."

I smiled in the darkness of my bedroom.

"But you don't have to do it if you don't want to."

"Why wouldn't I want to?" I asked.

"You may decide you don't feel like working and just want to go to school. That's okay too," he said pointedly.

"Why can't I do both? I went back to school after we did the show this time. Mom says I'm going back to work after the summer. Why can't I do both?"

Dad patted my arm. "You can do both. But school is the most important thing. Someday you will go to college. So you can't forget about doing your schoolwork. I know you won't."

"Of course I won't," I said.

"Listen to me." He paused again to make sure I stayed silent. "You can act when you grow up, but you also might want to do something else."

"I'm going to be the first lady president."

"Yes, you can be the first lady president. Or whatever you want. Whatever makes you happy. That's what is so great about our country. It's a free society with a free market."

"What's a free market?" I asked.

"It's the reason why President Reagan stands up to the Soviets. So everyone in America can go to college and work hard and become whatever they want to be. You can work hard and move up in the world. Just because someone is born into a poor family, there's no reason they can't end up wealthy. It's not the same in the Soviet Union. The people there don't have the freedom to become anything they want if they work hard enough."

I tried to imagine what he meant.

"My parents were very poor, okay? My shoes had holes in them."

Here we go with the shoes, I thought.

"My dad bought one new car in his whole life. One. A four-hundred-dollar Chevy. He loved it. But my point is, we lived on the South Side of Chicago and we didn't have a lot of stuff, like our family has now. My brother and I barely had any toys." He paused for effect.

"But my parents worked hard and told me that I could go to college and have a much better life, and they were right. I went to college and became an engineer and now I own my own business. It's a small business, but I'm my own boss. And we own our own home and have cars and a nice life. I want you to know that you will go to college, no matter what. And then you can choose to stay in showbiz, or you can choose to be a doctor, or the first lady president. Or an astronaut."

"First lady president," I repeated.

He laughed. "Someday I will tell you about Adam Smith and *The Wealth of Nations*."

"Is that a book? Can you read it to me now?"

"No. It's too late." I could hear the smile in his voice. "But I will tell you now that it's about the Invisible Hand."

"Why is the hand invisible?" I was partly curious, partly stalling.

"Because you don't need to see it to know it's working," he said wistfully.

"How do you know it's there?"

"Because there's evidence everywhere you look. It's another way of saying market forces work when they are left alone. And it makes sense. It's logical. That's enough for tonight. Time to close your eyes, and think of something nice but sort of boring, like baseball. And you'll fall asleep."

He kissed my forehead gently, and I pictured this giant Invisible Hand throwing a baseball. I was watching the whole thing, as First Lady President.

By the time the next season of *Little House on the Prairie* began airing, my life had changed in a very specific way. Everywhere I went, people recognized me from the show.

I could feel the attention unfolding. A stranger would look in my direction, the way a person's eyes naturally move over a face that passes in front of him. Then a flicker of recognition. The eyes dart back. They search my face, trying to place me. Then the shock of full recognition. A smile. Followed by a quick turn to the person next to them. A loud whisper, the other person looking confused. Their eyes find my face. The same process, the same jolt.

At first, I enjoyed the novelty of being recognized by strangers. Then the attention made me terribly self-conscious. I started to hide my face or turn away when a stranger started to recognize me. If they got up the nerve to ask, "Are you Cassandra from *Little House on the Prairie?*" I liked to say no. But I felt guilty when I did this because I knew I was being rude. I didn't want to be mean or lie, but all the attention was just too much even though I had recently turned nine years old. I was still a kid, and it was an invasion.

In general, I could handle attention, but the kind that could be turned on and off like a light. This was a pulsating strobe I had no power to dim.

When the filming of *Little House* resumed in the fall, one of the more pleasant changes on the set was the addition of the character Nancy. Her real name was Allison Balson. The writers were reincarnating the original show by positioning me as the New Laura and giving me a New Nellie, or archenemy. Naturally the script called for Allison and me to loathe each other on sight, and just like the first pair of girls on the show, we ended up rolling in the mud, trying to scratch each other's eyes out.

Allison had stunning pale blonde ringlets trimmed with bows and gorgeous dresses that I coveted. The wardrobe team decorated her each day like an exquisite, expensive doll. But playing the most elaborately bedecked character meant Allison got tortured in hair and makeup for two long hours every day, and she schlepped the heaviest ruffled petticoat around under her ornate dresses to keep them fluffed, even in the hundred-degree heat of the San Fernando Valley.

I also found a friend in Rachel, one of the twins who played

Carrie, my adopted sister. Rachel was easygoing and relaxed, always happy to hang out on one of the unlit sets that wasn't being used, or court trouble around the property truck. I'd latch on to her and her twin sister. The twins' professional names were Lindsay and Sidney. From the back, we looked like triplets, with our long brown braids and prairie dresses. We'd steal into the fake Mercantile Exchange and snag candy from the set. Then we'd bite into the candy only to find out it had been aging on the set since the show started eight years earlier. But in a few days, we'd go back for more, hoping some set designer had restocked the shelves, though they never did.

Much to my dismay, Jason wanted to hang out with the older kids. But no matter what, a pack of kids, regulars or extras, roamed around the set when we weren't in the schoolroom logging hours with our books. Still every grip, assistant director, and makeup artist looked out for the kids and doted on us.

Michael expected us to work like adults, but he also engineered horseplay in between shots. On rare occasion, he even wasted film. One blazing hot day in the Valley, I said my line, and when he turned to answer, he opened his mouth and a live bullfrog jumped out. This was no prop or product of Hollywood special effects. It was a filthy toad he'd found on the ground in between takes. I screamed in terror, no doubt only slightly less afraid than the poor frog who thought he'd turned into Michael's lunch.

Another time Michael put a tarantula under his hat, then removed it and delivered his lines as if he didn't know a huge furry black spider was perched on his head, slowly climbing through his bangs. When it stepped on his forehead with its long fuzzy creepy legs, we all screamed bloody murder. He was so pleased with the effect, he never seemed to consider the potential downside of recruiting a random desert tarantula to stroll on his face.

During one of the last weeks of the season on *Little House,* Mom invited my Brownie troop to take a field trip to the set. "Every single one replied yes," she'd said smugly.

Eighteen third graders showed up with their moms. I ran to them excitedly when they arrived, but Jennifer and Marybeth stood a little stiffly as if they didn't recognize me in my costume.

"Hey, guys!" I boomed.

Christy bounded over to me, but most of the others just stood silently, their heads swiveling as they tried to take in everything from the rafters to the blinding lights to the cable-covered floors.

"This . . . is where they shoot the interior shots," Mom explained authoritatively as she walked the group around the set, displaying impressive leadership skills, especially for someone who had flatly refused to ever host a Brownie troop meeting at our house.

We'd been shooting a winter episode, and the set designers had stapled white foam sheets to all the wooden buildings and window frames to make it look like snow. The magic of the set, layered on top of the general wizardry of creating a television show, enchanted Brownie Troop 407.

The *Little House on the Prairie* set was without question a magical place to work. Which was why the end of the run crushed Mom's spirit. She went from being on top of the world, bragging loudly wherever she went, to housebound and brooding.

The mini-Laura and mini-Nellie gambit had worked for a time to boost ratings and reignite the American heartland's interest in a show that was getting long in the tooth, but then Michael decided the whole family had to go. The nineteenth-century well had finally run dry. His creative energies were turning to a new show, *Highway to Heaven,* in which he would play the role of an angel, no matter how improbable this might seem to television viewers who had read about his serial womanizing in the *National Enquirer*.

In the spring of 1982, I was sad to leave my new friends, but happy enough to go back to school and have more time to ride my horse. Besides, every job I had ever had had come to an end. Why would this one be any different? But Mom reacted as if someone close to her had died. After receiving the phone call informing us that the show was over, she didn't answer the phone for days. She didn't want to talk to anyone, including me.

"Why's Mom so sad?" I asked Dad while we were both sitting on the couch in the living room. "Is she mad at me?"

"No, honey," he said soothingly, stroking my hair. "She's just really disappointed you guys aren't working on *Little House* together any longer."

"But I'll get something else," I said. "Is she going to stay in her room until I get something else?"

"I don't know," he replied. "It's possible."

"How will I get home from school?" I asked.

"Don't worry, we'll figure it out," he offered.

"How will I go on auditions after school?" I asked.

"Oh, that. Yeah, she'll leave her room for that."

Dad always said those years on the Prairie were the happiest of Mom's life.

CHAPTER SEVEN

I waited at the curb in front of the school for Mom to drive up in her little white Porsche. The benches were empty, except for a couple of lingering strays like myself. I gamed how long I should wait before I went into the front office and asked them to call Mom and confirm that she'd forgotten me.

The more time that went by, the heavier my chest felt. I wondered if she had decided not to come get me, or if I was just no longer a priority.

I could see Mrs. Nan peering out from the office, watching the second-to-last straggler climb into a car, leaving only me. My gut told me to hide. Every moment that passed increased the likelihood that Mrs. Nan would have to take action. I hoped she wouldn't come out and bear witness to my embarrassment at being the sole forgotten child. I checked the Peanuts watch I had received a few months back for my tenth birthday; it was now almost forty minutes past pickup time.

Life had slowed to a mundane pace over the past year. We still rushed on auditions, but I didn't have a regular gig any longer.

I felt more comfortable, at least when I wasn't abandoned at school. But the less demanding schedule also meant Mom had less direction. On the days when she picked me up from school in the same housedress she'd been wearing when I walked out the door that morning, I knew I was alone.

She had gained a fair amount of weight, though I had no idea how much. Her weight problem seemed to flourish in this climate of malaise. She'd talk about the latest Hollywood diet, then I'd find empty snack bags littering her room.

Finally, her Porsche peeled into the parking lot, taking the turn to the pickup area with a little too much speed. I could see her glance at the vacant benches that seemed to condemn her tardiness, but she dismissed them without changing expression.

"Hey," she said through the open window. I silently picked up my lunchbox and my backpack and tried to look as lonely and exhausted as I felt. She usually offered an excuse as to why I'd been forced to wonder if I were an orphan. Today, she didn't bother.

I yanked the door open and saw she had changed into jeans and a blouse. She had half a face of makeup, foundation but no eye makeup, and her hair looked slept on, either from last night, or maybe that afternoon. Either way, it didn't seem as if she'd been busy enough since I'd left for school with Dad seven hours earlier to justify her forgetting to pick me up. But who was I to judge?

"I brought your clothes. You want to go riding? It's Thursday we can make the five o'clock lesson."

"Did you pick up Tiffany?" I asked. She shot me an angry look as if she hadn't failed to pick up Tiffany's carpool two days earlier. That day she'd stranded four kids.

"She's changing at home. I told her we'd come back around and pick her up."

* * *

When Tiffany came out of the house, she was wearing her beige riding britches and a gray concert T-shirt. Now fourteen, she cultivated a rocker style that stood in sharp contrast to the riding pants and boots. She looked like a British headbanger out for a quick fox hunt. Her shoulder-length brown hair was pulled back in a ponytail to combat the heat. The temperature had risen into the eighties, which was unusual for so late into the fall, and it would feel even hotter at the barn.

I climbed through the center console of the car into the tiny backseat to let Tiffany ride up front. She opened the front door and sat down and then immediately adjusted the radio to her favorite station, which blasted Billy Idol's "Rebel Yell."

"Turn that down. Or I will sing," Mom threatened.

Mom had grabbed a pair of britches for me. I slid off my shorts in the backseat and pulled on the riding pants, contorting my body to get enough leverage to yank on the stretchy leggings that fit like a second skin. Mom had also brought a few needlepoint belts that I loved to match to my polo shirts and ribbons. I chose the pink belt to match my pink and green polo and slid it through the belt loops of my britches.

I counted the signs on the 118 Freeway as we snaked around the belly of the San Fernando Valley, approaching Hidden Valley from the back, rather than confronting the traffic directly via the 101. Tiffany and I had started riding at Foxfield about a year earlier and we'd timed every possible approach to find the quickest one. We arrived in a little more than thirty minutes, and from this approach, the rows of stables and adjoining hunt fields looked like a more arid version of the English countryside tucked into the outskirts of Westlake Village.

Mom had taken us out there to start riding about the time *Little House* went off the air, highlighting one of the biggest differences between us and other kids in the industry. Tiffany and I didn't support our family financially. The vast majority of kids in the business had parents who had also tried, with varying degrees of success, to make a living as actors. Those parents understood show business well and doubled as expert acting coaches for their children. That certainly gave those kids a huge advantage over us. But those families lived on the paycheck of whoever was working. Sometimes, that was no one. When a job ran out, it was time to cut back in a big way. Most families went from feast to famine almost overnight, never having saved or made enough for the inevitable rainy day.

Even when times were good, a lot of these kids did without the basics, like an education. Their parents "homeschooled" them, which was usually a euphemism for blowing off education altogether so the kids would be available for any bit of work, or an audition. I was amazed by how many smart young actors I saw in set schoolrooms who couldn't sound out a three-syllable word. I'd met a fifth grader who'd never heard of long division but went on to earn an Academy Award nomination. One of the girls on *Little House* wasn't allowed to leave the classroom until she could spell *prairie*. She had to have lunch brought in. It was an unusual life, and one that I had only one foot in, I realized, by comparison.

Mom, on the other hand, took a two-pronged approach to the lull in my work life. She'd either take to her bed in a fit of depression or throw us headlong into a hobby. Right now, she was doing a bit of both.

In the meantime, Tiffany had checked out of most of the activities we used to do together, except riding, which she passionately loved. She had graduated to ninth grade, where she exercised her independence and grappled with the awkwardness that came with being a teenager. I had grown almost as tall as her, but she had fully developed, which only added to her shyness. Her posture had changed. She seemed to have rolled inward, physically and mentally, withdrawing from our family.

Tiffany rarely went on auditions anymore. It had been ages since she'd really worked. I hadn't considered that there'd come a time when she wouldn't act at all, and I was alarmed to see show business evaporating from her life, which I hadn't thought possible for either of us. Riding felt like the last thing we shared.

When we got to Foxfield, Tiffany and I took off for Pony Island to get our horses. Pony Island was a series of barns on the other side of a ravine. To get there we walked down a path to the water and jumped from rock to rock. When it rained heavily, the ravine turned into a roaring river that surrounded the barns, hence the name. We liked to imagine that someday we'd get stranded there indefinitely with our horses, unable to cross back to the mainland.

Mom had bought me a huge chestnut mare named Alondra with a stunning flaxen mane and tail. She had also bought a gorgeous Palomino mare for Tiffany a few years earlier, but Alondra was the first horse that was really all mine. She had tall white socks and big white stripe down the center of her face. Alondra was both spirited and spectacular, and turned out to be way too much horse for me, but I'd loved her from the moment I laid eyes on her at a show in Santa Barbara. She would gallop and stretch out her neck while shaking her head to loosen my grip on the reins, and though it sometimes felt as if she were out of control, I never got too scared because I knew deep down she loved me too and wouldn't hurt me. Unlike most horses, she came when I called her. We had an understanding.

Tiffany grabbed the lanky bay she'd been riding lately when she wasn't working out Duchess. She rode stronger and jumped more bravely than I did, but I rode in a younger age group with less competition, so I'd won more ribbons by now. Tiffany didn't seem to care. She'd gravitated to a faster, more rebellious crowd at Chaminade Prep, the Catholic high school she attended, and suddenly wanted to do things with friends on Friday and Saturday nights rather than have dinner at home or ride horses with me. Recently Mom had forced her to take me along on one such weekend outing. That's when I realized there was more going on than I'd imagined.

Mom had dropped us off at Magic Mountain with Tiffany's new friend Dina. Tiffany said that Dina, who had a pretty face, wheat-blond hair, and an hourglass shape, rated among the popular kids at their school. I still went to elementary school and didn't really get what that meant, but I could tell it was something valuable that Tiffany wanted. We ducked into the bathroom inside the park gates to fix our hair and figure out what we wanted to carry around the park with us and what we wanted to shove in a locker.

"So what's it like to be on TV? I used to always watch *Little House*," Dina gushed. Unlike most girls stuck with their friend's little sisters, she doted on me and I immediately felt lucky to be there. Maybe I could just slide into Tiffany's older life and mooch off her fun. I'd done it before.

"Oh, I don't know. It's fun," I responded.

Meanwhile Tiffany seemed to be inspecting the bathroom. She peered under the door of each stall then wandered back to where Dina and I were standing near the sinks.

"What did you bring?" Tiffany asked, looking in Dina's backpack. Dina slid the pack off her shoulder and pulled out a wild berry Bartles & Jaymes wine cooler. I hadn't seen one before, and I didn't realize at first that it contained alcohol.

"Is she going to tell on us?" Dina asked, pointing to me.

"Nah, she's fine. Right?" Tiffany looked at me hard.

Of course I wasn't going to say anything to Mom or Dad.

They were the other team. But I couldn't really figure out why the girls wanted to drink at Magic Mountain. Just being here was exciting—going on the rides and pigging out on the food that Mom wouldn't let us have if she were there.

We crowded into a handicapped stall so no one could walk in and see what we were doing. I worried some park worker would discover us there and hustle us off to the police, who would immediately call our parents. Then Mom would show up and beat us, probably to death.

Leaning against the green metal stall door, Tiffany took a big swig from the bottle and handed it to Dina, who took a few gulps and handed it back. Tiffany pounded the rest and Dina broke out the second bottle. She opened it and handed it to me.

"You want some?" Dina asked.

"She's ten." Tiffany looked dubious.

"I've let my little sister have some."

I immediately took the bottle from Dina's hand before Tiffany could stop me and took a sip. The drink was sugary sweet, with a weird medicine-like aftertaste. As soon as I brought the bottle down from my lips, Tiffany snatched it away. I stood there and waited to feel different.

I liked taking part in Tiffany and Dina's mischief. I felt older and very cool, especially for a ten-year-old. At the same time, I wanted to know when it would end and we'd go back to the park.

Tiffany tossed back the rest of the drink with an abandon that made me nervous. She looked willfully out of control. I didn't like that. As the older sister, she was supposed to be worried and in charge at all times. That was her job. I had no idea where this left me. I certainly couldn't be in charge if something terrible happened tonight.

They polished off the second wine cooler without offering me another sip, and stuffed the evidence in the sanitary napkin bin inside the stall. Then we all walked out of the bathroom into the night.

"Wow, I'm buzzed," Dina laughed.

"Me too. Totally," Tiffany said.

I wanted to feel the sensation and join their club, but I had no idea how it was supposed to feel. How can you tell if you're drunk if you've never been drunk before? I gave up trying and got in line for the Swashbuckler. Tiffany and Dina followed me on the ride and laughed too loud each time the giant ship shot up in the air and stalled, only to switch directions and freefall back to earth.

When Mom picked us up at the end of the evening, she failed to detect any evidence of our misbehavior. This shocked me. In addition to the wine coolers, Dina and Tiffany had spent the night smoking clove cigarettes, which had a sweet, sickening smell to them. We'd doused our hair with Aqua Net hair spray to mask all the different illicit odors, but I never thought the trick would work.

After our riding lesson, Tiffany and I walked our horses around the field to cool them down. I patted Alondra's muscular neck, and she snorted and tossed her head. Like a child who had spent an entire hot day in the pool, Alondra was gloriously worn out.

"Hey, so I saved you from spending the night at school today," Tiffany said.

"Yeah?"

"Mom was lying on her bed eating chips and I asked her who was driving you home. She shot to her feet like I'd lit something on fire. So classic," Tiffany said shaking her head in disdain.

"Yeah, I could tell she just completely forgot to come get me," I said, stroking Alondra's blonde mane. I hadn't fully recovered from being abandoned at school. The helplessness I'd felt while sitting alone on the bench still stung.

"Don't feel bad, I'm going to get thrown out of my carpool, she's forgotten us so many times. Maybe I could set a timer for her in the morning. She does absolutely nothing all day long. All she has to do is pick us up!" Tiffany laughed, though neither of us really thought it was funny.

"I just don't get it," Tiffany continued. "I would be bored watching TV all day. There's nothing on. Dina loves *Days of Our Lives*, but seriously, nothing happens on that show. You could miss it for two weeks and come back and they are all still in the same clothes, doing the same scene."

"It would be awful to be on that show," I agreed. "They do totally wear the same clothes for weeks. How do they keep the wardrobe clean that long? I guess they must have a dozen sets of the same outfit for emergencies or spills or whatever. And do they never get their hair cut? The continuity person must go crazy. It's like that movie I did where it was the same day for the entire shoot. *Scavenger Hunt*. I spent weeks and weeks in the same pants and T-shirt. I never wanted to see that outfit again when that movie ended."

Tiffany looked thoughtful as our horses ambled next to each other. "The cute guy from *The A-Team* was in that movie. What was his name? Dirk Benedict! Is that a real name? Either way, he was super hot. That movie kind of sucked though."

"I know. It seemed like it was going to be funny."

"I remember Mom laughing nonstop when she read the script. No one laughed in the theater though. But you were cute in it." Tiffany dropped her reins altogether and her horse's head sank almost to the dirt bridle path in front of us. "Mom is only happy when you're working," she said.

"I know."

"She says, 'We're making money, not spending money.'"

"I wonder how much money we've made. Like, all together. Both us. Our whole lives? It must be millions."

"She'll never tell us." Tiffany's voice filled with contempt.

More and more often these days I heard that tone in her voice whenever she talked about Mom.

"Do you have any idea how much we make a day? Or a week? Maybe we could add up how many days we've worked?" I wondered aloud.

"No idea. I'm not even sure Dad knows. Mom puts all the checks into our accounts at Security Pacific Bank. I wonder if the tellers would tell us if we went in?"

"Probably not. Ah, who cares." I let Alondra's head sink and dropped my feet from my stirrups, letting my calves stretch after the ride. I stretched my arms over my head, trusting Alondra not to run off while I twisted my tired back, vulnerably off balance.

Our horses lengthened their strides as we turned back toward the barn. The sun sank low behind the rolling hills and a gentle breeze blew in from the ocean on the other side of the mountains. The peace and tranquility of the night enveloped us.

"We'd better put them back in their stalls for the night. I'm sure Mom's getting antsy," Tiffany said as we reluctantly made the final turn and headed in.

When we pulled up to the house, our cocker spaniel, KC, did not come out to greet us. Usually when we pulled into the driveway, the headlights caught him hopping out of his dog bed, tucked into the protection of our front porch. He never failed to greet us.

I got out of the car and went over to the porch to see if he was there, just moving more slowly than usual. Nothing. Then I circled around the back of the house to see if he'd been accidentally locked in the backyard. He wasn't there either.

"There's a note," Tiffany said, returning from inside the house. "Dad went to go get him from the pound."

"The pound?" Mom sounded alarmed.

When Dad pulled up, KC jumped out of the passenger seat, his tail already wagging. He jogged over to us as we ran through the front door toward him. Mom stopped in the doorway.

"What happened? Why was he at the pound? Did he get lost?" she asked.

"Let's go inside," Dad said, looking over the fence into the neighbor's yard below.

KC followed us inside the house, which Mom never, ever allowed. This was a special circumstance since we'd nearly lost him. He didn't know what to do first, but rather than pee on the furniture, he wisely chose to head for the kitchen.

"Come here big guy," Dad said, pouring dog food in a dish on the kitchen floor. KC looked no worse for wear, just shocked to be in the house. He wagged enthusiastically at the attention and wolfed down the food.

"The neighbors in front called the pound about the cats," Dad explained.

We had a stray cat population gathering on the side of our house. I'd started feeding a few strays, and apparently they'd told every cat in the neighborhood, and the population exploded. They fought and made noise. Mom didn't allow pets inside the house for more than a visit, so I couldn't really separate the few cats that were ours and bring them inside to feed them. I kept putting food outside because I didn't know what else to do, and the problem ballooned.

Our neighbors left a note complaining about the infestation. Then they came by to talk to Mom. She basically told them to get lost, but the truth was, we had no idea what to do now that the problem was out of control. The cats had congregated on our property and they weren't leaving.

The neighbors threatened to call the animal pound, and frankly, we welcomed the help.

"The animal catcher decided the best way to get our attention was to take the dog," Dad explained. "He's groomed and fat and wearing a collar with his name on it. Clearly we'd miss him. They wanted to get our attention, but I guess they didn't want to actually help with the cat problem. Or they couldn't catch the cats, since most of them are wild." Dad smoked a cigarette while he told the story.

My mouth opened in shock. They'd stolen the dog to punish us. It was my fault for enabling the cat population to flourish.

Mom's face burned red with anger. "How dare they."

"Who? The pound? It was actually pretty smart," Dad said, taking another drag. "I asked them what they wanted us to do. I told them they weren't ours. They just showed up looking for food."

"And what did those assholes say?" Mom didn't swear very often and when she did, she sort of tripped on the words as if she had a hard time forming them.

"They said the neighbors said they *were* ours. And it doesn't matter what we say anyway because when the pound came by, all the cats were here looking for food." He picked up a gallon jug of wine from where he kept it under the kitchen counter and poured a glass.

"Apparently, it's not legal to have more than three cats or something," he continued. "We need to have them fixed. I said they aren't ours, and we can't catch them anyway! I'll pay to fix them, or whatever. That's not the problem. We can't *catch* them to do it. They didn't give a shit. They don't know what to do and they're the fucking *animal control*. That's their whole job! I told them to take them, and they basically ignored me. Fucking bureaucrats. They don't have a clue."

I hugged KC, feeling very lucky to get him back and frightened that I had put him in jeopardy.

"The Parkers. It's their fault. How dare they call the pound. They'll pay," Mom warned ominously. She grabbed her purse and her keys and walked out the front door without saying another word.

We watched her headlights pull out silently, all wondering the same thing.

"What's she going to do?" Tiffany finally asked.

"I don't know," Dad confessed.

"I saw her take a hammer and hit someone's car in the parking lot outside the mall last week," I said.

"What?" Their heads swiveled toward me and Dad looked shocked. Finally. He never seemed surprised when I told him about the scrapes Mom got into.

"Some guy beat her to a spot, and when she pulled up and yelled at him, he just cursed at her and went inside the mall. So she got a hammer out of the trunk and smashed it into his door, making a huge dent," I said. I let the shock sink in.

"I was so scared someone was going to come and arrest us," I added, reliving the incident.

"She had a hammer in the trunk?" Dad asked, as if that were the most shocking part.

"Yeah, she said she put it there for that reason. Because of the last fight she got into in a parking lot."

Dad shook his head and then started laughing at the absurdity of the story. Then Tiffany and I started laughing too. Who ever heard of a suburban mom carrying around a hammer to punish her competitors in the parking lot? You had to laugh.

A few hours later, I heard Mom pull back into the garage and come inside the house. She went directly upstairs into her room.

Dad huddled in front of the television downstairs in the den, where he spent almost every night, watching television until way after we all fell asleep.

I got out of bed and stole into Tiffany's room, which was right next to mine. "What happened?" I whispered. Her light was off but I knew she was still awake.

"I have no idea. I don't care. Go to bed."

I couldn't stand it. I went down the hall into Mom's room. I crept in and sat on the edge of the bed. She saw me, but didn't look directly at me or say anything. I knew something bad had happened, because she just stared at the TV and didn't meet my eyes.

When she didn't say anything for a while, I stood up preparing to leave.

Then I saw the collar in front of the TV, reflecting the light. I took a step closer to get a better look at it. I felt my mom studying my face while I tried to work out what had happened.

"It's Coco's. The Parkers' dog. I took her in my car, and I drove her out to the pound in Simi Valley. And I turned her in. A lost dog. Like KC."

I calculated what that meant in the silence that followed. She had the collar, so the pound had no idea whose dog it was.

"But they don't know who to call to rescue Coco," I said, looking at the collar.

"That's right." There was an edge to her voice I rarely heard, but I knew enough to get away as fast as I could when I heard it.

Without the collar, the pound had no idea who the dog belonged to, no name, no one to call. And Simi Valley was miles away, much farther than a dog could go on foot. The Parkers would never think to look all the way out there. They'd assume Coco got lost on her own, and they'd drive through the neighborhood or go to the dog pounds nearby.

They'd never find her, and the pound would eventually kill her with the other strays that weren't lucky enough to find a home.

Coco was a sweet dog, but old and kind of matted. She loved a nice pat on the head or one of KC's dog treats. She was friendly but reserved now that she had aged. She was not the kind of dog that would ever get adopted by a family looking to rescue a pet. She would never speak up and save her own life.

Mom had effectively murdered our neighbors' dog as revenge.

I got in bed and cried into my pillow. I wanted to tell the neighbors, leave them a note, so they could save Coco's life. But I was so scared of what Mom would do to me. The Parkers would confront her or report her, and she'd know who had told on her. Who knew what she'd do to me then?

Coco was going to die. And, one way or another, the situation was completely my fault. I'd created the problem by feeding the cats, and now I was too frightened for myself to stop the consequences. I wanted to help Coco—how could I live with myself if I didn't? But if I saved that poor helpless dog, and Mom found out I'd betrayed her, as she inevitably would, who would save me?

No one. I couldn't risk it. Poor Coco.

CHAPTER EIGHT

I went into Tiffany's room and sort of wandered around, looking at her things. She'd plastered her walls with posters of her favorite bands like a typical fifteen year old. Billy Idol made three appearances around the room, clenching his fist and snarling his lip on the cover of his trademark album *Rebel Yell*. He was by far her favorite. But other superstars of 1984 also made the cut: U2, Madonna, Adam Ant, the Psychedelic Furs, and a few throwbacks like the Sex Pistols. She'd recently developed a strong taste for punk mainly because the wild look and frenzied beats made Mom nervous.

She'd long ago traded in her youthful pink, green, and white bed linens for solid royal blue sheets and blankets that made the room more mature and less color coordinated. Various necklaces and bracelets spilled out across the top of her wooden dresser, interlaced with hoop earrings and chunky, gothic rings. She'd started wearing crosses, which I thought was odd, since she reviled Catholic school. She'd always had a problem with religion, but much more so now that it was a mandatory part of her day. I found organized religion comforting at almost twelve, but she wouldn't give it a chance. Wearing a cross like Madonna was her way of mocking Christ and the flock of sheep who followed him.

Tiffany walked in behind me. "What are you doing?" she asked, grabbing from my hand the tape that I had picked up from her desk.

"I'm getting ready to go riding. Want to come?" I asked.

"No, I have plans."

"Where are you going?" I asked.

"I'm going to hang out with Chris and some friends, maybe Laura. We'll probably go to Magic Mountain," she said checking her makeup in the mirror over her dresser.

Tiffany and her best friend, Laura, were currently dating twins, Chris and John, cute bleached-blonde boys from the public school in our neighborhood. Conveniently enough, the brothers looked a little like Billy Idol. Or David Bowie. The two singers seemed to be the same, as far as I could tell.

Tiffany and Laura were in tenth grade now and though neither of them had a driver's license yet, many of their friends did, which opened up a whole new world of freedom to them. Mom made anyone who came to give Tiffany a ride come in the house to say hello. She'd grill them on their plans and give everyone a once-over, but I wasn't convinced of how effective that was. I knew from experience anything could happen once we got out the door and down the street.

Tiffany had on about six pounds of navy blue eyeliner and pearly pink lip gloss, both of which happened to be in high pop/rock fashion. She was channeling Madonna, circa *Like a Virgin*. She'd cut her hair to shoulder-length and had streaked it blonde to complete the transformation. She teased her bangs to the sky, and we both covered our wrists with rows and rows of intertwined black rubber bracelets we'd bought at the mall.

She had just had her ears double pierced, and now she put enormous hoops in every hole in preparation for a big night. Her look ventured closer and closer to the edge of full rebellion, but her face looked so pretty in the midst of it, Mom wrote it off as more fashion than a statement.

"Ouch," Tiffany said after she put in the last hoop.

I thought she was talking about her ears, but when she stopped primping she wiped a few drops of blood from her forearm. I looked at the cut on her arm. It was a perfect lowercase *t*. She dried it with a tissue and left the room before I could ask why in the world she had cut herself.

Tiffany and Mom's bickering had become an almost constant din that kept the atmosphere around the house tense. Tiffany's attitude exacerbated Mom's dark moods and each one's negative energy fueled the other's. Tiffany would make an unnecessary, snide remark to Mom, and the back-and-forth would escalate until Mom was confiscating her favorite jeans, taking away her phone, or just hitting her with the closest object, like a hanger or a belt.

Many times I would try to defuse the situation before it boiled over, interrupting the action and distracting Mom with a positive bit of information, like a high test score, or a bit a new information about the audition I'd just been on. But Tiffany wouldn't always take the opportunity to retreat. There was only so much I could do when they were determined to battle. I could take refuge in a forgotten corner of the house, but when they were done, Mom would be so agitated, she'd turn her sights on me.

Just when I was sure one of them might kill the other, I went back to work and the clouds parted. I got cast in an ABC Movie of the Week that my agent described as "groundbreaking."

When we went on the audition, Mom kept me in the car for a chat before we went inside to get the script. I thought she was gearing up for a pep talk, which by this point, I didn't need.

"This is a kind of weird topic. You know how TV tries to be more and more outrageous to grab viewers and shock people? Well this is about incest. Do you know what that is?"

I shook my head. Mom looked very uncomfortable. She had the pained expression she got when anyone talked about sex, so I had some idea, but I hadn't heard that particular word.

"It's when a parent has sex with their child." We both recoiled in disgust.

"Yuck."

"Exactly," she said. "But the truth is, it happens. And no one talks about it. So these producers want to talk about it, hoping that maybe it will inspire kids who are victims to speak up against their parents, and get help. The kids I guess feel helpless and powerless because they are being hurt by a parent, who after all, is supposed to be protecting and loving them. Do you understand?"

"So who . . ." I asked slowly.

"Not you," she jumped in. "It doesn't happen to your character. It happens to your older sister. The parents are already cast. The dad is Ted Danson, from *Cheers*. The mom is a really famous actress, very serious, not sure if you have heard of her, Glenn Close. What would you have seen that she's been in? I'm not sure I would let you see anything she's been in. She does a lot of adult dramas."

I shook my head. I didn't know her.

"They are really solid, well-known actors, so as your agent said, you know the producers will treat this tactfully with class, nothing salacious. They are really trying to help kids. And I'm sure the shock value won't be bad for ratings. Once you say incest, you don't have to go much further to shock people. There's no nudity or anything; you don't see anything happen."

I was on board if Mom was, so I went in and read my lines. The key to bagging this job, once again, was crying on command. I still had that skill down cold.

I got the job, which was good, because the competition had taken it up a notch. Now that I was in sixth grade, the kids I auditioned with were on the ball. They were trained actors, serious athletes in what used to be just a pickup game of kickball. It used to be that I knew when I had won a job, and I'd come out and brag to Mom that I'd gotten it before my agent even called with the news.

Now the victories were a little fewer and little farther between, and my swagger had lost a bit of its bounce. This victory came at a time when we all needed a lift.

When it was time for the show to air, I felt slightly embarrassed about the topic. The newspapers and magazine shows did features about the show breaking new ground and talking about a taboo subject. They inevitably featured a real-life victim who before then had felt too ashamed to speak up. I wanted to be proud to help, but I didn't feel like I'd done anything special, beyond showing up and doing my job like a good professional actor. I was always proud of that.

The show was called *Something About Amelia*, named for the victim in the story. Roxana Zal played Amelia and won a well-deserved Emmy. Mom said Ted Danson had deliberately played the creepy part of the dad to break out of his image as a sexy, lovable guy on *Cheers*. And by all accounts, he did just that. He was funny and goofy on the set, so I wasn't sure how he was going to sell creepy, but the topic did the work for him. Glenn Close played our mother, which gave the movie some real dramatic heft.

A few days after the show aired, a girl at school came and told me her dad did it to her. I just stared. I didn't know what to say. She didn't explain. Just said, the same thing happened at her house, with her dad. I'm not sure I even responded. Luckily for me, she also told our teacher.

We graduated from elementary school shortly after that and I never knew what happened to her. I had always thought she was different, and Mom, for some reason, had never let me play at her house. She'd always had a weird feeling about the girl's dad. He was an artist of some type, who did his own hair and his daughters in a '70s Farrah Fawcett style. Mom called him a creep and said sort of cryptically, "Stay away from him."

Still, when the girl told everyone, Mom said, "You can't always believe what kids say. Who knows what really happened."

I was shocked that she would cast doubt on the girl's admission. She probably just wanted to end the conversation. After all, we'd done the whole movie so kids would feel confident enough to speak out. You can't do that, and then dismiss what they have to say when they finally say it.

"Missy, wake up!"

I heard the voice but I couldn't pull myself out of deep sleep.

A moment passed, and I slipped back into unconsciousness. I thought I was dreaming when I heard the voice again.

My father put his hand on my shoulder and shook me gently.

"Missy, wake up. Your sister has been in a car accident. She's in the hospital. Mom and I are going to see her. Do you want to come? You don't have to, I guess. You can stay here. We'll lock all the doors. It's almost morning anyway, and we've got to go right now." Dad's voice was calm, but urgent.

"I want to stay. I'm too tired."

"That's fine." He was gone.

The next time I woke up, it was light out. I heard voices downstairs in the kitchen. I heard Mom, so I assumed I had dreamt the whole thing.

I walked into the kitchen and sat down at the table. I quickly understood that I hadn't been dreaming. Mom's face was tear-stained and tired. Aunt Marilyn was still crying.

"What happened?" I asked, now shocked to attention.

"Your sister was in a car accident last night. Dad came in and told you but you didn't want to wake up."

Immediately, I felt overwhelmed with guilt.

"I came home to get you. He's still there with her." Mom looked at the clock. "We have to go back to the hospital. Put on some clothes and let's go. Hurry!"

"Is she okay?" I asked, now drowning in the news.

Her voice tightened. "We don't really know. She's conscious now so that's a good sign, the doctors say. She and Chris were in the back of a pickup truck of all things, riding home from Magic Mountain. They'd all been drinking. The truck hit some gravel and flipped and they all flew out. There were three other kids in the back with them. Chris is hurt much worse than Tiffany. The doctors say he'll need a metal plate in his skull and he almost lost his eye."

At this, she broke down and started whimpering, which made Marilyn cry even harder. I sat at the table in shock. I was supposed to be heading upstairs to change, but I couldn't make my legs work.

"When they left the house, she was in the cab of the truck. She promised me she wouldn't get in the back. Frankly, I didn't

even consider the possibility. There were only three of them."
Mom choked back tears, then waved her arm at me irritably.

"Go change! Or go like that. I don't care."

I went up and changed into something that didn't match
and we raced to Holy Cross Hospital. It wasn't the closest hospital to the site of the accident, but the first paramedic on the
scene thought the impact had torn up the kids too much to just
move them. He'd found most of them unconscious and a few
moaning, and had radioed for a medevac helicopter to fly in and
rush them to a special trauma center. The chopper landed in the
desert nearby, and whisked them away.

Dad stood outside the intensive-care room where Tiffany
lay, wrapped in bandages. Blood and guts made me woozy, so I
could force myself only as far as the doorway. I could see from
a few feet away that she had her eyes closed and that there was
a huge bandage around her skull and forehead, padded with
gauze and soaked with iodine and blood. Her face was swollen
and purple. I couldn't tell if it was really her.

She was sleeping, dressed in a white hospital gown. Her
hands, also wrapped in bandages, lay motionless on top of the
blanket.

Mom came up next to Dad and he put his arm around her
as she melted into him, crying again. A doctor approached them
as they swayed together in the hallway.

"I think she's going to be okay," the doctor told them. He
was an older man with wavy graying hair and glasses. He was still
wearing his scrubs, and a silly little blue hat that rode down on
his forehead and tied behind his head. A matching mask dangled loosely from his neck.

His tone was matter-of-fact. "Most of the damage is cosmetic. She's lost a lot of skin all over her body. We had a plastic surgeon stitch up her forehead and scalp, but the impact with

the road and the gravel did a lot of damage, burning and tearing the skin. There's part of her scalp where her hair will probably not grow back."

"What about brain damage?" Dad asked in a voice that tried to stifle his emotions.

"We'll have to see. She was awake at a few points, although not that lucid. It was hard to assess her mental state because her blood alcohol level was so high. In a way, that helped. Because the kids were so drunk, they bounced on impact. They might have been worse off sober. Then again she might not have been in the back of a speeding pickup with an intoxicated driver if she were sober," the doctor said.

I couldn't absorb the words he was saying. I'd been at Magic Mountain drinking with Tiffany not too long ago. But that time all she had had was two syrupy wine coolers, and Mom had done the driving. Tiffany had graduated to a whole new level in the year or so that had passed.

After the doctor left us we crept into the room, and my parents took turns whispering soothing words to Tiffany while I hovered as close as I could to the door. We waited endlessly for her to regain consciousness in what became one of the longest days of my life. As the hours ticked by we heard reports of the other passengers in the truck from the doctors and the other parents. Chris had sustained many more injuries. He'd had his arms wrapped around her when they flew out of the truck, so he bore the brunt of the impact. He'd lost many of the brilliant white teeth Tiffany and I had admired together when he smiled.

The driver, the oldest in the group, was beat up the least. He'd been inside wearing a seat belt. Though they were all drunk, Mom blamed him. He'd driven, and he was an adult, so the police would hold him responsible as well.

Chris's twin brother, John, and Tiffany's best friend, Laura, had skipped the evening and avoided disaster.

I sat quietly in the corner. My sister, the only child I'd known my entire life, my partner really, looked like a mummy. This was without question the worst thing that had ever happened to our little family.

I flashed back to how pretty she'd looked leaving the house with Chris just the night before, and what a picture-perfect couple they made. I could see them walking down the Spanish tile path, away from the front door, so happy. Too young for a real date, just off to Magic Mountain with friends.

If this nightmare could follow so closely on the heels of that happy moment, the world was a horrible and dangerous place.

Tiffany woke up and began to heal over the next week. I brought her some of her favorite items from her room. Some books and magazines, the pillow off her bed to replace the foam one the hospital gave her. Friends from school stopped by and dropped off flowers or cookies. She didn't have much of appetite, but at least the gifts made the room seem less sterile.

As a few days passed, Mom's sorrow eventually ripened into anger. The reality of the disaster as an avoidable occurrence took hold.

"What were you guys thinking? Why did you get into the *back* of the truck?" Mom asked. We'd all avoided discussing the night of the accident. Tiffany looked so helpless, that pressing for an explanation seemed cruel. But Mom was ready to rip off the Band-Aid. She wouldn't be satisfied until she had it out with Tiffany.

"Mom, I don't know. There was no room in the cab," Tiffany said, eyes fixed on the television overhead in the hospital room.

Mom sat in a chair next to the bed, her anger having pushed her to the edge of her seat. I moved farther back in my chair in the corner, hiding behind my book, not wanting to participate or even listen to this conversation. Distracting Mom with an A on an algebra test was hopeless this time. If I could have left the room to go to the bathroom, I would have, but that would have drawn too much attention.

"But when you left the house, there were three of you. And you all got in front. Look what you've done to yourself! You're going to have scars for the rest of your life! On your face! You could have died. From your own stupidity," she railed.

"Mom, I have a headache," Tiffany said, a tear dropping onto her pillow.

Doctor Barnhard entered the room with a big smile, breaking the tension. He had been our pediatrician since birth. He'd brought a doctor's bag full of banal, reassuring words for Tiffany: she was lucky, all would be well.

After spending time with her he stepped outside the room to talk to my parents. They discussed her case in low voices, forgetting that I was just inside the room and could hear them. Tiffany had fallen back to sleep, in large part because of the pain medication they had her on, which made her pretty loopy. And of course there was her desire not to have any more conversations with Mom.

"Neurologically, she got really lucky; she's going to be okay. It seems like all the damage is cosmetic."

I shifted and peered out the door, trying not to be noticed.

Mom hugged Dad. She was once again in tears. I wasn't sure at this point how she had any left. We were all exhausted from the stress and the long hours at the hospital. Tiffany was now lucid and in one scarred piece. So much of the initial drama had faded, and the soul searching had started.

"I think you should consider finding her some good counseling," Dr. Barnhard said gently. He was slightly older than my parents, always perfectly groomed with shiny tasseled loafers and a dark tie peeking out of his doctor's coat. He had a way of giving advice that made most people take him at his word.

"Because of the trauma?" Dad asked.

"Yes, in part. She's bound to have flashbacks. It was a terrifying experience. What she'll remember of it. She was very drunk when they brought her in. I would call it pickled. So luckily, most of the worst memories won't exist. But we don't know what will crop up. Her clothes were torn off by the impact. It was a very serious accident."

Mom hiccupped a cry again.

"Beyond that though, you've said this isn't her first run-in with alcohol. She's relatively young to be acting out this aggressively."

He looked at Mom now, and must have noticed the expression in her eyes shift from weepy to defensive. I'd seen him cajole her before, and he tried it again.

"You've told me many times over the years how much you lock horns with her in particular. I've known your kids since they were both born. She's been a tough nut to crack. I think maybe this is a wake-up call, an opportunity to dig down a little deeper, and make sure you get through to her before this turns into a full-blown problem with alcohol. Or maybe drugs. Perhaps this was an attempt to get your attention."

Dad shifted his weight to his other foot. I knew he did not believe in therapy. He was a classic tough guy. He thought therapists were expensive charlatans with fools for patients.

As for Mom, she loved to prattle on about her burdens,

but she didn't put a lot of stock in other people's opinions about how she might modify her behavior to make things better. I knew that the last thing she wanted to hear was how her caustic relationship with Tiffany could have played a role in this disaster.

"Doc," Mom chimed in. "I'm as furious with her as any parent in their right mind would be. And trust me, I'm going to straighten her out and wring her neck when she recovers. But this is normal teenage stuff."

Doctor Barnhard was amiable but persistent. "I don't know about that. It can't hurt to be thoughtful about this. These are the warning signs parents look back on later and wish they'd paid more attention to."

"That she got in the car with a drunk driver?" Dad asked.

"And that she got drunk herself," he corrected. "Maybe you both could use some help with a new approach. I know you are doing everything you can and you're great parents. But maybe it's time to ask someone else what to do with a particularly tough child. She's trying to get your attention. You have to ask yourselves why."

I thought of the cross Tiffany had carved into her arm, which was now hidden by bandages. I certainly didn't understand what she was doing. I wanted this situation to be a simple case of bad luck. But it felt more like a death wish.

Having pressed the issue of counseling as far as he could, Dr. Barnhard left and, eventually, it was time for us to go home. We each took a turn saying goodbye to Tiffany, petting her gently, and reassuring her that we'd be back tomorrow.

As we emerged from the hospital into the warm summer evening, tempers began to rise.

"What do you think?" Mom asked Dad.

"I don't know." He grimaced. "It's so hard to know what good counseling would do. I have no idea how much that costs.

How long it would take to see any progress. If ever. They're billing you the whole time. Who knows?"

Dad's body language said he knew. He unlocked the car and I tumbled into the backseat as my parents took their places in front. Dad rolled down the window and lit a cigarette and took a puff before turning the ignition.

"Maybe it's what she needs," Mom ventured.

"Maybe."

"Maybe that's what I need," she added ruefully.

"Maybe." He shrugged and turned, placing an arm behind her headrest as he backed the Mercedes they'd recently bought out of the parking space.

She didn't seem to like that response. "Maybe she's emulating your drinking."

"Right." He sounded as if he knew she would bring this up eventually.

"What do you mean, 'right'?"

"You're saying this is my fault?" he clarified.

"Well, I don't drink. Where did she learn it from?" Mom shot at him.

"Knock it off." Dad kept his eyes on the traffic ahead, his expression grim.

"Where then?" she attacked.

"Maybe you shouldn't pick on her so much."

"Pick on her? Yes. That's exactly what I do. How would you know? You spend all your time at the office. How do you know what I do?'

"I know this is what you do. To her. A lot. Let's stop this," Dad said, trying to turn down the temperature.

"No! Not if you are going to blame me now for her problems. This is not my fault. I've given my life to these children. Everything!"

"Cut it out. This isn't helping anything." No doubt he was

about to glance in the rearview mirror at me, so I stared out the window and tried to look like I wasn't listening.

"So you think we should go for counseling?" Mom challenged, daring him to say yes.

He tried a diversionary tactic. "I'd just like to know what it's going to cost up front. Or if the insurance will cover it. I don't think we can afford it, so it's a moot point."

Silence.

"The problem is," he continued more quietly, "they usually decide to become shrinks because they are crazy themselves. They are trying to figure out their own problems. And they aren't that smart anyway. If they were, they'd be surgeons making the big bucks. It's easy to trick them. I've had so many evaluations and aptitude tests and IQ tests. You can always tell what the right answer is. What they want to hear. So really, it's pointless," he said, shutting the door on Dr. Barnhard's advice.

A few weeks went by before the doctors released Tiffany from the hospital. When she came home, she moved gingerly around the house like a wounded cat. She still had some stitches in her hands and arms. Looking at her skin held together with wiry thread turned my stomach. She lacked energy, but when she smiled and asked if the shirt I had on was actually hers, I knew she was essentially the same.

Tiffany wasn't home twenty-four hours before she started mixing it up with Mom. They picked at each other and bickered over the small stuff, like rinsing the dishes.

"Your legs still work, you can carry your dishes to the kitchen and put them in the dishwasher rather than letting them pile up," Mom said.

Tiffany rolled her eyes. "I was doing that. I'm getting to it. I'm tired," she said.

The pressure would build up periodically and explode, with Mom yelling and insulting Tiffany, who would then look either dejected, or furious like a cornered bull.

They were like two warring drug cartels trying to live in the same town.

"You have no one to blame for this but yourself!" Mom would inevitably conclude.

"I know! I'm ruining my life. You're ashamed of me," Tiffany fired back.

"Now you're going to feel sorry for yourself! Wallowing around in self-pity!"

One issue at the forefront was the hesitation of Tiffany's Catholic high school to let her return to school. Mom and Dad went in for a conference, and returned visibly stressed.

"Well, that was fun," Mom said, dropping her purse on the counter.

Tiffany and I were in the kitchen making dinner. I stood in front of the stove, mixing hamburger into a pan filled with Rice-a-Roni. Tiffany, still weak from surgery and so much time lying down, sat at the kitchen table reading *Cosmo*, which Mom had brought home for her. Evidently Mom had never read the magazine. She thought it was mainly about beauty and fashion rather than tips on keeping a boyfriend's sexual interest piqued.

"Brother Bill doesn't want you back at school. We had to beg, which I of course loved doing," Mom said, sitting down at the square table next to Tiffany. "He said that drinking alcohol was against school policy and the law at your age. And of course, we said you were not drinking."

"They'd need your medical records to know if you'd been drinking," Dad added. "And the police report isn't public information since you guys are minors. Unless we tell them, they won't know what happened. Although everyone has heard through the grapevine. All they know for sure though is just that you were in an accident, and that's why you're not at school. So they can't really throw you out of school based on something they suspect but can't prove happened . . . off school property on a weekend. They need more to go on and we didn't give them anything."

"So don't say a word to anyone. I think we saved you. Again. *By lying*," Mom said.

On the last word she pounded her balled-up fists on the table and cocked her head to the right, looking hard into Tiffany's face. Tiffany had been looking vaguely in Mom's direction while she spoke. Now her eyes went back to her magazine and she essentially acted as if she didn't hear Mom any longer.

Clearly in the mood for another fight, Mom pushed harder. "'Thanks, Mom'? 'Thanks for going in and lying for me'?"

"Thanks," Tiffany said as insincerely as she could.

Normally, this would have been Mom's cue to attack and Tiffany would have immediately taken up arms. The drama would have escalated until Mom pulled out Tiffany's chair and screamed at her to get out of the room. I could see the scene unfolding and I just kept browning the beef. I was starting to feel like getting involved was fruitless if Tiffany didn't want to pitch in and do at least *some* of the appeasing. She never even tried to turn Mom's mood anymore; she seemed to prefer fanning the flames

But this time instead of pouncing and attacking, Mom paused. Her eyes got stuck on the stitches in Tiffany's forehead and the anger drained from her face. She studied the scars setting in, Tiffany's skin dotted with purple here and there. Then she leaned forward and her head fell into the palms of her hands.

I looked over from the pan I was stirring. Dad hung in the doorway, still looking at the ceiling. Mom's eyes were hidden in her hands, and I couldn't tell if she was crying or just exhausted into silence. Tiffany had returned to her magazine, her feet tucked underneath her and her shoulders rolled forward, her whole body curved protectively into a ball. I turned off the burner, and as the gas flame popped and went out, the room fell silent.

CHAPTER NINE

I walked down the hallway, tugging at the hem of my navy blue pleated skirt. I wondered if I'd shortened my new school uniform a little too much, since it fell to about the same length as my cheerleading skirt. I tucked in the hem of my blue collared shirt as I neared the classroom. The taskmasters at my new school were fanatics about the dress code.

Two girls stood at their locker. One said, "That's her!" Then they turned back just as quickly and started whispering.

I'd graduated from elementary school to Chaminade College Prep, the Catholic coed school where Tiffany went. Everyone on campus knew me as the girl from *Little House on the Prairie*. When I'd gone to cheerleading camp the summer before school started with the other girls who'd made the Chaminade squad, twelve- and thirteen-year-old cheerleaders had mobbed my room looking for Cassandra.

"Is she in there?" I'd heard a girl say in the hall while I stayed hidden in my room, tired of being a spectacle. The girl knocked, and I could see through the peephole that she'd brought half a dozen friends in matching blue and white cheerleading uniforms and pigtails that bounced as they turned their heads to one another.

"I'm going to slide this program under the door. Maybe she'll sign it if I put a note on it. Let's come back after lunch," the leader of the group said. She turned and left as the rest of her squad trailed after her.

Little House on the Prairie had been out of the primetime lineup for almost three years, but the fervor around the show had yet to die down. It still ran every day in reruns on the syndicated channels, in more than one language, so they'd cycle through the seasons pretty quickly. You could always tell when they'd gotten to my years, because more people would stop me on the street than usual.

For the first half of seventh grade, I was so distracted by a new middle school and a huge batch of new classmates and friends that I barely noticed that I hadn't worked much. I was grateful not to be working, in fact, because I didn't want to miss a minute of my new life. I moved from class to class, mixing with different kids every period. I had eight teachers instead of one, a whole range of new subjects to dig into, like chemistry and Spanish. And then there was a brand-new selection of boys. The student body was almost ten times the size of my old school.

I'd scored a handful of meaty commercials during the summer and the fall, national spots that ran often and filled the mailbox with checks. Every afternoon my mom brought in the mail, quickly sifting the junk mail and tucking the envelopes with checks in a neat stack inside her purse.

But while commercials still seemed a dependable "get," the theatrical roles were proving to be more of a challenge. Fellow veterans were no longer peers but major roadblocks, Sydney Penny in particular. She was petite and absolutely gorgeous with dark skin and shiny dark eyes that set off her sparkling white teeth and pink nail-beds. Mom said she looked "ethnic," but casting directors who would normally complain about the challenge of matching someone with Cherokee roots to a set of fictional parents didn't seem to mind. Even though she was a couple of years older than I, her smaller frame helped her pass for my age and thus take my roles as well as the ones in her age bracket.

She wasn't the only problem. There were too many other girls like her. The field had simply gotten a lot more competitive now that we were all young teens who knew the drill, understood the value of working, and showed up at auditions hungry.

But a few months into seventh grade, just when I was starting to really worry I was washing up as an actress, I somehow landed a big one. This was the perfect role to end a dry patch, the lead on a new series on NBC. The creators had already sold a slate of episodes to the network, and the first one was centered on my character and a little brother.

The premise was wildly improbable. The show focused on a combined orphanage and old-age home. I was pretty sure orphanages didn't exist anymore, although this would be my third or fourth time inhabiting a fictional one on TV. The show was called *Morningstar, Eveningstar* just in case the viewer missed the juxtaposition of the oldies and the kids, all left for dead by their biological families. The script and the dialogue were saccharine sweet, but then again I had come from the corniest family drama ever to enthrall viewers.

The new show was even shot on the MGM lot where we did *Little House*. Returning to work on the lot was like going home, if home was a place where you'd find a new crew of kids in your bedroom every time you returned.

The producers cast Fred Savage, a boy out of Chicago, to be my little brother. Fred was short and round, with a pudgy nose, dark eyes, and a mop of coarse curly dark hair that fell in his eyes when it got too long. We didn't actually match that well physically since my eyes and hair were both lighter, but the producers figured it was close enough. Fred had come out to L.A. with his mom for the job and brought a midwestern accent with him.

The show had seven adults and seven kids for balance. Tammy Lauren played one of the older girls. She was about six years older than I and a veteran like myself. Like so many successful child actors, Tammy was fit and had a compact frame, and was pretty but not stunning. She had bouncy blonde blunt-cut hair that fell to her shoulders and swung when she walked, and bright blue eyes. All her features were bigger than the space they filled: eyes, nose, teeth and lips, which was also a common trait among actors. Mom always said successful actors had little bodies and huge heads and even bigger facial features because that's what the camera liked.

Tammy's loud, friendly, funny demeanor made almost everyone like her immediately. Like a true workhorse, she showed up every day, lines learned, acting choices made, hoping to stand out and outshine the rest of us or prove to the writers the next episode should be based on her. She was competitive, but only with herself, never the rest of us, which was rare in our business.

The boy closest to my age was Joaquin Phoenix. He'd decided to call himself Leaf, though, to fit in with his older siblings who had the woodsy names, River and Rain. Rain, however, was currently calling herself Rainbow, so who knew what anyone's real name was in that family. River never came to the set, but Rainbow hung around all the time, and I took to her immediately because of her free-spirited friendliness. With her round face and warm smile, she loved life and lacked the bitchiness girls my age were already developing. She and Leaf had two younger sisters as well, Liberty and Summer, who looked like twins to me but weren't.

Leaf was younger than me but handsome in a rough way

with wavy brown hair, light eyes and red lips. He was born in Puerto Rico to parents who were missionaries for the Church of God, which explained a lot. The whole family could sing and play instruments, and they'd traveled through Central and South America in a van, singing in tiny town squares for donations to buy food. On the set, Leaf had declined to eat a Caesar salad because it had egg in it and he was vegan, a practice I'd never heard of.

In spite of this perceived worldliness, a lot of basic stuff I took for granted was brand-new to him because Leaf's parents homeschooled their children, regardless of whether they were traveling or in one place. The birthday party we threw for him in the studio schoolroom turned out to be the first one he'd ever had.

"Happy birthday, Leaf!" the teacher chimed in when we finished the song. She presented him with a cake that craft services had made without eggs.

We crowded in to hug him and pat him on the back, and his eyes welled up with tears. Then he hugged the set teacher as if she'd given him a kidney.

"I haven't had a party like this before," he said quietly, now suddenly shy.

I couldn't believe he'd missed the gravy train of presents all those years, but he seemed more struck by the gesture. I was charmed by the idea that he'd seen so much of the world and also so little.

Two older boys and a young black girl who wasn't even in school yet filled out the seven, but I stuck mostly to the Phoenix clan or Tammy.

On *Little House*, we'd spent half our days on the lot, and the other half outdoors in Simi Valley, and on the Simi days, the show runner would hand out per diems. A per diem consisted of a little yellow envelope filled with cash that was supposed to cover our gas and expenses for not being on the lot. Ironically, on the per diem days, they also fed you from the world-class catering truck in addition to doling out gas money. The per diem equaled twenty-seven bucks a day, which Mom let me keep. That kind of cash really stacked up in my piggy bank at home.

But on this new show, we spent every day on the lot, so no per diem. And on the lot, the cast had to fend for themselves when it came to food and buy what was available out of their own pocket. We could leave the property, though we only had an hour.

I loved to eat at the studio commissary. Mom said it was expensive, but they had crackers on the table and you got to see many of the other actors who were on the lot shooting different shows, so we became regulars. I always ordered a BLT sandwich. Leaf's mom thought the commissary was pricey too, so her brood rarely visited, but Tammy and her mom often joined us.

When the show started, Mom finally told me what I was getting paid. I was making five thousand dollars per episode, which was great money for a fourteen-year-old girl in the late '80s. I think she couldn't help herself this time. She was brimming with the news. She'd fired my agent and hired a new one who had brokered this deal. She'd lined up Harry Gold, Missy and Tracey Gold's father. They were both very successful child actors with regular shows and their dad had managed their careers so well he decided to make managing kids his business.

"See," Mom told Dad. "Jack wouldn't have gotten this much money." Jack was the agent she'd fired.

Dad was standing at the sink shaving, and she was sitting on the edge of their bed, where she could look into the bathroom and talk to his reflection in the mirror.

"How much money?" I piped in. No one had noticed that I'd entered the bedroom.

"You don't need to worry about that," she said.

"Come on," I pressed.

"Five thousand dollars an episode," she boasted.

I was dazzled. Five grand went a long way back then. It took a week and a half to do an episode so I calculated I'd be rich by the end of the year. She quickly straightened me out.

"They only sold seven episodes. So you're getting $35,000 for the whole thing until they rerun it, and the government takes about half."

"What?" That seemed illegal to me.

"I know. I always fill out the form that you have ten dependents so they don't take the money right away, but we have to pay the IRS at the end of the year anyway, so they get you one way or the other."

I put the fact that I had to give away half my earnings to the government on the back burner and started to plan for the other part. "What are we buying? Can I have a new horse?"

"No. It all goes into the bank for college. You know that."

"That account must have a bazillion dollars in it by now," I said.

"I'll never tell," Mom said.

After the first episode aired, I got the sense the show was a clunker. Even though I was only fourteen and probably didn't have the most sophisticated taste, I knew *Morningstar* was hokey beyond belief. There was a catchphrase we all said at the end of the first episode, "Rain on you!" which made absolutely no sense to me. When we all delivered the punch line together, I hoped I was the only one who didn't get it.

Unfortunately, the critics didn't get it either. Somehow hitting the audience over the head with obvious moral lessons had worked for *Little House* but failed miserably for this show. We were in the midst of shooting the third episode when the first one aired to mostly crickets. It was a blow. Everyone hoped for a miracle, but there are few miracles in TV land. If no one watches, and the critics don't encourage people to tune in, it's pretty much hopeless.

They'd hired an acting coach to work with the kids, which I immediately resented. I'd never been coached, never taken a single acting class, and had always won praise on the set. To motivate me, Mom shared that the consensus among the writers was that Leaf was the best actor in the bunch. That certainly irked me.

"I'm going to tell you what Sherry said, but this is meant to make you better," Mom said. Sherry was the new acting coach. We were in the car, and I kept my eyes on the road. Directors and casting agents had always said my acting was authentic, that I didn't overact or sing my lines like so many kids who thought they were way up onstage in the school pageant playing to the last row of seats.

"They all think Leaf walks on water of course. Probably because of his older brother. But I have to say, the kid's a good little actor. Tammy's a hard worker; she's always thinking about the scene that came before the one she's in, where her character is emotionally, sort of where she's been and where she's going. But she can overact," she said, shrugging her shoulders.

Mom had paid keen attention to the comments from the writers and directors over the years. Her on-the-job training had transformed her into a spot-on critic.

"David," she continued, referring to one of the older boys, "David is hopeless. He's never worked before and it shows. He's in way over his head and the episode they did around him is tragic." She ticked down the list.

"Freddy's got good potential they say, but he's hammy. He's always rolling his eyes. He puts in a bit of a canned performance, like his mom spends all her time telling him exactly how to say each line. He can do a take ten times, and the words will come out the same, every single time. Nothing real about it."

She paused.

Here it comes, I thought. I could feel my temperature rise, and the backs of my legs start to stick to the leather of the car seat. She glanced at me briefly, but delivered most of her critique to the traffic in front of her.

"And you. Sometimes you're engaged, and sometimes you throw away your lines. Leaf is focused and every performance is real. He beat the hell out of you in that scene where the two of you were supposed to get in a fistfight, and he was right to do it. I know he hurt you, just like he would have in real life. You and Allison used to do that fake fighting on *Little House*, and I should have stepped in and told you it looked staged and silly. Someone should have pointed it out. I was counting on Michael or someone to say something if it wasn't right. I thought I knew the least of everyone there, but I should have told you." She shook her head.

"They say Leaf's committed, every single time. Do you understand what that means? To commit to the character? You have to get into her shoes and really believe you are her and believe what are you saying. Not thinking about getting back to the schoolroom to finish your math work. Not thinking about what you want for lunch. I've always left the acting to you. Just taught you the lines and left the way you said it up to you. That's worked for fourteen years. But this is what Sherry and the writers are saying. In fact, they told me to talk to you because they don't think you are taking Sherry seriously."

I hadn't moved a muscle during the lecture, hadn't made a sound. I hated what she was saying, hated what I was hearing, hated what I knew to be true. But that wasn't slowing her down.

"You are not always disciplined about acting. You are not taking your craft seriously enough. I think you take it for granted. You have to get serious *now* and work harder. If this show doesn't get picked up, you only have these performances, and every single one is a precious gift. You need to work like every performance could be your last. Because it could be. I am seriously afraid it could be."

We rode the rest of the way home in silence. The message burned like a block of dry ice I had tried to grab out of an Igloo cooler on the set. It seemed harmless at first, but before I knew what was happening, it was stuck to my hand, searing the skin until I could figure out how to scrape it off.

The last episode we shot of *Morningstar* was ripped right out of the *Little House* playbook. A fictional family came to visit the orphanage and wanted to adopt my little brother, Fred Savage's character, but not me. Freddy and I were the only pair who had two shows centered on them in the original seven-episode slate.

I wanted to make the most of this opportunity, since Mom had told me so pointedly that this could be my last shot for a while. But when we rehearsed the scene, my voice came out sounding as if someone else were talking. I tried again, but every line sounded wrong, and I couldn't imagine what would make them sound right. I was so focused on doing the best I could, I had lost my footing and was floundering. Now I just wanted to get through the scene alive.

Just to make life a little more interesting, Mom had pointed out that the Levi's they had bought for me to wear in the first episode were now snug. I assumed they'd shrunk, but Mom reminded me that they'd washed the hell out of them before we started shooting since we were all supposed to be orphans with handed-down clothes. She told me I'd made too many trips to the craft services snack table in the afternoon when they put out all the cookies and candies.

"Tammy never eats that junk. Look how disciplined she is. Meanwhile, you've packed on the pounds. Look at that rubber tire around your waist! And now those jeans are tight on your thighs too," Mom pointed out after rehearsal.

Once again, she was right, and my confidence sank yet another notch.

The scene was between me and Kate Reid, an older actress who played the character from the nursing home gang that had been paired with Freddy and me during the story arcs. She was an acclaimed British actress with two Golden Globe nominations and very little affinity for or patience with children. I got the impression she thought we all sucked at acting and our lack of talent might be contagious.

We walked through the rehearsal. I was sitting at a table doing homework; she came in and sat by me, and gently explained that the couple who had visited wanted to adopt Freddy but not me.

Now we were going to do one for real.

"Rolling. Speed? Speed. Marker! Action!"

Kate started on her speech.

"Sarah, I know this is hard to hear. It doesn't make you any less special. They just want a boy. They want Alan. And only Alan," she explained.

The script called for me to wait until the end of her speech and then tell her that was fine. They could take Alan, who was Freddy's character, and I would make the supreme sisterly sacrifice.

But I couldn't meet her eyes. She told me that they didn't want me, didn't like me. I had just heard this speech from Mom in the car the night before. Kate tried to take my hand and my back stiffened. A reluctant messenger, sticking me with pins, delivering the news she was sent to convey, barely comforting me. I was embarrassed by all that I lacked, ashamed that someone had been sent to tell me about it, and then sorry for her discomfort at being forced to do it.

Kate wasn't halfway through her speech, and without ever looking at her, I just started to cry silently. I tried to stop, but I couldn't. I cried for my character, and for myself. We were both barely teenagers, and this was just a little too much weight for us. Girls our age were supposed to be learning how to put on lipgloss in a middle school bathroom somewhere. Instead, we were being judged as deficient, and cast aside.

Kate got to the end of her lines, and it was time for me to respond. I couldn't find my voice. I said something like, "I understand. I'm glad for him. He should go and be happy." But the words barely came out. I paused and gathered my breath to try to give the last line more volume while wiping away the tears. I was trying to be brave for both of us, but I could barely get the air to speak.

"I'll be okay. Really. I want him to be happy." The script didn't even call for me to cry, but I just couldn't help it. I was involved in the scene and the larger drama swirling around it. I couldn't tell which was which.

Kate leaned in and hugged me and started crying herself. And the director just let the scene go. When he finally said cut, the whole crew started clapping.

As so many of us suspected, when the final show aired, the network pulled the plug. Once again, I was out of work and back at school. When I went riding, my friends' moms liked to ask if we'd heard if the show was being picked up. The families at the stable all lived in and around the television industry and were pretty savvy about the business. They knew the show was a dud and they wanted to rub it in because Mom had been fairly unbearable when I was cast.

"Did you hear about the show yet? Did they order more episodes?" Shannon's mom, Megan, asked. She was an oddly shaped woman who always wore light-colored sweatpants that accentuated her enormous hips and butt. Her hair was dark at the roots but orange and red at the tips and she had problem skin. In the solitude of our car, my dad would say Megan looked like a pear with acne, and Tiffany and I would bust up laughing.

"Hi, Meg," my mom drawled reluctantly. She knew Megan had read the news somewhere and had shown up only to turn the knife.

"Did they order more? I hope, I hope!"

I thought Megan needed Sherry, the acting coach. I slipped into my horse's stall before Mom answered. I knew she'd come up with something, and I didn't want my face to reveal that we felt bad about the cancellation of the show.

"Nope. Oh well. The show stank. Can only do so much with bad writing. Just frees Missy up to do something better," she tried.

Needless to say, Mom was in a bad mood.

No matter how she spun it, the show's being canceled was a defeat.

Tiffany and I were back to our normal routines, which included a fair amount of head-butting. After all, we were two teenage girls living under the same roof. Most of the discord emerged from the borrowing or outright stealing of clothes.

Tiffany had adopted a pink and white striped Guess blouse as part of her weekend uniform. She wore it a million different ways, open with a camisole underneath, closed and belted over tight jeans. She'd tease and spike her bangs, put on a knotted hairband ripped right from Madonna's *Material Girl* album, and look like a million bucks.

It wasn't long before I started slipping into her room and pillaging the pink and white shirt, and other key items, from her closet. I'd sneak in while she was in the shower, snag something, and hide the item in the part of my closet where the sliding doors overlapped, so you couldn't find it unless you already knew it was there.

She'd retaliate by coming into my room, trying on something fresh from the cleaners, and then dumping the shirt or dress in a heap in the middle of the floor, leaving it rumpled, even though it hadn't yet seen the light of day.

I would enter my room, find the heap of fresh clothes, and scream her name at the top of my lungs.

One Friday night Tiffany was getting ready to go out, but she couldn't find the pink and white shirt. She charged into my room, wearing only a bra and her jeans, and flung the mirrored doors of my closet open with all her might, frantically searching piece by piece through the closet.

Confident my hiding spot would remain undetected, I calmly lay across my bed, watching Don Johnson prance around in a linen blazer on that night's episode of *Miami Vice*.

Then she found it.

"Ha!" she barked as she gripped the hanger in her fist, her face candy-apple red from the search and agitation.

"That's mine actually," I lied coolly, not budging from my position on the bed.

"You're a liar!" she yelled. And with that she turned and slammed my closet door so hard, it bounced back off the frame with equal force.

"What are you doing!" I yelled, finally jumping to my feet.

"You're right!" She stopped, breathing heavily, and narrowed her eyes. "Why would I close that? I bet there's more of my stuff in here!" She turned back to the closet and started rooting through the hangers again.

"This is mine. And this," she said, plucking out my favorite items, one by one.

I grabbed the shoulder of a dress and we began wrestling over it.

"Stop it! I'm so sick of both of you!" Mom barked behind us.

We both jumped. Neither of us had seen her come in.

She picked up the pink shirt that had started the fight and left the room. Instinctively sensing disaster, we both trailed her down the hall and into her room, where she ducked into her bathroom and then reemerged with a huge pair of scissors that she held up like a sword.

We gasped.

"You'll never fight over this shirt again!" she said, slicing through the shirt with her shears as we watched in horror. I waited for the fabric of our most beloved shirt to bleed. Then Mom threw down the scissors and just started tearing our treasure to shreds.

"I hate you!" Tiffany screamed.

Mom threw down what remained of the shirt and charged her, grabbing her by the shoulders, shaking her. Then she turned toward the door, dragging Tiffany's body violently alongside her as if she were a rag doll.

They disappeared through the door and after a frightened beat, I followed them into the hallway where I saw my mom drag Tiffany down the flight of stairs while Tiffany scratched and clawed to get away.

Resistance was hopeless. Mom was stronger than any wrestler when she was fueled by rage.

When they reached the bottom of the stairs, still entangled, Mom grabbed Tiffany's arm with one hand and reached for the front door with the other hand. Tiffany was still naked from the waist up, except for a bra, and I could see the red marks on her arms and shoulders where Mom's fingers had been gripping her.

Mom opened the door and flung Tiffany out into the night, slamming the door with so much force, the picture windows that lined the front of the house shook. She bolted the top lock and came stomping back up the stairs, where I was watching the scene, gape-mouthed.

"You can't leave her out there. She has no shirt on," I reasoned when Mom reached the top.

"You want to go with her?" she shouted, eyes wide with anger, teeth clenched.

"I'm letting her back in!" I said, sliding past her.

But as I moved past her, she grabbed me by the shoulders and threw me down the stairs, headfirst.

I tumbled forward, the carpet on the stairs burning the skin on my face. I stuck my arm out to brace for the fall, but my legs caught on the banister first, my shins slamming painfully into the wood. But, at least, this slowed my fall.

I slipped the rest of the way to the bottom, just as Dad finally emerged from the den downstairs. I was amazed it took this long for him to come out.

"What's going on?" he yelled.

He turned his head to the window and saw Tiffany shivering outside, half naked. He turned back to Mom and glared at her.

She was indignant. "You want to deal with them! Fine! Get involved! For once! You deal with them, for once!" she screamed, thundering into her bedroom and slamming the door.

I was still on the ground, assessing my limbs for damage, when Dad went to the front door and unlocked it.

"Get back in here," he said to Tiffany, who was now bewildered and tearful.

"I don't know what you two did, and I don't fucking care. I'm sure it was something. Get upstairs to your rooms! Both of you! Jesus Christ!" he cursed, returning to the den as the mayhem in the house ended, leaving only silent rancor and the hum of the television in the den.

A few months after NBC canceled *Morningstar* I got a postcard in the mail from the Academy of Television Arts and Sciences, saying that the show's producers had submitted my performance in the final episode for Emmy consideration. I didn't get a nomination, but I saved the postcard in my room, taping it to the mirror.

At least they reran the show, and more checks arrived in the mail. I rode with Mom to the bank, where she left me in the car and went inside to deposit them. She came back with the printed receipt and I decided to quietly pick up my financial investigation. After all, she'd told me that I was making five grand an episode. That meant she was weakening. Now was the time to strike and get more information.

"So how much is in that account now?" I inquired.

She stopped adjusting her seat belt and let her hands drop to her lap. "Why do you want to know?"

"Because I work hard. I'm excited. I want to know. There's got to be more than I need for college. Come on. Tell me. I'm fourteen. I can take it."

"But I don't want you telling everyone. The reason I've never told you is because this is what everyone wants to know. They always ask you, 'How much money have you made?' like a bunch of low-class people. It's so rude and none of their business. And I didn't tell you so you could honestly say, 'I don't know.' Will you be able to keep your mouth shut?"

"Yep."

She waited for what seemed like a year. I didn't budge. Finally, she handed me the slip.

It was over a quarter million, a lot of money, but not what I expected. I'd done a lot of math since she'd told me I was making five thousand an episode for *Morningstar*. I knew you got paid a large percentage of the original fee every time a show re-ran. It was called a residual. And I knew my quote hadn't been much lower on *Little House*. Even if it was half of what I'd been paid per episode for *Morningstar*, the show had run about fifty million times. Plus I had heard Mom tell my dad that each cycle of a national commercial brought in about ten grand. Those could pay out for years. I'd done dozens. More than fifty. Maybe seventy-five. We'd lost count. I'd been in two movies, which had shot for months at a time. The number I'd come up with was much bigger.

"Is that it?" I finally said.

Her face fell.

"Is that the only account?"

Mom's shocked expression flushed with anger and her face darkened. Then just as quickly, she looked defeated.

" 'Is that it?' Is that really all you have to say?" She sucked in a mouthful of air and made a noise like a wounded animal.

"I've devoted my entire life, selflessly, to taking you to interview after interview, callbacks, and so many times you've come up empty. I've sat on set after set for hours, bored. To tears! Taught you a million lines. Driven hours in traffic, packed clothes, sacrificed all my time! The things I could have been doing for myself all that time! I could have gone back to college, improved myself like so many moms. Selfish moms. But instead what have I done? I've made *you* a star. I've made *you* rich. And that's the thanks I get?"

She started to cry, not even stopping to breathe as she unloaded her frustration on me.

"What an ungrateful, selfish brat you turned out to be! I might expect this from your sister. But not you. Never in a million years did I think you would look at all I've done for you and say that!" A man walking by looked in the car, but it didn't slow Mom down. She just rolled up the window and kept going.

"My mom never lifted a finger for me. It was all about my brother, her beloved Sonny! Or Marilyn, the pretty one. My father wouldn't send me to college. Just a waste of money, he said, when you'll go get married and get pregnant. The day I graduated from high school, no thanks to them, by the way, he told me to go out and get a job and start paying him back for raising me." She sniffled angrily.

"If I'd had half the support from my parents that you get from me, who knows what I'd be today! But I didn't get an ounce of anything from them, and I've poured my life into you and this is the thanks I get!" She pulled the slip out of my hand and crumpled it into a ball.

"My friends have always told me that I shouldn't do so much for you when I get nothing in return. You get all the fame and fortune and I'm just the hated stage mom. What do I get? Nothing. But I always did it, I was happy to do it because I love you and we're a team. I never thought you were the type of kid who would turn on me and bite the hand that's feeding you, that's made everything possible. My friends warned me, but I didn't believe them."

We sat in silence for a while, then she finally put the car in gear and headed home. When we got home, she got out of the car and slammed the door so hard the window should have shattered. Then she went into the house and up into her room and slammed that door so hard I expected the big picture windows at the front of our house to crash in next.

I tiptoed up to my room and lay down on my bed and stared at the ceiling.

I had the distinct feeling my mom was lying.

About what, I had no idea. I felt guilty for being an ingrate, but I couldn't think of what friends she would have had that conversation with. She didn't have any friends she confided in. None. Just her sister, Marilyn. But that's not who she'd quoted. Why would she lie about that if she wasn't compensating for another stretch of the truth.

Then again, what did I really know about how much money had come in? I could be wrong. I'd been kept in the dark so long, I had so little information. I couldn't tell.

I looked at the framed picture of Grandpa, her father, that I kept next to my bed. A tiny three-by-five, black-and-white of him in a Yankees uniform. I'd put it in a gold frame and set it next to my bed after he'd died two years earlier.

He'd played on the Yankees' farm team, or at least had tried out for it, depending on who was telling the story. He was up at bat, smiling but looking serious at the same time. Tall, handsome, and slender, it was the 1930s version of the man I adored.

He was always my favorite grandparent, ready to play catch in our cul-de-sac at any moment, even in his dress shoes, which he always wore. Endlessly patient, he never turned me down for a game of Monopoly. So many times, I'd run down the hallway to build up a head of steam, then fly through the air and crash down onto his stomach as he snored unsuspectingly on our guest room bed. He'd nearly have a heart attack from the shock, but he never got angry. He'd chuckle and fall back to sleep, or rouse himself and play whatever game I wanted.

When he walked in the front door of our house, Tiffany and I would attack him and turn out his pockets, looting him for gum, candy, or spare change. We'd even go visit the little candy store he owned in downtown L.A. and pillage the shelves there, taking a year's supply of chocolate and candy. And he'd just laugh as Mom tried to rein us in.

This was the man who had demanded payment when Mom graduated from high school? This was the miser who had terrorized their household? I'd heard the story a million times, but it still didn't ring true.

Mom had said a lot that didn't add up and tried to cover it all with outrage. I knew something wasn't right, but I wasn't going to solve the mystery that day.

CHAPTER TEN

When Tiffany walked in the door from school, there was a thick envelope sitting in the middle of the kitchen table. Mom was standing next to the table with her hands on her hips, shifting from foot to foot. She had somehow stopped herself from opening the envelope since the mailman dropped it off hours earlier. I had to give her credit. Normally Mom didn't hesitate to open our mail. She said we were minors living in her home, so she had every right to monitor our communications.

But this was special. Tiffany had been waiting to hear back from colleges and we all knew what a thick envelope meant, versus a skinny one. This one seemed to hold a whole registration packet and had been sent by one of the most prestigious schools in the state, the University of California, Berkeley.

The college admission process had been a tense time in our house. Tiffany's SAT scores were very good, but even though I was only in eighth grade, I could see her that track record in the classroom had a few potholes. She'd opted to take the hardest Advanced Placement classes but had settled for mostly B's along the way, plus many of her after-school activities, like getting into trouble with her friends, weren't the kind you'd list on a college application. Her transcript read smart with a bit of a lazy streak.

In a fit of crisis management, Mom had hired a college consultant to dress up Tiffany's applications and improve her odds, and he'd said she'd be a stretch for anything Ivy League, but there was a back door she could use to make sure she got into UC Berkeley. She could apply directly to the College of Forestry and then switch out once she got there. Stanford, everyone's first choice, remained a long shot. In 1987, Stanford had been the premier school in the state for years.

The consultant turned out to be right on every count. Tiffany got into UCLA, and Penn State, and rejected by Stanford. But now Berkeley seemed to be calling.

"Open it already!" Mom squealed.

Tiffany's face broke out into a huge smile. She laughed nervously. I wasn't sure I'd ever seen her this elated. She tore through the envelope and read the first sentence.

"They are pleased to offer me admission!" she laughed. Both Mom and I rushed over to hug her.

"That's huge!" I said. "You are so smart! Wow! I'm so proud to be your little sister, smarty pants!"

"I'm really proud of you," Mom said hugging her. "This is a real feather in your cap! What an achievement. Of course UCLA is right here, though. We could still see you all the time," she added.

"Oh, God!" Tiffany laughed, as if that wasn't entirely a selling point. Mom got the message and rolled her eyes, letting the comment go by.

Mom, who hadn't gone to college, wanted Tiffany to go to UCLA and become a sleek blonde sorority sister. Over the past year, Tiffany had turned eighteen and come as close to Mom's ideal as was humanly possible for her. She'd picked up a seemingly preppy boyfriend, grown her hair long and blonde, and acquired a wardrobe that was mainstream with a little edge. At five feet two, she'd slimmed down to a hundred pounds, and she looked gorgeous. Overall, she was finally well behaved, at least on the surface. The last step in a full transformation would have been to go to UCLA, which was known for its population of perfectly toned, blonde California girls.

To the naked eye, Tiffany had grown up and calmed down. I wanted to believe she'd put her passion for backlash to rest. But I knew my sister better than anyone else did, and I could tell that something under the lovely new mask she was wearing was itching her. She couldn't relax. She'd burn through a pack of cigarettes when she left the house and douse herself in perfume before she returned to cover the giveaway scent. She'd hide all the contraband in her purse, never letting the bag out of her sight for fear that Mom would riffle through it.

I also guessed some part of her felt like a sellout compared to the rebellious spirit she'd embraced for years. She'd always made fun of the girls who looked exactly like she did now. She'd traded black nail polish for bubblegum pink, but I suspected it was a costume she was trying on and could easily shed. I also thought the majority of her new image had more to do with keeping her new boyfriend, Cliff, happy and interested, than her own personal preference.

We'd visited Berkeley a few weeks earlier, and it had something for everyone. A healthy streak of anti-establishment fervor for Tiffany, even if the school's tradition of activism and the local hippie culture seemed tired and threadbare by the end of the '80s. The brilliance of all the math and science geniuses that had come out of the school dazzled Dad. Mom liked the prestige, even if it didn't measure up to Stanford, a fact she didn't hesitate to communicate to Tiffany. And I think everyone longed to put a bit of distance between Tiffany and Mom. I didn't believe their recent, fragile truce could last. A lifetime of battles versus just months of relative quiet seemed more like a break in the action than an end to the conflict. A six-hour car ride seemed ideal. Close enough to visit, far enough not to.

"I've decided to go to Berkeley," she announced one morning when she was getting ready to go to school. We were all in the kitchen, Tiffany standing at the door fidgeting with her car keys, the three of us around the table reading the paper and eating.

Everyone smiled and nodded approval, even Mom. Deep down she knew the more she'd pushed for UCLA, the less likely Tiffany would go. This outcome seemed inevitable.

"Let's all go to dinner tonight and celebrate!" Dad suggested.

That night we went to Tiffany's favorite Chinese restaurant, the Mandarin Gardens. We walked in on our best group behavior, which couldn't last.

"You look so pretty tonight with your hair like that," Mom said, pushing a few strands of Tiffany's hair back behind her shoulder.

The compliment was too solicitous for Tiffany. Her shoulders tensed as she rolled her eyes. "I need to get my roots done," she said, nervously running her fingers through her bangs.

"I say you look pretty and you immediately say something negative," Mom pouted.

"Mom. Come on," Tiffany sighed, shoving her hands into her pockets.

"What? I was trying to give you a compliment! Can't I say your hair looks nice?" Mom's voice was too loud, amping up the level of discomfort.

As we took our seats in a deep red leather booth, I tried to lighten the mood. "I went through your closet and took out the clothes I wanted to keep," I said, trying to divert attention. Tiffany pretended to scowl at me and shoved my arm.

We ordered a tray of satay and some egg rolls, but by the time the main dishes arrived, the banter at our table was edging toward a throwdown.

"We've driven past those houses next to UCLA. It looks like so much fun! Berkeley has sororities too. You should be sure to join. You could make friends and meet boys," Mom purred.

"I don't know," Tiffany said, looking down and picking at her acrylic nails. I wondered if they filled acrylic nails in downtown Berkeley. Seemed unlikely.

"Well, it just seems like a great way to meet people! You shouldn't knock it until you try it. At least try it! Promise me you will try it," Mom pressed.

"We'll see," Tiffany said pointedly.

"A group of girls would be a great way not to put on that famous freshman ten. You look so fantastic right now. The last thing you want to do is go away to college and get fat, eating pizza and drinking beer. That's what everyone does. They always say girls look their best in high school and it's downhill from there. So you have to stay on top of it. And being with a bunch of other pretty girls, the competition, will keep you on your toes," Mom preached.

Tiffany looked sideways and met my eyes. I shook my head, willing her to just let it pass. I wanted to eat my beef and broccoli without an explosion.

"Now what? What are you two looking at each other for?" Mom said tersely.

"Jeez! Nothing, Mom! I just don't know if I want to join a sorority! It seems really fake and I'm terrible at that," Tiffany said.

"Don't call them fake. You don't even know anyone in a sorority and already you've decided they are fake! Why don't you turn over a new leaf. It's a fresh start! I wish I had the opportunities you have! Going off to a nice college, all paid for, the ability to join anything, be anyone I want, parents footing the bill and supporting me! You're so ungrateful!" Mom charged, raising her voice now.

"So why don't you go to college?" Tiffany said, throwing down the gauntlet. In other families you could get away with a little talk back like that. It wasn't a big deal. But challenging Mom like that was pulling the pin on a grenade.

Right on cue, Mom got vicious. "We had to lie to get you in. Unless you *want* to be a park ranger."

And, scene . . . I thought. Happy family movie officially over. I felt angry with both of them. Why couldn't Mom leave her alone, but really, why couldn't Tiffany just play along and keep dinner civil? They both made life so complicated.

"Just go! Get out of here," Mom said, shoving Tiffany's shoulder. Demanding Tiffany now leave was a complete overreaction, but it was also predictable. "Why don't you just leave for college now. We'll all be so much happier when you're gone."

The couple at the next table looked over uncomfortably. I studied my plate, suddenly absorbed by the consistency of my rice.

Tiffany stormed out. She had driven to dinner separately. I looked out the window and watched the rear bumper of her red Jeep speed out of the parking lot, tires screeching as she bumped up over the curb and cut off the oncoming traffic. Her license plate, H8SKOOL, disappeared into a sea of taillights.

Dad drank his wine and shook his head, looking down at the tablecloth and frowning. I digested the silence, until Mom started tearing up and muttering quietly, kicking off a self-pitying monologue about all she had done for Tiffany, and how ungrateful she was. Neither Dad nor I jumped in, but our lack of participation seemed to have little impact on what she was saying.

We sat around the table, inhabiting three separate worlds. The waitress took pity on us and brought the bill quickly, disappearing and reappearing with Dad's credit card. Dad signed the check and we walked out, a defeated and deflated group, smaller than when we had walked in.

I sat in the backseat on the way home, ready for Tiffany to leave for college. I liked spending time with her alone, going for a quick meal or even to the beach for some sun, but it was hard to ever have her to myself since Cliff soaked up so much of her time. And tonight she proved she couldn't help herself when it came to Mom. Why she had to constantly lock horns with Mom boggled my mind. Why bother to expend so much energy for nothing? What was there to win? Did she think Mom was going to have an epiphany and suddenly realize she had been too hard on Tiffany her whole life, then fall to the ground and beg for forgiveness? They were eighteen years into the game.

Mom had started the night being as nice as she could. Playing along would have required so little effort from Tiffany. Yes, talking with Mom, especially when she got so pretentious, could be grating. But ruining a perfectly good dinner was worse. I loved Tiffany dearly, but I was ready to be an only child.

We all got a little breathing room when Tiffany moved into the college dorm a few months later. Mom, Dad, and I drove up to drop her off. I met her roommate, Candice, who had black hair and Goth makeup and seemed to be channeling the devil, or maybe she was a witch. Beyond that, she seemed quite smart and certainly nice enough. She and Tiffany did the first few freshman mixers together before my parents and I drove back to L.A. Tiffany said after that, though, they went their separate ways more or less, as Candice found her own coven of friends and Tiffany looked for hers.

* * *

I started ninth grade as the only child at home, which certainly made life a lot more peaceful. The bathroom I'd shared with Tiffany was finally fully mine. We weren't fighting about clothes, and there were no more quarrels with Mom about how late Tiffany could stay out with Cliff or the best way to be or dress. But my new status as the only child made me the sole focus of Mom's attention, which was a little much for a fifteen-year-old yearning instead for some independence.

Around this time, Mom and I both realized that I hadn't worked in about a year. It was the longest dry spell I'd ever endured. I didn't notice until it hit me that so long had gone by. I'd been busy cheerleading, riding my horse, and, of course, trying to jockey and manage the fights between Tiffany and Mom, hoping that they wouldn't kill each other before she left for college.

Many of the roles I auditioned for went to girls who were over eighteen. They didn't have to go to school on the set or abide by any of the child labor laws that regulated how long kids could work in a given day. Plenty of eighteen-year-old girls who looked sixteen or even fifteen could be hired by production companies with a lot less hassle and at a lower cost than girls who were still minors. That made an already competitive market downright cutthroat.

To battle back, Mom had me legally emancipated. She'd heard about another young actress working without the impediments of the child labor laws, and when she asked my agent about it, she was told it was as easy as hiring a lawyer and going to court.

We booked a date and went to court, asking the judge to make me an adult. The law existed to help kids get away from dangerous and harmful parents.

"Why are you petitioning for this?" the judge asked as we both stood before the bench. He was bald with reading glasses perched on top of his smooth, shiny head.

"I'd like the ability to work more hours when I'm hired. I will not let my education suffer. As you can see from my transcript, I'm a serious student. I have straight A's and I'm ranked second in my class. This is the only way I can compete with girls over eighteen who are trying out for the same roles."

The judge's clerk took my transcript from my hands and delivered it to the bench. The judge looked it over and his expression softened.

"This is impressive. Straight A's and all honors classes. Very well done for any student, much less someone who is also a professional actress," the judge said. His tone had changed, and now he studied both of us closely, his focus shifting to Mom.

"And, Mom, does this have anything to do with money?" he asked.

Mom cleared her throat the way she always did before she announced something she was trying to sell but personally didn't buy.

"No, your honor. My husband owns his own company. The money is there for her. It is hers. She'll use it for college. This is about leveling the playing field so she can continue to work," Mom said.

"Do you like to work?" the judge asked me. He took his glasses from the top of his head and placed one stem in his mouth, chewing on the end.

"I do. It gives me a sense of purpose. It's what I have always done," I said earnestly.

"When did you start? Whose idea was it?" he probed further. "Missy was discovered as an infant at a Johnson & Johnson baby shampoo commercial her sister was doing. Missy's worked steadily ever since," Mom said.

"Are you a Stage Mother?" the judge asked provocatively, employing a buzzword riddled with negative beauty pageant connotations.

Mom stiffened but her voice was steady and calm. She smiled faintly and replied, "Are you asking if I spend my free time driving her to interviews and sitting on the set all day while she works and becomes a star and I'm not paid a dime? Do I deal with her agent and contracts, buy her clothes and pay for her haircuts so she can work and have a successful career? Am I the only one protecting her on the set, and looking out for her interests, all for free? Do I do these things for her while people call me names and treat me like a hanger-on while I'm on the set? And she becomes rich and famous? If that's what you mean by a Stage Mother, then yes, I am that."

She was right, I'd heard that speech before, and every word of it was true. Still, the speech seemed to go against our best interests at the moment.

"Sounds like she needs you. Why should I emancipate her?" the judge responded.

"Because I will always do those things, whether she's emancipated or not. Because I'm her mom. She'll be free to work as long as she likes, but nothing else will change."

"You sold me. Missy Francis, you are now an emancipated minor."

I was legally free to live however I liked, but once again, Mom was right—nothing else would change. I still needed someone to manage my life, enroll me in school, make sure I had health insurance. But I did wonder, for how long?

* * *

The first job I did as an emancipated minor was a Kmart commercial. The next project, though, put the work back in working. I was cast in a blood-and-guts slasher movie about a cult that commits mass suicide in a house fire. I played the female lead, Jennifer Rubin, in all her flashback sequences. Her character, the only survivor of the house fire, constantly relives her time with the cult in her dreams, hence the title, *Bad Dreams*.

In the first scene, the leader of the cult, a very scary-looking Bruce Abbott, baptized me in a filthy lake out behind Magic Mountain. Bruce had white hair and startling blue eyes and looked like a burn victim, which could have been a result of the way the makeup artists painted him, but I wasn't sure. Either way, he was fairly terrifying.

The lake was covered with slime, and I couldn't see my hand below the surface. I could not believe that they wanted me to stick my head into that disgusting water. There was no way they had the budget to test it to see what toxins or deadly bacteria lived underneath the blanket of sludge that coated the top.

They blew out my hair and applied my makeup, which made me hope that somehow I wasn't getting dunked. Maybe they'd cut away and replace me with a stunt double. Although I doubted they had the budget for that either. When I noticed all the exact replicas of my outfit stocked in the wardrobe truck, I knew I was getting slimed.

The director explained that the senior cult members would walk me to the edge of the lake, then Bruce would come take my hand and lead me in until I was about waist deep in the water. Bruce would say a few lines and guide my head underwater.

I wanted to run. I knew from past experience, there was no escape. I needed to just man up.

"Are we going to rehearse?" I asked the director, trying to buy time.

"That was your rehearsal. We can't get you all wet if we aren't rolling."

I took a deep breath and prayed for a miracle, but instead, he yelled, "Action!"

I walked to the edge of the lake, and Scary Bruce met me and dragged me in. The thick, putrid water filled my shoes and clung to my calves, and I fought back the urge to vomit as I got deeper and deeper in what felt like quicksand.

Bruce chanted his lines, looking possessed. Every muscle in my body seized up. Finally the moment of truth arrived and he shoved my head underneath the water and into certain bacterial infection.

I guess I didn't really allow him to push my head all the way under, but just sort of fought away from him as the water started to fill my ears. It all happened so fast. When I came up, slimed and embarrassed, I was hoping that somehow my flailing had looked normal, and I was done. The crew groaned.

"Cut."

Bruce waded back to shore and wandered off, adjusting his burned skin, and I quickly scrambled to safety. They rushed me inside a trailer, threw me a robe, and started combing the slime out of my hair and blowing the ends with a hair dryer.

The director came into the trailer.

"So *this* time . . ."

Oh my God, I thought. We're doing it again.

They finished drying me off and restyling my hair in silence. And all the while I knew that this effort to get me warm and clean was leading me closer to having my nostrils refilled with slime.

As the hum of the hair dryer insulated me, I steeled my insides against the inevitable. I had to just go out and do it right, or I'd be marching into stagnant mosquito larva for the next three days. It was certainly getting harder to earn a buck in this town.

They delivered me to the set, and this time the crew looked at me with annoyance. They were clearly put out. I was costing everyone time, and until I did my job, no one was going anywhere.

That was it. I refused to be unprofessional. No matter how inhumane the task was, I was going to do the job I was hired to do. I had hoped that Mom would somehow save me from this, but she hadn't said a word since the first take. She just frowned in pain, offering no alternative, no relief. I was alone in this torture, and there didn't appear to be any way out.

"Action!" the director yelled with extra force, willing me to do it right this time.

I let the extras lead me to the edge of the water, and in my mind, I left my body, disconnecting myself from the horror of the experience.

I felt the water once again rise to my waist as Bruce led me back to the middle of the swamp. As my body began to shake with panic, I just let go. I let go of my fear, my sanity, my inclination to vomit. If I could disconnect long enough, it would be over.

I pressed my mouth and eyes closed tightly, hoping I could vacuum seal myself against the sludge. If I could have sucked my ears closed, I would have.

Scary Bruce dunked me, and held me under for good measure. Then he brought me up, and I broke free and stumbled to the edge, as the director yelled, "Cut!"

I'd done it. It was over. I hadn't done it well, no awards would roll my way as a result, but I least I'd let myself be baptized as directed, and we could move on.

When the movie hit the theaters, the kids from school went together to the Northridge Mall to see it. I didn't go along. I was mortified that the movie was completely silly and I wasn't at all good in it. Now a huge group of my peers were going together to sit in judgment of the production and make fun of me.

"They'd all give their eyeteeth to be in it," Mom said, trying to make me feel better. I was sure that she was right, but it didn't really help. I knew they were going to give me the hazing of a lifetime after they saw it. I looked ridiculous gulping for air, eyes big and wide as the moon during the fake baptism. The last thing I wanted was to go along and witness the snickering and mocking firsthand.

Besides, it was impossible to watch myself in any production, must less this one. I hated watching myself on television or on a screen of any type. I'd focus on any physical flaw, any bulge of fat or the bump in my nose, and every line I delivered made me cringe. I don't know why I couldn't enjoy watching myself. Lots of other performers did. All I ever saw was the faults.

I tried to see being in a horror flick as a good time, but in my heart, I was struggling. Was this the kind of work I had to look forward to? Fifteen was a tough age to be embarking on a midlife crisis, but no matter how much I focused on school or anything else, I couldn't escape the thought that my career was stalling.

Agents and casting directors expected successful child actors to fail to make the transition to working adult actors, and they didn't hesitate to speculate about it right in front of me. It seemed to be all that I heard. Other parents seemed to derive glee from my cresting professional failure. I didn't understand how people could be so hard on someone who hadn't even achieved her full height yet, but the swords were out and no one seemed to care that I was basically still prepubescent.

"Right! The kid from *Little House on the Prairie*! Has she done anything lately?" another cheerleading mom asked my mom. I was standing right there, and the woman insulted me, in the third person nonetheless. I wanted to ask her if her kid had worked lately, but then she would know she got to me. It was easier to just silently lick the wound.

I tried to act as if I didn't care, but that made things worse. Mom would accuse me of not caring, which was so far from the truth. I desperately wanted to stop the slide to failure, but I had no idea how. I didn't even love acting that much any longer. I felt like a puppet mouthing someone else's words. But I missed the sense of achievement, the sensation of winning, and the pride I'd see in Mom's eyes that came with completing a job successfully. Getting straight A's at school was a feather in my cap, but being a successful actress had been a diamond-encrusted crown almost no one else had been privileged to wear.

When summer rolled around Tiffany didn't come home from Berkeley. She decided to stay up in northern California, to get a jump on the required classes for sophomore year by knocking out a few over the summer.

The decision felt like a wise move. When she'd come home for holidays, at first, she'd seemed like a new person, free and happy. She'd slept in late, and we'd hung out having coffee and toast until we decided to get manicures and pedicures together or go to the mall shopping. I loved having a pal around the house, and Mom doted on her, at least initially.

But after a few days, Mom was picking at her, criticizing her sloppier appearance or where she threw her dirty clothes, and it seemed to me they couldn't coexist under the same roof for longer than a week.

"It might be time for you to go back to the dorm," Mom growled over a heap of wet towels on the rug in Tiffany's room.

"I will pick them up! Jeez! I'm still using them," she said

from other end of her closet, where she surveyed what little she'd left behind.

Still, Mom didn't like to be left out of what Tiffany and I did. So she'd come to the mall but quickly wear out her welcome.

"Those pants look tight," she said from the couch outside the dressing rooms where Tiffany was trying on some new Guess jeans.

"Well, I'm not starving like I was at the end of last year. I could stop eating if you think that would be better," Tiffany said while fixing her eyeliner in the mirror.

"I'm sure there's a middle ground between starving and eating pizza and drinking beer. I just don't want you to gain all the weight you lost. Have you gained the freshman ten? Have you weighed yourself lately?" Mom pressed.

It wasn't the best conversation to have in the middle of a store. I knew Mom road us about weight because of her own struggles with a fluctuating figure, but inflicting pain on Tiffany right on the spot wasn't the way to make a visit home a pleasant one. I gave Mom a pleading look.

"What?" she snapped.

"I don't know," I said quietly when Tiffany went back into the dressing room. "Maybe go easy on her?"

"Oh, of course. It's all me. I'm the bad guy. You guys gang up on me and I'm the bad guy. You only bring me along for my wallet. That's all I'm good for. Pay for your clothes and keep my mouth shut! Why don't I just take my wallet and go home and see how you two like it!"

Her response was so disproportional to what had come before it, but there was no reasoning with her.

So Tiffany's decision to get ahead of the course load was brilliant, no matter how thin that excuse sounded.

* * *

To my own surprise, I started to strain and blister under Mom's totalitarian rule. I had always faulted Tiffany for not simply following the party line and promoting harmony. But now that I was carrying out that mandate alone, I realized what a burden it was. It was exhausting to constantly manage Mom's mood. When she picked me up from school she'd show up angry, and I'd have to cajole her with gossip from school. On a whim, she'd suddenly ground me and stop me from going to the movies with my friends because I had looked at her the wrong way. Sometimes she'd just say she didn't like my attitude and would refuse to tell me why. She was wildly unpredictable, striking out at me, even hitting me, with almost no warning or provocation.

"Get off the phone," she said one day, storming into my room unannounced. "Laura, hang on . . . ," I said, not hanging up right away. She took the cordless phone out of my hand and threw it against the wall.

"How do you like *that*!" she said before stomping out. I never found out what got the ball rolling.

Other times she'd be quiet and sullen for days, and then suddenly turn sunny on a dime. I had no idea what to expect, and having Mom as a constant variable in the equation made life even more complicated than it needed to be.

Around this time, Mom let the house slowly go to hell. I noticed half-empty boxes and shopping bags filled with papers piling up in the family room. They'd appear one day, seemingly for no reason or purpose, and blend in with the furniture, taking up permanent residence.

Lulu, the housekeeper who had been with us for years, continued to come by on Fridays, but cleaned only the middle of each room while clutter piled up around the edges, like snow being pushed to the side of the road.

In the formal sitting room, which we'd never been allowed

to use, the fabric and carpet had faded under the sun's glare, frozen in time, like an abandoned dollhouse. The once bright and cheery Kelly green carpet that ran through the house now looked tired and tattered.

While Mom gained weight and lost energy, I assumed she didn't notice or didn't mind our home's deterioration. Until I tried to invite my friend Cori over to go swimming.

"The house is a mess; you can't have anyone over with it looking like this, for God's sake," she said, lying on her bed, her left arm curled under her head while she rested. She was wearing stretch pants and the same shirt she'd worn the day before.

"Okay, I'll clean up," I offered.

I scurried around the house with Ajax, cleaning the sinks and tub in my bathroom, finding the smell of the toxic cleaner oddly refreshing. I polished the faucets with Windex for good measure, and the bathroom sparkled when I finished. Then I vacuumed the halls to make the carpet—where it wasn't worn down—stand up at attention like freshly mowed grass. I tucked as many bags and boxes behind the couch as possible, and scrubbed the kitchen with a mixture of Fantastic and Ajax as warranted. I was efficient and motivated, and the whole exercise took about ninety minutes.

I returned to Mom's room, where she hadn't moved.

"House is clean," I said hopefully. "Can I tell Cori to come over?"

"No," she said without moving her eyes off the small color television that sat on the table next to her bed.

"Why not? The house looks great."

"There's too much crap in the family room," she said with an edge in her voice.

"Okay, where do you want me to put it? I could move it all out to the garage. Would that be good?" I offered.

"Don't touch it. I have a lot of important papers in those bags. I'll never find anything again if you move it," she said.

I stood there silently, trying to figure out how to move this discussion forward.

"What if we don't go through the family room at all? I'll make sure we only go to the pool through the kitchen. Please? I kind of already invited her."

"That was stupid of you. You didn't ask *me*. The carpet is torn. We cannot have people in the house until we replace the carpet. And the walls need to be painted. You can't have anyone over," she ruled.

I stood there trying to wrap my head around the idea that I was basically never having anyone over ever again. I was the only one taking any action around the house, but I didn't have the ability to reweave the carpet. That one was beyond me.

I left the room crestfallen, and went to my room to call Cori. I couldn't figure out how I was going to explain this. I was embarrassed to disinvite her and ashamed that Mom thought our house was too much of a shambles to have friends over. It was worn, but who cared? Certainly not Cori. She was the nicest, least judgmental person I knew. She just wanted to hang out and swim.

I picked up the cordless phone, which I'd duct-taped back together, and dialed slowly. It rang twice and then I heard Cori's voice on the other end.

"Hello?" she said.

"Hey, it's me. You aren't going to believe this. My mom says I can't have anyone over. She's mad at me for something, I don't know what. I live in hell. She's insane and I don't want to subject you to it anyway. She says our house is a mess or something and not suitable for company," I said.

"That's okay. Our house is immaculate. I just squeegeed the

shower. I'm not sure my mom's beating yours on the sanity scale," Cori said.

"I love your house. It's so clean. I'd like to move in," I replied.

"Bring a squeegee if you want to shower. Wait, scratch that. We've got like six."

"I'm so sorry about today," I said truthfully.

"Oh my God, don't sweat it. You're welcome to come over here if you want to swim. We'll eat lunch, we can eat off the floor. I'm pretty sure my mom just bleached it," she offered.

"Yeah, I don't know. I'm not sure I can even get out of the house now. I will keep you posted," I said and hung up.

When I went back to school in the fall for my sophomore year, I was on the cusp of getting my driver's license, which meant real freedom, and Mom knew it. The day I got the precious document, I borrowed her car and barreled off to an interview.

"This doesn't mean you can go where you want, when you want, you know," she threatened.

But, of course, that's exactly what it meant. I had been dating a boy who lived on the other side of L.A. in Beverly Hills, and if I had my own transportation, I could see Oscar anytime I wanted as long as I had a good cover story, another fact that set Mom and me up to battle.

Tiffany had gotten a car for her sixteenth birthday, so in the months preceding my birthday I fantasized about owning the ultimate teenage dream car: a brand-new red BMW convertible. In what seemed like an act of extreme generosity, Mom went ahead and ordered it for me. The car was about to arrive when Tiffany came home from college for winter break, and I suddenly felt awkward knowing that she had a utilitarian Jeep and I was getting an expensive sports car.

Me around age four in my audition uniform. Boy, did I get sick of those overalls and puff sleeves. Don't forget the bows!

Photo courtesy of the author

Tiffany, with her signature shy smile, at around five years old when she became a Barbie commercial favorite.

Photo courtesy of the author

Missy Francis

BIRTHDATE: December 12, 1972
HEIGHT: 42½"
WEIGHT: 38 lbs.
HAIR: Brown
EYES: Hazel

Missy Muffin has a personality perfectly suited to her nickname. She is affectionate, effervescent and a constant joy. Missy has already earned fine commercial, photographic and modeling credits, attesting to her self-confidence and ability to take direction.

She has appeared on "The Young and The Restless" and was featured in "The Ghost on Flight 401". Missy also appeared in the television special "I Love You".

She enjoys her dancing classes and playing with her big sister Tiffany-Ann and together they swim, horseback ride, ice skate and love animals.

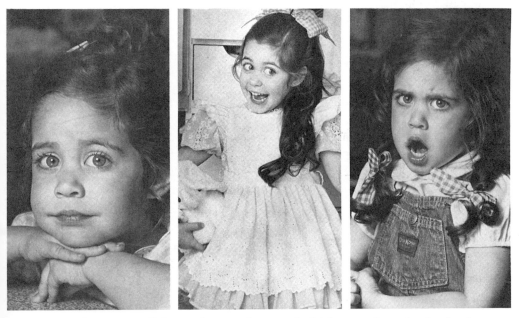

My "composite" for auditions, boxes of which were kept in the back of the station wagon at all times. The photos were meant to show a full range of emotions so the casting agents could envision me in any role, from drama to comedy. Plus, I had a sister, just in case the production needed another kid!

Photo courtesy of the author

The cast of *Little House on the Prairie* when Jason and I joined the show. Melissa Gilbert's character, Laura, was already the school-teacher. Both Grace (the blond girl in front) and Carrie (next to me) were played by sets of twins, and I have no idea which twin of each set is actually in the photo.

Photo by: NBCU Photo Bank

Me with my fictional brother (Jason Bateman) and adoptive father
(Michael Landon) on a rare day when I wasn't in those Ingalls braids.
The smiles are real; we had a lot of laughs.

Photo by: NBCU Photo Bank

Fake snow falling indoors on the studio set in Culver City, on the magical day my Brownie troop came to visit the show. On the show, it was Christmas Day, and the Ingallses couldn't get to the barn to get their gifts because they were snowed in by the blizzard.
Photo by: NBCU Photo Bank

The scene where Michael Landon (as Charles Ingalls) stopped the train and climbed aboard after deciding to adopt Jason Bateman (as my brother James) and I, rather than sending us off to an orphanage. We were rehearsing, so I hadn't turned on the tears, yet.
Photo by: NBCU Photo Bank

A glamour shot of me and Tiffany right after I started at Chaminade. That's my cheerleading uniform. Tiffany's spiky hairdo covered the scars on her forehead from the accident.

Photo courtesy of the author

Taken just before I left
for Stanford summer
school; the torn jeans
were my new uniform
of choice.
*Photo courtesy
of the author*

Marrying Wray, in 1999 at Sherwood Country Club.
Photo courtesy of the author

"You realize you're paying for that car, right?" Tiffany said to me when she came into my room and saw the brochure.

I just raised my eyebrows and shrugged. I'd realized by now that Mom was controlling every dime that came in. She collected everything my father, Tiffany, or I made and doled it out as if it were hers. I'd seen her write checks out of the account that was supposed to be my trust fund.

"Isn't that account for college?" I'd asked when I saw my name at the top of the check. She paused initially, like she'd been caught with her hand in the cookie jar, but then explained that she was writing a check for my private school tution.

"It's for your education. You don't want to pay for Chaminade? That's not your bill? That's mine? How about your clothes? Your horses? Your head shots? Your hair appointments? All mine? I don't have furs or big diamonds! I barely have clothes! You wear designer everything! What a spoiled monster you are!"

She'd attack with such vehemence anyone who dared to probe into how she was handling the money that each of us soon gave up. It was exhausting.

The irony was that, now that I was emancipated, anything I made was supposed to be my own. Those checks no longer had to go into a "trust." But gaining control of my money never seemed like a real possibility to me.

Still, I began to worry that Mom saw herself as the family banker, and she didn't seem like much of a long-term investor, or even fiscally responsible.

I tried to talk to Dad about it the next time we were alone.

"You certainly don't have to have a BMW," he said. "You could be sensible and buy yourself a gently used Honda. That's what I would do. I think that car you're buying is silly and a waste of money."

The severity of his tone panicked me. Was there reason to

worry? Was money running out? In my most adult voice I said, "I'd like to know how much money I have left."

Dad put down the paper he'd been reading and said, "Look, college will be paid for, no matter what. Everything that comes in is spent on you and Tiffany. You should have quit riding horses earlier if you were worried about saving money. You should get a good used car. Don't blame your mom for decisions you're making. You wanted us to spend family money on clothes and horses and private schools and save your own earnings off to the side? Well, I guess that would nice. If you had spent less that could have happened. Everyone's spending has gotten way out of control, and you don't make the same bread you used to. I mean, that's fine. You don't need to work. Other kids aren't out there earning money like you. You just need to understand the math."

I got his logic. And I couldn't disagree. I just would have liked to have been informed when we officially started spending what I had thought was my trust fund for later. Had I known the money I was making wasn't just going into a pot somewhere, waiting until I turned eighteen, I might have made different decisions.

That assertion made me seem pretty selfish. I would have spent differently the last few years if I knew I was spending the money *I* was making? Now I felt guilty on top of everything else.

When the red BMW arrived from the factory, Mom brought it to school with a huge red bow on the roof and parked it in the faculty parking lot. I immediately got detention for leaving my car in the faculty lot, even though the principal, Brother Bill, knew I'd had nothing to do with it. He had to punish someone for the obnoxious behavior and he didn't have jurisdiction over Mom. I'm not sure anyone did.

In a single move, Mom pissed off my teachers and alienated my friends, all to show off. Then she wanted a debt of gratitude from me for giving me such a great birthday gift. I spent the next few days doing damage control at school.

"I really got in a lot of trouble over the car," I grumbled after dinner one night.

She laughed in disbelief. "You're so ungrateful! I bought you a beautiful red BMW convertible for your birthday! Name one other parent you know who did that!"

It wasn't worth pointing out that most parents wouldn't handle all of our finances the way she was. She would just hit me and ground me, and never cede the point anyway.

We were in the kitchen. I was washing the dishes, having made chicken and rice for the two of us. Dad was still at his office, hiding from the rancor that had taken over the house lately. Mom was standing at the tile island in the middle of the room sorting bills and reading the junk mail.

"I know. It's just that we aren't allowed to park in the faculty lot." That was hardly the issue and we both knew it.

She shrugged. "They are all just jealous because it's such a nice car. You don't have to have nice things if you don't want to."

"Even still, I'm not sure hitting them over the head with it is the way to go."

"Great." She sighed and threw the junk mail in the trash. "If that's how you feel, I'll drive the car tomorrow. You can ride to school with Cori."

The only way I had of escaping my mom was to get out of the house. Once I had a car, I'd use any excuse to go out. There was always a price to pay once I got home—she would be suspicious of my whereabouts, or irritated by my increasing independence, or both—but evading her grasp for an afternoon or evening was worth it.

I joined the track team, which annoyed Mom to no end. I'd never been allowed to participate in a team sport because the practices would place time demands on my schedule. Mom always said there was nothing special about being part of a team. But by high school, I wanted to be part of a group, not always an individual. Track wasn't exactly a team sport the way basketball was, but by this point, all of my classmates had laid claim to various sports and track was the only sports team I could join this late in life and do decently.

I loved having a uniform and going to meets. I could run relatively fast and placed well in the hurdles, and I somehow showed promise at the field events, like javelin and triple jump. Plus track was a positive way to shape up or lose weight without starving. But Mom hated that someone other than her was managing my time.

One day after a track meet I walked into the house with a medal I'd won. Even though we'd come in second, I was proud that the coach had let me run with the 440-yard relay team. My hands shook before the race, but I ran my heart out, and I still glowed with the feeling of winning a ribbon with three other girls at my side.

"Check it out. We got second in the relay. I ran the first leg," I told Mom as I entered her room. She was lying on her bed, watching the local news. Her eyes were narrow. She didn't turn to respond or look at me. I thought maybe she was just feeling down.

After a few moments of silence, I turned and started to walk out of the room.

"Where were you really?"

"At a track meet," I said, wondering what this was going to be about.

"Against whom?" she said coldly.

"Beverly Hills High School. I told you that this morning."

"I went to Beverly Hills High. You weren't there. You're lying."

It took me a moment to realize she was serious. I had been at the meet for hours. I had no idea where she was going with this.

"I was at the meet. You can call Coach Ryan. I got third in the shot put," I said, my feelings hurt.

"I went there. It was empty. There was no track meet. Beverly Hill High on Wilshire."

"It's on Moreno. It's not on Wilshire. You went to the wrong place. I could have told you where it was if you wanted to come watch. We all took the bus, but it would have been great to see you there. I'm actually pretty good," I said.

"I don't believe you," she said, holding her ground.

I couldn't believe she was accusing me of lying about going to a track meet. I knew she didn't support my foray into high school athletics, but this charge really burned. Other parents proudly supported their kids' athletic achievements. I wasn't that good, but I was working really hard and getting a boost from sticking with the commitment I'd made to the track team.

"If you don't believe me, let me dial Coach Ryan right now. Right now. Ask him. I won't say a word. You ask him! Or come next time," I insisted. I wasn't lying and I wasn't going to let this go, even if this time she threw me against the wall instead of the phone.

"It's a waste of your time. You should take an acting class if you need something to do. What's the point of being one in a sea of millions? Are you going to run track for a living when you grow up?"

I left and went into my room and threw myself on the bed. She was acting as if I were doing something dirty by joining a team. I guess I understood her suspicions. I was making it my job to get away with everything I could, pushing the envelope as far as I could without getting caught. But she didn't really know what I was up to and she had no proof even if she was suspicious.

I'd crawled out my window a few times to meet Oscar. I had a fake ID so I could go out in Westwood to the hangout spots by UCLA. But she knew about that and didn't care as long as I didn't drink, which she'd never caught me doing.

I drank wine coolers with my friends at parties, but everyone did that, and it had never amounted to any trouble. I cut some classes, but I always had a well-forged note, and she'd never gotten a call from school. The bottom line was that I had straight A's and every academic honor possible. I'd barely received a detention. My record was perfect and clean.

She just sensed that I usually wasn't where I said I was, which was pretty accurate. My goal was to get beyond her reach, and we both knew it.

I called Tiffany to commiserate. This year she'd moved into a house off campus with a girlfriend, Molly, and a bunch of guys. I called the phone in their living room and it took them a few minutes to track her down.

"Hey, what's up?" she said.

"Mom is driving me nuts."

"That's her specialty," she chuckled.

I heard people yelling and laughing in the background.

"You need to just keep her happy. It's the only way to survive. I've got my hands full here. Trying to get Thor to clean up the kitchen and not leave his dishes everywhere. Collecting rent. Dealing with the landlord who doesn't like the renovations Chris made in his room. I've got to find time to go to class. You've got it good at home."

Tiffany had been the one to find the house, so she had taken on the role of den mom. She was complaining but I could tell she relished being in charge.

"Can I come up for a weekend?"

"Of course. That would be fun. If Mom will let you."

*   *   *

It took a lot of finesse—I had to find a way to suggest the idea without seeming overly interested in going, which would've made Mom suspicious—but Mom actually let me drive up alone to stay with Tiffany. In the end, she probably just wanted me to go and report back on what Tiffany was doing.

I drove five hours alone, stopping only once to go the bathroom and get a Diet Coke. I felt compelled to make good time, for no real reason. I had made the drive a number of times with Tiffany, or with Mom and Dad, but never alone. I wasn't nervous really, just eager to do it efficiently and get to Tiffany's house without incident, plus I enjoyed the solitude of the drive.

When I got to her place, I hoped I had the wrong address. The faded tan house looked like it might collapse into a heap of dust at any moment. The bushes in the front yard were gnarled and dusty, roots gripping the dry earth beneath them for dear life. A driveway ran from the street to the backyard, loaded with dilapidated cars. Tiffany's red Jeep, now dinged up and road worn, sat at the front of the pack.

I walked over the threshold with my duffel bag full of clothes. A dirty, tattooed guy with piercings dotting his ears and nose stumbled down the stairs and looked at me warily before turning the corner into the kitchen. Another group of guys slumped together lazily on a cluster of mismatched, dusty recliners in the living room. I tried not to touch anything while I scanned the room, looking for any sign of my sister.

My pink cable-knit sweater glowed against the faded khaki backdrop of the room. I couldn't tell what color the walls and floors had been originally, but now they just blended together into a universal shade of grunge.

"Hello!" Tiffany smiled, bounding down the stairs. "What

do you think? Mom would hate it, I know. But it's ours! And I'm in charge."

She was bursting with pride, so I tried to look positive.

"Oh, you're such a princess. You hate it, right?" Suddenly she looked crestfallen.

"No!" I said. "It's really cute. Hey, I'd love to live anywhere but home. I'm completely jealous."

"Molly is still at class. This is Dave, Chad, and Thor," she said, gesturing to the lumps in the living room. "Did you guys say hello to my little baby sister?" She always got a kick out of calling me that since the top of her head barely cleared my shoulder.

"Come on up to my room and put your stuff down. I have the master bedroom."

We walked up the creaky stairs and past a few doors to the room at the end of the hall. It was the same size as my room at home, with two old-fashioned double-paned windows that slid up and now hung open without screens.

The comforter that Mom bought her for the dorm stretched across the bed, stained and tattered from abuse. Dresses and a slew of collared shirts and sweaters hung in the open closet next to a row of pants and short skirts, while still more clothes lay in a heap on the worn carpet. A mountain of shoes and boots, most of which I recognized, covered the floor of the closet. Posters of various Seattle grunge rock bands covered the walls. Heaps of funky jewelry she'd probably bought on the street covered the top of the natural pine dresser.

"I've got a wine-making chemistry class in about thirty minutes. We could go on campus for that and then grab some dinner. There's a great vegetarian place on Telegraph."

I had forgotten she had become a vegetarian, while fully embracing the hippie-chic lifestyle that still had a grip on Berkeley. She'd even registered as a Democrat to stick it to our conservative parents. Still, I knew the act was just for show, because she snuck a cheeseburger the last time we drove through Jack in the Box in L.A.

We went to class, which was more chemistry than wine-making, and put me to sleep after the long drive, then we strolled back through the sprawling campus before settling into a table at the Grove.

"So what's new at home? Dad still miserable? I have no idea why he doesn't leave Mom. She treats him so badly," Tiffany said, picking at her roasted vegetables. I had ordered a salad, but I could already tell I was going to need a pizza chaser.

"Yeah, I have no idea why he puts up with it. Inertia I guess. Maybe when I go to college he'll bail," I said.

The waitress stopped by the table and dropped off two fresh Diet Cokes.

"This is pretty cool," I said, gesturing to the atmosphere around us. "I could see myself at Cal."

"Oh, no. Mom and Dad expect you to go to Stanford. At least," she said, dissecting an enormous eggplant on her plate.

"Like Cal isn't a great school?" I said brightly, eager to undo the damage Mom had done denigrating Berkeley. In millions of other families, Tiffany wouldn't be second-rate.

"You can't choose a college just to spite Mom."

We spent the next day walking around downtown Berkeley, shopping, talking, and laughing. This was the Tiffany I loved. Calm, happy, funny. Wearing jeans and pink Birkenstocks with a Clockwork Orange T-shirt, she picked out oversized earrings and handwoven sweaters for me to take home.

The girl who had graduated from high school and left our house had quietly vanished: stick skinny, blonde, beautifully made-up, but reined in and tugging at the bit. Her new messier, more relaxed look matched her demeanor and it suited her. It seemed as if she could finally breathe.

We walked down Telegraph, moving in and out of shops, trying on things, chatting. I wanted to stay for a week and see what this relationship could be.

When we got back to her place a few hours later, I changed into tight Guess jeans and a black Lycra top. She told me she and Molly had planned a house party in my honor, though I got the sense from the keg on the counter they did this whether a special guest was in town or not.

By ten the place had filled with twenty-somethings in rumpled shirts and torn jeans. Talking to people and listening to their conversations, I quickly realized that most of the people at the party didn't go to Berkeley, or any college for that matter. Neither did the guys who lived in the house. They were all locals, friends of friends, musicians, waiters, bartenders, bouncers. Tiffany's off–campus house was an off-campus life. She had tried to fit into the sorority scene, but couldn't wear the costume of a perky coed. She was too shy and insecure to make it in that *Lord of the Flies* culture. She found a spot to fit in, but it wasn't terribly collegiate.

I wandered around the party, not having much in common with most of the people I bumped into, making it hard to keep a conversation going. They were deep into liberal politics, and as they talked about the evils of corporate America, I wondered if anyone had ever received a paycheck and seen the difference between their gross income and what was left after taxes.

Nursing a wine cooler, I went upstairs and found Tiffany and a handful of people sitting in a circle on the floor in one of the other bedrooms.

A guy with long brown hair tied back in a ponytail used a lighter to ignite a whitish ball that sat on a piece of tin foil on the ground. As he lit it, another guy in a black Metallica T-shirt leaned in and inhaled the vapor with a pipe.

A girl with blue hair and thick black eyeliner walked in next. "Oh, speedballs. Yes!" she said as she took a seat. I'd never seen anything like this before. I'd seen cocaine at parties, but I'd never tried it. Flaming balls of speed and coke were far beyond my comfort level.

Metallica handed the pipe to Tiffany, and she inhaled deeply. She took one more hit, and then passed the pipe to the blue-haired girl. I faded to the back of the group and then slid out of the room.

I stood at the top of the stairs and looked down at the living room, where the music had taken a loud, manic turn. People stood around, more than a few in a bleary haze.

I backed away from the landing and instead wandered down the hall to Tiffany's room and lay down on the bed. The alcohol weighed on me as I turned out the light and tried to pull the shade on what I'd seen.

The next morning, I woke up alone to a quiet house. I had no idea what time the party had ended, but as I walked silently down the hall to the bathroom, I could see sleeping bodies on couches and even the floor.

I didn't want to talk to Tiffany about what I'd seen her and her friends doing the night before. I was embarrassed about being frightened by the drugs and the whole scene I'd witnessed in that upstairs bedroom. I just wanted to go, so I grabbed my bag and wrote a note to Tiffany, thanking her for the fun weekend and explaining that I had to get back home to get organized for the week at school. I got in the front seat of my red BMW, a standout on the shabby street, and sped off.

CHAPTER ELEVEN

I walked into the audition and straight to the sign-in sheet. Old framed movie posters hung along the faded red walls, and beneath them chairs were lined up in rows for actors to sit in while they waited to be called into another room, where we'd stand in front of a white paper backdrop and read the lines to a video camera on a tripod.

I picked up a chewed pencil and started to fill out the empty line beneath the names of everyone who had come before me that afternoon. By now I could do the drill in my sleep: name, birthdate, Social Security number, union membership, agent, audition time. I filled it out, grabbed a Xerox copy of the sides (the scene we were expected to perform) and took a seat.

In the last six months, I'd worked only on a Frosted Flakes commercial. In that one, I'd raced over hurdles, fueled by sugary cereal. Improbable, but a jackpot nonetheless. Even with that money rolling in, I needed to work again. I had a plan. I'd been sneaking down the driveway to the mailbox and intercepting residual checks as they rolled in. Then stopping by the bank on the way home from school to deposit what I could glean into an account that no one else knew anything about.

The balance was growing pretty quickly. I had worked so much over the course of my life that checks rolled in all the time. I could skim enough off to make a difference without Mom realizing it.

I needed to stockpile about ten grand to pay the tuition and board at Stanford summer school. I had floated the idea of going away for the summer to my parents, and not surprisingly, my proposal was greeted like burnt toast. I casually agreed with my parents' reasons why I shouldn't go so that Mom and Dad wouldn't realize I was going no matter what. I was only gauging their participation.

Dad said summer school away was too expensive, and Mom immediately sniffed it out for what it was, a plan to get out of her reach. She couldn't grill me, control me, pull my hair to get my attention from four hundred miles away.

I looked at the sides. "Tampax, so I feel confident no matter what time of the month it is." How am I going to sell that pitch, knowing every guy at school will see it? Nightmare.

It didn't help that I felt huge in my jeans. I remembered what another hot agent had said when I went to talk to her about representing me earlier that week: "I don't want you to be anorexic, obviously, but you need to try to be as small as you can possibly be."

What did that mean? Could I take a knife and slice off the meat that had shown up on either side of my thighs? I could stop eating, but that would be tough if I wanted to stay awake and avoid a migraine.

I had to find a way to say the lines believably. A national commercial like this would easily net ten to twelve thousand dollars in the first cycle. That's the kind of check that Mom would miss if I took it out of the mailbox. But the second-cycle check could get derailed into my stash without her noticing.

Two months alone was a dream. I could study, date, go out. See what it could be like to live Mom-free.

"Missy Francis?" the casting lady called.

I walked into the audition room and stood in front of the small video camera. A cue card blurted out the simple, mortifying line.

"Tampax, so I feel confident, no matter what time of the month it is."

I said the words three times, three different ways, and then practically ran to the car. There had to be a better way to escape from Mom. There were thousands if not millions of people who would scream that line from the top of a building to be on TV. I knew that was true. I just didn't happen to be one of them anymore.

When I walked in the door Mom was waiting in her room, watching TV and listening closely for the sound of the garage door opening. She'd been monitoring me closely since I'd blown off an interview the previous month. I'd decided to spend the whole afternoon with Oscar while she thought I was on a casting call. I figured she'd think it was just another audition I didn't get. Too bad my agent reported the no-show to the authorities. She'd driven my car for a week just to make me feel what it would be like for her to have it instead of me. It seemed like she'd bought me the car for my birthday only so she could take it away and make it hers on a whim. The convertible was more an instrument of torture than a gift.

As I climbed the green-carpet stairs, I kept my eyes on the bright frayed strands. When I got to the top, I could see her sitting on the edge of her bed. She held my report card between her fingers, studying it, lips pursed, eyebrows raised. I knew exactly what it said. I always reviewed my grades with each individual teacher long before the school printed them out and sent them home. I knew I had carefully cultivated straight A's like always.

I couldn't walk by now without stopping, so I entered her room.

"I have to say, I'm disappointed," Mom said with a frown.

What? My turn to raise an eyebrow. She went on.

"You got an A minus in AP Chemistry." Disgust filled her voice. She may well have said the dog peed on the carpet.

"Right." Incredible!

"That's almost a B plus."

I laughed, outraged. She stood up and slapped me across the face so hard I thought a few of my teeth might have flown out.

I laughed again, regaining my balance, and left.

That's the best she can muster to hold me down? In the hunt to drum up evidence to justify clipping my wings, an A– in AP Chemistry was her smoking gun. Ludicrous. But then again, as long as I lived there, she was the judge and jury. And apparently Dad wasn't going to do anything to stop her, so what did it matter how weak her case was?

The truth is I hadn't brought home a B+ since eighth grade. I drove myself relentlessly to keep her off my back but also because I believed what she told me in the beginning: if I wasn't first; if I didn't get an A, it was simply because I wasn't trying hard enough. I was born at least as smart and as good as anyone, she always said.

She had drummed that into me daily from birth, and I

believed it then as I believed it now, and it made me bulletproof. Every setback was temporary. Success was only a matter of will and effort.

I cheated on a typing test once because I hadn't practiced enough, and it was a physical skill I couldn't think my way out of. (That was the lone B+, the lone blemish on my academic record.) When I got busted, the teacher, Mrs. Valentine, begged me to confess. I wouldn't dream of it. She said "I understand why you would do this given the tremendous pressure you obviously get from your mom to be perfect."

Fuck her.

I got straight A's, I drove myself because I was worth it. I was worth the sleepless, ceaseless effort. In the beginning, it was about the fire-breathing dragon waiting at home. But not anymore.

I took an F on that typing test, and got an A on the rest. Even though it all averaged out to an A–, Mrs. Valentine gave me a B+ to prove her point. "I can't let you have an A– when I know you cheated. Even if you won't admit it."

Ironically, I proved Mom right. I got a B+ because I didn't try hard enough that one time. The mediocre grade was my fault. I had no one to blame but myself, and I would never let it happen again.

Now this A– in AP Chemistry was one the toughest grades I'd ever earned. I'd struggled, and had even found a tutor at UCLA to help me, and Mom was looking down on the grade with disdain. A red mark splashed across my cheek as my reward.

It was insane. I had to go.

A few weeks later, a thick envelope arrived postmarked from Stanford, and I thought I'd explode. I tore it open, slicing my finger on the thick paper near the seal, and sure enough, it held the magic acceptance letter and registration packet. I just stood next to the mailbox in silent shock, one hand over my gaping mouth, the other clutching the stack of mail. My heart pounded in my throat.

During an open house night, the assistant principal, Ms. Corbett, had told Mom that spending a summer at Stanford, and doing well, would demonstrate I could carry the load and would go a long way to helping me get in to any college. Ms. Corbett had taken on the job of mentoring me after I'd been in her Honors Literature class. She said I had a knack for writing and analytical thinking, and a wisdom beyond my seventeen years. I think she suspected I might need a break from home. Though Mom had originally resisted, she and Dad couldn't say no to at least letting me apply when the recommendation came from the assistant principal.

I flipped through the registration booklet and stopped at a picture of the dorm I would be living in with the other summer students. Brown bricks, modest, sort of '70s, devoid of Mom. This was complete genius. I had engineered a way to live on my own, without parents, all summer. I couldn't believe none of my friends had thought of this. I'd actually never heard of anyone attending a university summer program. I didn't even know enrollment was possible until Ms. Corbett mentioned it.

I went in the house and showed Mom. She read and reread the letter. She couldn't help but be proud of the achievement. An acceptance letter from Stanford reflected well on her.

"Well, if you go, you can still come home for auditions," she said, studying the catalog at the kitchen table.

I doubt that, I thought.

"Of course," I said.

* * *

We went to dinner at our favorite Italian restaurant, Giuseppe's. I figured a public setting would be the best location to reveal the second part of my escape plan, the money I'd stashed away to make the whole thing work.

Mom and I walked through the swinging glass door of the restaurant. The black plastic blinds that blocked out the blinding setting sun jumped and slapped against the glass door as it shut. Mom and I stood by the hostess stand, waiting for a petite brunette to take us to a table.

The hostess deposited us at a round booth with a view of the strip mall parking lot. An upscale wine store and a nail salon filled out the rest of the mall.

Dad's white Chrysler pulled into the lot. About a month before, he had traded in his troublesome silver Mercedes for this car, much to Mom's dismay. He'd said he was sick of paying to keep the Mercedes running. He'd looked quietly gleeful as Mom had yelled that he couldn't make these types of decisions without consulting her.

Dad opened the door to the restaurant, letting in a flood of light. He saw us by the window and came over to sit at the end of the booth. His leg dangled out into the aisle as he flagged down a waitress and asked for a glass of Chablis. He had on his signature faded Levis and blue and white striped button-down, with a pack of cigarettes in the breast pocket. His hair, now almost completely white and thicker than ever, covered his forehead in a fluffy wave.

"Hey, baby. How was school today?" he said, patting my arm as his drink arrived.

"Great. I got into Stanford," I said, peeking up from my menu.

"That's great," he said with a smile.

"So can I go?" I pushed on.

"I wish you could," he said easily. "It would be great. But we don't have the money for that right now. How much is it again?"

"It's about ten grand with everything. Food and room and board," Mom said.

This didn't seem like the type of opportunity that should be evaluated on the basis of a price tag. Going to Stanford was exactly why I'd worked so hard in school for eleven years plus. Spending this money would be without question an investment in my future.

Luckily I'd planned for their collective unpredictability.

"I'm saving up for new tires for the Chrysler," Dad said. I let the absurdity of that statement go.

"I've been saving too. I've got it covered. So, no worries," I ventured.

"Well, I don't know about that," Mom laughed lightly. "But I'm sure I can find the money somehow."

She was about to tick off her demands in exchange for letting me enroll, then it would be impossible to thank her enough. I'd owe her for the rest of my life. Again.

"I've saved some money in an account at the bank. From tutoring the neighbors, and that Frosted Flakes commercial. Now I've got about twelve thousand. Maybe thirteen."

Electricity gripped the table. I'd done the unthinkable. I'd moved the pea before she could palm it. No one had ever dared to screw with her shell game before.

"You *what?*" she said. They were both looking directly into my eyes, the three of us suddenly wide awake and connected.

"My paychecks, some residuals. And the money from tutoring Kiera. For the SAT. And then I saw the latest cycle check from the Frosted Flakes commercial in the mailbox and I just put that in too." I said it like I'd just found a discarded piece of paper on the ground and picked it up.

"You stole a check from the mailbox?" Mom demanded, her voice so sharp it could have shaved ice.

"It was made out to me," I continued. "What difference does it make which account it goes into?" If we weren't sitting in a public restaurant, she would have grabbed me.

"Right," she said slowly. Ever the shell man, she wouldn't admit she'd lost control of the game even for a minute.

"I mean, I will write the check to Stanford. Isn't that great? I've got enough set aside. You both just said it's a great idea but we don't have the cash. Now we do. Problem solved. I planned ahead," I said.

"Set aside? You've got it *set aside*. Well, why don't you take care of *all* of it then? There's a tuition check due at Chaminade. You're welcome to pay that. And there's your car payment. Go ahead and write that one too. And the car insurance. I've got a bill from Allstate in my purse. How's the balance now?"

"What about all the rest of the money?" I asked, picking the shell she'd led me to.

"What *rest* of the money?" she said, laughing that I'd fallen into the trap. "You have more than spent every dime you have *ever* made, and don't you dare kid yourself otherwise. Don't you ever say, *I* spent it. *You* spent it, my dear. Every single penny. You don't see *me* in jewels and furs, do you? You're the one driving the expensive sports car. You're the one attending the private schools, you're the one dressed to the nines. Not me. Not him. Certainly not your sister. She has never had half of what you've had. And you know it. You've worked hard, and you've spent hard, and don't you dare ever say otherwise."

She pushed out of the booth and got up, knocking over an empty glass which rolled across the table. She dragged her oversized leather purse with her, and sniffed as she strode to the door and threw it open, letting it slam behind her with another slap of the shades.

Dad and I just silently watched. It was the millionth time she'd shot up and stormed out during a meal, leaving only a cloud of dust and drama in her wake. One time she made a production of departing in a huff, and walked all the way home, which took an hour. The problem was that she had forgotten that she'd driven herself. She had to get a ride back to the restaurant the next day to pick up her car. Sometimes she'd speed off in the only car we'd brought, stranding the rest of us in the process. Dad had taken to driving separately and keeping his keys in his pockets to be safe.

"Well, you've done it now." Dad laughed, a little gleeful. "Did you really open an account and siphon off money as it came in?"

"Yep."

"It is yours, I guess. You've got a right to it. But everything else she said is true too. You earned it. And you've spent almost all of it. There's enough left for college, and if there isn't, we'll find a way to pay for that. But that'll be a stretch. Beyond that, you'll have to go out and get a job. But that won't be a problem for you. You're a smart girl. You can do anything you want."

He smiled to himself and took a sip of wine. "She does like to control every last nickel that rolls in, no matter how it arrived in the mailbox. You've really done it this time." He laughed ruefully.

We both knew we were on borrowed time until we had to go home and face the music.

When we got home, the house was dark, except for the glow from the television set that constantly hummed on Mom's side of the bed. I crept past her door, quickly and quietly, trying to get the floorboards to keep the secret of our arrival to themselves. Then I changed rapidly in the dark into my pajamas and slid under the blankets almost without disturbing them, stealing off to sleep before anything more could transpire. I'd had enough excitement for one day.

The next day, Mom went down to the bank and closed the account, getting a cashier's check for the full amount. She read the teller the riot act for letting a child open an account alone without a parent on it. And somehow, even though mine was the only name on the record, they let her walk out with the balance. And she didn't even bring a gun.

CHAPTER TWELVE

By the time the airport came into view, I'd nearly lost hope. The flight would take off in about thirty minutes, with or without us.

"Look, you guys get out and check in," Dad said. "Dump the bags. I will park the car and meet you at the gate."

We'd all gone silent amid the tension, although Mom had spent a good part of the trip berating Dad as he dodged in and out of cars in the heavy traffic that clogged the length of the 405 freeway.

In truth, he deserved the abuse. Mom and I had been ready to go for hours. Our destination: Boston. Harvard was holding a weekend of spirited events for prospective freshmen who had already been accepted, and I was one of them.

Stanford summer school had been even more fantastic than I'd imagined. Not only did I have total freedom and control over my life and my time, but I was introduced to a whole world beyond Hollywood, where intellectual curiosity and the ability to reason were the main values, not body type and how convincingly I could pretend to be someone else. I hadn't realized that school could be more than figuring out how to crush a test. I had just seen school as a competition and a means to an end. I had a lot more in common with this group of people than the kids I saw on auditions. I hungrily consumed the opportunity to find my own way without Mom steering me toward what *she* valued.

Now I couldn't wait to see what it would be like if I were to move all the way across the country pursuing the same dream on my own. I'd never been to Boston, and it was hard to believe that the ivy-covered old buildings depicted in the catalog really existed. The pictures of the campus looked like Paul Revere might canter through one of the courtyards on a snorting bay stallion just in time for lunch.

I'd packed for any weather possibility, from flurries to subtropical heat. I didn't want to take any chances. Mom, insecure about having gained more weight, packed a wardrobe of black pants, tops, and sweaters. She threatened not to go on the trip, since she had failed at another crash diet, but we convinced her no one cared, which was the truth.

Dad on the other hand had waited until the morning to pack. Then as we rushed around him in a buzz of activity, he calmly drank his coffee and watched the morning news. Slower than the grass grew out front, he'd climbed the stairs to their bathroom and started his morning ritual, which included a twenty-minute shower, complete with multiple verses of multiple songs, and a thirty-plus-minute tour of the sink area, where he'd polish every tooth individually, shave, and then slowly blow his hair dry with a fifteen-year-old hair dryer that had a comb attached to the vent so he could smooth his hair as it dried.

By the time he came downstairs with his bag, Mom and I were sweating with panic.

"Dad, seriously. We have to go," I pushed.

We hadn't waited for him to load our bags into the car.

Now we rushed out and threw ourselves into our seats, slamming the doors, while he slowly circled the house, closing the wrought iron gate and tugging on each individual sliding glass door and entry to make sure it was locked. He worked slowly and deliberately while we lost our minds waiting.

By the time we hit the highway, I realized we'd have to be the only car on the road in order to speed down to LAX in time, and in L.A., gridlock was the norm. Indeed lines of cars inched forward like endless armies of crawling ants, as frustrated drivers tried to push into the next lane, which wasn't moving any faster anyway.

At the curb in front of the terminal, Mom jumped out and waved frantically to a United skycap, who wheeled a cart over and started unloading. I headed to the outdoor counter to speed things along before the bags could be wheeled over.

"We're on the three PM to Boston. The last name is Francis," I said.

"Oh, boy. You guys are cutting it close. You better run," the second skycap said as he pulled the plastic off the back of our baggage labels and slapped them onto the bags. He checked his watch and confirmed that we were screwed.

"You hear that!" Mom shouted at Dad breathlessly.

"I will just go park the car," Dad said, still calm, as if the pilot would simply wait.

"Don't go to some bargain lot. We don't have time! Just park nearby and come right back. We'll wait for you inside," Mom said.

"Dad. *Hurry*," I begged.

"Don't worry." He laughed nervously, finally realizing the gravity of the situation.

Mom and I went inside the terminal and rushed to the gate. We swam upstream through a school of travelers who'd just gotten off a long flight from overseas. They all looked tired and rumpled, speaking an Asian language I didn't recognize. I envied them because they'd arrived at their destination, while we were still struggling so mightily to get off the ground.

We pushed our way through the crowd to gate 71. A tall woman stood at the gate in a blue uniform. She wore a tight smile as she scanned the waiting area. Her eyes landed on us, and she smiled through her irritation.

"You must be my stragglers," she said as we approached.

"We're on this flight, but we're waiting for one more person. My dad," I said. My heart pounded in my chest and I could feel my blood pressure rising.

"Oh, sweetie. There's no time to wait. I suggest you board. We're closing the door," she said as if she'd seen this scene before.

"Not without my dad. We're visiting Harvard. He's parking the car. He's right behind us," I said, panting from our rush to the gate.

"Please," Mom begged. "He's coming."

"You two should wait for him on board," she warned.

"We can't. We're all together," I said. "We can't go without him."

"Does he have his boarding pass?" she asked.

"Yes," Mom said.

"Then you should definitely get on," she said.

I looked at Mom. "Let's just run back and tell him to run. I'm sure he's coming."

The flight attendant shook her head, washing her hands of the matter, as we rushed back to the main artery of the terminal, which was still flooded with hundreds of people moving in every direction. I stood on my toes, trying to see over the crowd, and I realized we didn't even know for sure what direction he was coming from. I picked up the pace and broke into a run, heading back toward the door to the street, weaving in and out of the crowd, while Mom tried to hurry behind me.

I reached the doors and pushed through to the curb. My eyes swept the long line of cars pulling up to drop off passengers. I looked through the crowds, face by face, and came up empty.

"Let's go back to the gate and see if he passed us somehow," I said when Mom caught up.

"You go. I'll come as quickly as I can behind you," she huffed, breathing hard from the stress and exertion.

I ran back to the gate now, darting through the families pushing carts piled high with luggage ready to topple at the slightest bump. Children trailed their families, dragging backpacks and dolls. A pack of teenagers sat cross-legged at another gate area, passing magazines back and forth.

I raced all the way back to the gate without encountering Dad. When I reached the door to our flight, it was closed. They'd finished boarding without us. I had no idea if Dad had gotten on without us, or never made it inside. But our luggage was taking off for Harvard without us.

Defeated, I collapsed into a seat and watched Mom slowly amble up. The corners of her mouth turned down into a frown.

"What do we do now?" I asked, trying not to cry.

"I wish I knew what happened to your father. For all we know, he had a heart attack in the parking lot," she said.

I hadn't even thought about that possibility. The new dimension of worry was more than I could take. Tears rolled down my cheeks as Mom looked around the terminal, searching.

After a minute or two, we rose to our feet and walked back to the ticket counter, combing the masses that came toward us, still looking for any sign of Dad. By then, searching felt hopeless.

When we reached the counter, Mom cut the line and stepped up to a haggard but capable-looking agent with graying hair and heavy eyelids. I stood by her side, holding my breath to stop crying. Another man at the front of the line looked peeved, but saw my tears and didn't have the nerve to complain aloud.

"We were supposed to be on the flight that just left for Boston. We lost my husband on the way to the gate. Is there any way to page him?" she asked.

"Of course. Give me his details. We can page him and call security. And I can help you get another flight if you still want to go today. There's one on American that leaves in about hour. I think there are a few seats left."

She paged Dad and booked us on the flight. We bought two seats for more than a thousand dollars. All the planning, buying our tickets in advance to save money, everything we'd done, down the drain.

Thirty minutes later, we sat at the new gate, silent and defeated. "What happened to Dad?" I asked.

"I have no idea. This is typical. If he's not lying dead somewhere, I'm going to kill him."

"You know, the real problem is that he doesn't want you to go to Harvard," she said. Mom always had a larger conspiracy theory to fit any crisis, no matter how accidental the situation seemed.

"Why?" I asked, unconvinced.

"He always said the UC schools were good enough. He doesn't have the same drive that I have. He wants you to go to Stanford because it's closer. I'd like you to stay too. But who gets into Harvard? You can't just turn it down. I don't know what you should do for sure, but this is sabotage on his part. Maybe he doesn't know that's what he's doing, but that's what he's doing."

When we arrived in Boston, Dad was waiting for us. We'd left a message with my aunt about the new flight information, and he'd thought to call her. He was sitting on a bench, hands folded in his lap, looking beaten and exhausted.

He'd somehow weaved past us in the crowd and boarded

the original flight. He assumed we'd boarded that flight ahead of him as planned, but when he saw the empty seats in our row, he kept going instead of getting off. That decision was logical, he explained. We were all heading to Harvard no matter what.

"I stuck with the plan," he said, a phrase he loved to hold over us. He constantly saw value in staying glued to whatever plan we'd made, not deviating, not flaking, no matter what circumstances arose.

I had been too worried about him to get on a plane and just ditch him. I wanted to make sure the whole team was okay and on board and count heads before moving forward. In retrospect, I should have just kept going east.

The weekend at Harvard turned out to be magical despite the rough start. The campus could have been a set for a movie about Colonial America, with centuries-old ivy-covered brick buildings at every turn. Each quadrangle of classrooms and dorms looked unlike anything I'd ever seen in California.

I'd picked up two new friends, Matt and Michelle, who were committed to enrolling at Harvard and immediately infected me with their unharnessed enthusiasm and momentum. They were shocked I'd even consider any other school, which was by definition second-rate.

Matt was a worldly, cerebral New York kid who I could tell would eventually own or at least finance most of the island of Manhattan. Michelle was pretty with long brown curls and a laugh that made you love her immediately. Plus she was one of the only girls on campus wearing makeup, so it made sense that we should team up. She had an older sister and brother already on campus, and they were both so welcoming. They adopted us and made the school irresistible.

I could see a window into my new life, controlled only by

me, and the thought of being a million miles from home and Hollywood morphed from frightening into freeing. If I left behind everything that tethered me to my past, I would fly or drown, but I would know for sure whether I could live without Mom or the business driving my life. Maybe there was another option, another path, another life. Maybe there wasn't. I hadn't really considered the possibility that there could be another way to live until that weekend. Once I opened the door to that possibility, it couldn't be closed.

I announced the news in the family room. I was going to Harvard. Mom sat on the corner of the fading green couch. Still in a housedress, she held a section of the *Los Angeles Times* in her lap, her bare feet on the coffee table and her eyes fixed on the television.

Dad sat upright in his chair, still in his sweats from the night before, deeply engrossed in the *Times* opinion section, which he never agreed with. He'd already swept through the sports pages. He sipped his second cup of coffee, still a good thirty minutes away from folding the pages and heading upstairs for his morning routine.

"I've decided. I'm going to Harvard.," I declared to the room.

Mom looked up and smiled slightly, her lips closed. She knew this was coming. It was hard for me to surprise her. Dad cleared his throat but didn't look up.

"Well, that's a nice idea. I don't know how you are going to pay for that," he said. "You guys never sweat the details," he laughed, but not happily. "But someone has to. Someone has to write the check. I don't know who that's going to be."

"They offered loans and financial aid if we can't swing it. I went to the financial aid office when we visited. They said that

I was in and there was always a package to make it work, no matter what," I said.

I had prepared for the standard dismissal: we can't afford it. Lunch? We can't afford it. Toast? No way. But I honestly didn't think he would go there this time. Harvard wasn't frivolous; it wasn't a pony. This is what the money I had earned was supposed to be saved for, and my father had always assured me that it would be there for this purpose. If the cash wasn't there anymore, it was hardly my fault, or my responsibility to replace it, no matter how the two of them justified its absence.

"Financial aid takes care of tuition, which is only half the battle, maybe less," Dad pointed out. "What about flying back and forth? What about winter clothes? That takes bread. All things you don't need if you go to Stanford. You get in your car and drive to Stanford, and wear the same clothes. It's closer, it makes sense. It's a fantastic school. You need to be practical. Like I am. It's hardly a sacrifice to go to Stanford, and it's probably a better school anyway."

With that, Dad turned his attention back to the opinions of the *Times* writers. I was stunned. Dad always seemed to be in my corner; he was the rational one. I looked at Mom, who shrugged. I knew she didn't want me to escape, but as she liked to say out loud, it was such a big deal to go to Harvard. I thought maybe I could swing her. I couldn't believe Dad was going to be the holdout.

I was already late for school because it had taken me so long to work up the nerve to walk in and make the proclamation. Now I stormed out of the house and got in my car, flying backward down the driveway, throwing the car into drive at the bottom the hill, zipping out of the cul-de-sac.

All day at school, I went through the motions of going to classes, still in disbelief at my parents' reactions. Who ever heard of a kid getting into Harvard and her parents not wanting her to go? It was astounding to me. Maybe I was making the wrong decision. Maybe they were right. Maybe I'd go thousands of miles away and fall off the other side of the continent.

I felt so confused I didn't raise my hand all day. Was I just trying to escape from my family and would I later regret that? Was I the rash one? My relationship with acting had turned sour. I needed some distance. I'd never known a life that didn't include it. I'd been an actress since my earliest memory. I'd taken for granted that acting would always be a part of my life. But then we'd had a falling-out. I started to feel silly playing dress-up. By the time I decided I wanted it back, it was too late. Like a spurned lover, it had moved on without me. I couldn't break back in. In the last year, I'd done a few commercials, but I was barely even getting called to audition for the good roles, and even then, I wasn't getting called back. I'd gotten close to landing a role on a new show, *Beverly Hills 90210*, but when that didn't happen, I was so frustrated at having my hopes raised and dashed again that I wanted to put acting in a closet, lock the door, and throw away the key.

"What's up with you?" Cori asked as we walked to AP Literature.

"My parents won't let me go to Harvard," I said.

She laughed. "That's fresh," she said.

"I know. It's a mess. I don't know what to do," I said. Cori was wearing a Northwestern sweatshirt, her fate signed, sealed, and delivered. I envied how certain her future looked. Everyone in her family rowed in the same direction.

"I guess I do know what to do. I'm going," I said.

I sat in last period Religion and filled out my acceptance card. I signed the bottom. Melissa Ann Francis. That was it. I was going no matter what. The response date was in a matter of days, and all that was left to do was get the card postmarked at the post office.

If the money really was gone, I would find a way to pay the tuition myself. I'd waitress. I'd save what I could to get going. I didn't care how Mom and Dad felt about it. I was making this decision for myself, and I'd see it through. I needed to see if I could leave behind the life I knew and still survive. I could always come back. If acting called, I could always give up and come back. But I had a feeling there was a whole other life out there, and I had to try it on for size.

Technically, I didn't need my parents' permission to go, but I wanted it. I decided to go by Dad's office and give him one more chance to get on the train before it pulled out of the station. Maybe he'd been thinking all day too. Maybe he regretted dismissing me that morning.

I pulled into the industrial park where his office was located and took a spot right across from the door. The company name, Theatre Products International, and the logo were painted on the glass door in hunter green. The facade was modest but respectable, like the occupant.

I pushed the door open and walked through the waiting area to his office. I stood in the doorway and watched as Dad rocked back in his large brown leather swivel chair, leaning in at various moments to scribble notes on a yellow pad with a sharpened pencil, phone cradled to his ear.

"I can get it to you by Monday, probably," he said into the phone. His eyes looked up from the paper and met mine briefly, then returned to the pad. I stood there, expecting him to excuse himself for a few minutes and talk to me. Then I gave up and walked back to the waiting area, collapsing into a chair.

I chipped the polish off my nail while I waited for him to wrap up. I figured he would speak first, make his argument more apologetically this time, and I'd stand firm, express my hurt, and tell him I was going no matter what. He'd laugh at my petulance, relent, and everything would be fine.

Another ten minutes went by, and it occurred to me that he was staying on the phone on purpose. As he continued to talk, I got angrier. He was intentionally letting me stew. I folded my arms across my chest and looked down at my watch. The post office was closing in fifteen minutes. I'd give him five more.

My watch ticked forward like a bomb waiting to explode. The moment the second hand swept over the numeral twelve signaling the allotted time had elapsed, I bolted.

I was angry as I gunned the engine and flew down the street, pounding the steering wheel with my fist, angry at myself that I'd shown up and created an opportunity to be blown off again. I didn't need his blessing, I didn't need anything. At the end of the day, I was even more alone than I'd expected.

When I arrived at the Northridge post office, I rushed inside and waited in line to hand over my acceptance letter. The hand-to-hand delivery might have been unnecessary, but I wasn't leaving my fate to chance any longer. I thrust the postcard at the clerk, and he smiled and raised his fuzzy eyebrows toward his receding hairline, knowing exactly what the card meant. It was that time of year. My eyes brimmed with tears, which confused him, so he simply took the letter without another word.

I rushed out the front door, having achieved my mission, and got into my car, throwing the gear into reverse and punching the gas.

Smash.

I didn't see the truck behind me until it was too late. The impact jarred my head forward, hurtling my forehead into the steering wheel, but I hadn't been going fast enough to really hurt myself. My heart jumped into my throat, and I burst into tears, now limp and defeated in the driver's seat.

The vehicle I had hit was a navy blue pickup truck with a Domino's sign on the roof. A Hispanic guy, no older than twenty, got out and came to my door.

"Didn't you even look behind you?" he said angrily.

"I'm sorry. It's been an awful day," I tried to explain.

He backed his truck up and parked at the side of the row of parked cars, then got out and inspected both of our bumpers to assess the damage. I watched him circle the car in my rearview mirror without getting out. I wasn't sure I could stand.

He returned to my door.

"Look, I don't see any real damage. It was your fault, but . . ." His voice trailed off for a moment. "I'm going to get fired for getting into an accident, even though this wasn't my fucking fault. How about we both just get out of here?"

I nodded in agreement, and he turned swiftly back to his truck and sped off, tires screeching as he peeled out of the parking lot.

I sat quietly for at least ten minutes, trying to collect myself. Finally, I put the car in drive and headed home.

When I told Mom what I'd done, she just nodded. Pretty soon, she was acting like sending the acceptance letter was her idea. I heard her tell another mom "we decided on Harvard." Turns out I had more power than I'd thought. Cognitive dissonance set in. Once it became clear that the plan was going forward no matter what, she took ownership of it and changed the script to make herself the driver of the action.

Dad, on the other hand, didn't talk to me for a while, which was fine with me. I figured he just didn't want me to leave. Without me in the house, he'd be forced to face what had become of his relationship with Mom. They hardly interacted any longer, sleeping on separate floors of the house, eating almost every meal apart. And while I understood the trepidation he might be feeling, clipping my wings was neither fair nor a solution.

The more I thought about it, the more I realized that I needed to make all of my own decisions from then on, and not let the potential backlash at home dictate my path. I was eighteen, and the rest of my life would be up to me.

CHAPTER THIRTEEN

I opened my eyes and looked at the ceiling, off-white and bumpy, as if cottage cheese had been spread evenly over the entire surface. Sunlight snuck in around the edges of the curtains. Judging from the brightness of the rays, and the temperature of the room, the sun had been baking the back of the house for a while.

I'd slept in later than I'd planned. The night before I'd been on a date with Patrick, a guy I'd met a few months earlier during a shift at Islands, a loud burger bar in Westwood, the college town that surrounded UCLA. My plan to man the hostess stand at the front of the restaurant and collect fraternity boys for the summer was a stroke of genius. I secured an apron and started working before graduation. Now my sore feet and meager paycheck reminded me why I was leaving for college in the fall.

I'd worked my shift the night before and then met Patrick for a late dinner. He'd graduated from UCLA a year earlier, so when he first came into the restaurant with a pack of friends and asked for my number on the way out, I lied to him.

I told him I was home from Stanford for the summer going on auditions, trying to decide if I wanted to go back. Since I'd been enrolled there the previous summer, I knew the lay of the land. I thought it was unlikely that at twenty-four, he'd date a high school senior, so I'd just invented the story on a whim.

He had a boyish, Woody Harrelson look and manner and a lean muscular build that made him seem very collegiate. But in a flash he'd expose a thoughtfulness and maturity that could calm the choppiest waters. I expected the relationship to run out of steam after a few dates like so many others had, so lying about my age seemed harmless. Now I was hooked on this guy, and leaving for Harvard in a little more than a month. I had no idea how to untangle the web of duplicity I'd woven around us. Perhaps the situation was doomed since I was moving thousands of miles away anyway. At least that's what I told myself to quell the remorse I felt for lying to him.

I rolled onto my side and heard chatter coming from the kitchen. Mom was talking louder and more feverishly than usual.

Then I heard it, Tiffany's voice. But not her voice. This voice was calm and in command.

Her flight had been delayed on its return from Europe last night, and I'd tried to wait up for her but couldn't keep my eyes open. She'd been gone for almost six months, riding on a Eurail pass to every corner of the continent with her boyfriend, Colin. She'd packed only what her backpack would carry, convincingly taking the role of Berkeley hippie on the road. They'd even traveled with tents, so they could camp out when they weren't near a youth hostel. The trip sounded bohemian-horrible to me.

I got out of bed and padded downstairs in my slippers, eager to see her after so long. I had thought the idea of spending a whole semester traveling without even getting course credit was indulgent and wasteful but I'd missed her all the same. Plus I was curious.

When I entered the kitchen, I was struck by the stranger sitting at the table. Six months of blackish brown roots grew from her scalp and abruptly turned blonde five or six inches from the ends. The hair was tangled and matted from the plane and so much time away from a salon. But even that couldn't distract from how thin she was, and how clear her eyes and skin looked. She shone.

"Look how skinny your sister is!" Mom exclaimed. Of course that would be the salient change in Mom's eyes. "She's a waif! I'm making bacon to put some meat back on her bones."

"Really? Has the fire started yet?" I said, looking directly at Tiffany. She laughed. Dad snorted from the far side of the table. I hadn't noticed him sitting there.

On the rare occasion that Mom made breakfast, she'd broil batch after batch of bacon in the oven without draining the boiling grease from the pan. Inevitably the crackling, bubbling fat would burst into flames, and one of us would have to pull out the rack and beat the fire into submission with a sacrificial dish towel that then ended up in the trash with gaping burn holes. We'd all played firefighter so many times, the ritual had simply morphed into part of the process.

Mom frowned, pretending to be offended, but unable to hide her delight at the daughter who had returned from Europe. This could be the Tiffany she'd always wanted.

She went to the counter and came back with a plate of bacon that was half blackened and half raw. Apparently I had slept though the fire.

"Aren't you a vegetarian?" I asked as Tiffany stuffed a piece of bacon in her mouth.

"We had to make our money last on the road. We sort of ate whatever was cheap and looked safe. I couldn't be that picky."

She picked up another piece of bacon and ate it, her shoulders relaxed, an easy smile on her face.

Dad got up from his seat and walked toward the coffee-maker on the counter to refill his mug.

"How did you lose so much weight?" I asked.

"Yeah, Tiff," Dad said. "You look so fit."

"Well, like I said. We only had so much money. Nothing for extras. Too much food meant less for something else. A museum, or a beer. And we certainly didn't spend money on cabs, or even buses really. We walked everywhere, carrying our packs," she said proudly.

The notion of being too poor for food was laughable. She'd had one of Mom's credit cards the whole time. Does Europe not take Visa? She certainly wasn't going to starve. But if they were sincerely on a budget, God bless them. She did seem to have the body to prove it.

We ate the rest of the charred bacon and she announced that she needed a long bath.

"Yes, you do!" I said teasingly.

She rolled her eyes. "What are you doing later?" she asked.

I was surprised by the question. She had stopped asking me about my plans years ago. "I was going to go the gym to work out before my shift at Islands." I hesitated before adding, "Do you want to come? I have some guest passes."

She shrugged her shoulders, but looked directly in my eyes when she answered. "Sure."

When we arrived at the gym, I took her over to a machine that was supposed to tone thighs. I'd been a slave to this machine all summer and was on the cusp of abandoning it as a cruel hoax.

I did one set and then got up and wiped the seat. "Want to try?" I suggested.

"Sure. Maybe a little less weight. I'm not as strong as you are," she said.

She sat down on the machine, wearing a pair of black bicycle shorts I'd loaned her and a white tank top. She stood nearly six inches shorter than me and now she was so thin, I thought I could fold her up and just slip her in my purse.

"Hey, Melissa. Who is this?" Eric asked. He was a personal trainer I'd agreed to go on a few dates with in the spring. I'd stopped retuning his calls, but it hadn't made a dent in his resolve.

"This is my sister, Tiffany," I said with a guilty smile. She immediately sized up the situation.

"Hi," she said.

"Your sister's been very busy lately," he chided. "Maybe you want to get some dinner sometime?" he said, pretending to joke around, though I had the feeling he'd turn very serious if she expressed interest in his offer.

"Oh, well, that doesn't seem like a good idea," she demurred.

"She has a boyfriend she's been traveling around Europe with for the last six months. I don't think he would like it," I shot back, slightly annoyed.

"Well, there's nothing wrong with taking both of you out. We could all go to dinner," he persisted.

"I don't think so. You are so kind to offer. But I haven't seen my sister in so long, I'm not prepared to share her," I said firmly.

And with that I moved to another machine across the room, leaving Tiffany no choice but to follow me. Eric smiled and continued to the trainers' office, where he was already late picking up his next appointment.

"Oh my God. Are you dating that guy?" she teased.

"We went on a few dates. It was months and months ago and it was nothing serious. Didn't seem like a bad idea at the time. He's cute enough. And actually smart for a personal trainer. He goes to Pepperdine."

"So do you only date college guys?" she asked, eyebrows raised.

"Well, Patrick, the guy I really like, isn't in college anymore. He graduated. Now he works in banking. I have no idea what he does actually," I admitted.

"So do either of them know you are in high school?" she laughed.

"I'm only in high school for another week," I shot back.

"So they both know that?" she pressed.

"No."

She laughed as I lay back on the next machine, exposed.

That weekend the blistering heat of the San Fernando Valley forced us into her car and up over the Santa Monica Mountains to the beach. Tiffany had convinced Dad to remove the roof and the doors from her Jeep, so the wind whipped through the cab as we swept down the highway, tangling our hair and sending anything flying that wasn't secure. We blasted Nirvana's new hit, "Smells Like Teen Spirit," on the radio as we drove. Grunge rock dominated the airwaves in 1991, and we sang along at the top of our lungs.

When we got to the beach, we parked the car and walked to the end of the parking lot where the black tar met the golden sand. Then we threw our sandals in my tote bag and ran down the scorching beach to the edge of the water, where we dipped our toes in to cool them off and laughed at how silly we looked running down the beach like little kids.

The waves were powerful in this part of the Pacific Ocean, nearly knocking us down as they crashed into the shore and spraying our clothes before trying to drag us back out to sea in the undertow.

"Let's go back up over there and throw down our stuff and lay out the towels," Tiffany suggested.

"Yeah, that sounds good," I agreed. We made our way back out of the water to a spot a few yards back. The waves had soaked the bottoms of our shorts, but I knew they'd dry in minutes in the hot sun.

My towel fluttered in the breeze as I snapped it and then laid it flat on the sand. Tiffany did the same and we lay down, having taken off our shorts and T-shirts. The sun was hot on my face, but it felt good.

"Did you remember to grab those Cokes out of the car?" Tiffany asked.

"You bet," I said pulling two out of my bag.

Tiffany had carried a portable radio, and she tuned it to the same station we'd been listening to in the car. We lay back on the towels and let the hours pass, flipping over occasionally. An even tan was our only worry on that blissful day.

I spent the first few weeks after graduation feeling like an adult. I didn't have school anymore, I was eighteen, and I took as many shifts at Islands as I could stand. I thought the extra cash would come in handy when I left for Harvard at the end of the summer.

I still went on a few auditions, but I'd told my agent that I was leaving for Cambridge soon, and she'd pretty much given up on me. We both knew I wouldn't be flying home for auditions.

It was Thursday night, and I'd picked up the closing shift, which meant I'd be done a little after eleven. I liked that shift, since Thursday was the most popular night to go out at UCLA, and this kept me busy and awake until an acceptable time to arrive at any club or bar.

I'd told Tiffany to come before closing and have a salad so we could go to a bar in Westwood afterward. She walked into the restaurant, and I saw Gary, the bartender, take a second look. Mom had treated Tiffany to a whole head of light blonde highlights. She'd always had thicker, stronger hair than me. Now it was a golden color that caught the light and spilled all the way down her back.

She wore a pale pink cotton tank dress that showed off her tan, paired with a bangle earrings and studded belt to add an edge. With lots of black kohl eyeliner and a pale frosted lip, she looked sizzling. Gary's eyes didn't leave her as he mopped up a spilled drink and shoved a tip in his pocket.

I showed her to a table near my hostess stand, surprised by how excited I was to see her. I wanted to be around her more than anyone else. I hadn't felt that way since we were little kids.

"I highly recommend the Hawaiian salad. My friend Tory says it has the fewest calories if you get it without cheese. Or you could get it with cheese, and then it tastes really good."

"No cheese. I don't want to gain any weight before I get back up to Cal. Also, why the hell did you torture me on the treadmill this morning if we're just going to eat cheese?" She sighed.

"Excellent decision. I will let them know. You eat, I will clean up my station. We can close up and go in like fifteen minutes." I smiled.

A short time later, we were sitting at a bar a few blocks away known for loud music and careless bouncers.

"It never ceases to amaze me when we get into a bar with the same ID!" I laughed. I'd been using her ID since she turned twenty-one. It was guaranteed to work, except when we were together.

"How do they not notice it's the same name, the same birthday, and nearly the same picture?" Tiffany said.

"I don't know. The picture looks different. You have short hair on yours. Long hair on mine. That's something," I said, sipping a rum and Coke.

"Which one of us is driving home? I don't mind," she offered, pushing her drink away.

"Actually, I don't care either," I said quickly. I loved that she didn't feel compelled to get hammered. I'd seen her drink compulsively so many times, pouring drinks down her throat as quickly as they came. She had a casual relationship with this cocktail that I didn't want to upset.

"What are you going to do when you go back to school?" I said, changing the subject. "Are you going to apply to grad school?"

It was her fifth year at Berkeley, which was entirely normal in the University of California school system. Almost no one graduated in four years anymore. They either couldn't get the classes they needed because of overcrowding or they were just avoiding adulthood.

"I'm going to apply to law school and take the LSAT. I thought about doing psychology, but it's such a long road. Besides, I'd really like to be a lawyer," she said.

"I think you love *Law & Order*," I teased.

"Well that's true."

The thought of her going back to Berkeley unsettled me. I didn't want her to return to her old friends and her old self. This transformation seemed tenuous, and I wanted to hold on to her.

"Are you excited about Harvard? It's so far away," she asked with wide eyes.

"I know, isn't that fantastic? A whole plane ride away. No one can drive to see me. No pop-ins," I said.

I was thinking of Mom, but I suddenly realized that included her, and the distance bothered me unexpectedly.

"You can visit me," I offered. "Mom would buy you a ticket."

"Not without wanting to come," she said ruefully.

We hung out most the days and nights when I wasn't working for the next few weeks; Tiffany delayed going back up to Berkeley, but it couldn't last. She had to go back to school to register and get settled in after such a long time away traveling around Europe. The summer was fleeting.

One night, I took off by myself to see Patrick. He was two hours away in San Diego visiting his parents, and I drove down to meet them and go out to dinner. I still hadn't come clean to him about how old I was, and now I was getting in deeper by meeting his parents.

When we made the plan, I knew it was unrealistic to think I would drive all the way back to the Valley that night. But if I went with the premise that I would spend the night at his house, the idea would have provoked a huge fight with Mom.

Sure enough, when midnight rolled around, Patrick and I were entangled and exhausted in the room he'd grown up in and the last thing I could do was tear myself away from him and leave. He was going to vanish soon enough anyway.

I phoned Mom with some lame excuse about how I was too tired to drive safely, and instead of yelling, she just slammed down the phone. There was nothing she could do from a distance, and we both knew I would be dead when I finally turned up at home. I may have been eighteen, but not coming home was tantamount to an insurrection.

At six AM, Patrick rolled over in his bed and woke me.

"You'd better go. Both of our moms are going to kill us," he said without opening his eyes. He was even sexier in the morning, which I wouldn't have bet was possible. I rested my head on his bare, tanned chest and then tilted my head up and kissed him. He kissed me back before gently pushing me off him and onto the floor with a smile.

"I'm serious. You have to go."

"You're twenty-four," I said, very well aware of the difference between our ages. "I know why I'm in trouble, but why is your mom going to kill *you*?"

"Because this is her house, and not my apartment. My little sister still lives here. We're Catholic. I really can't have a girl stay over. You've got to go."

I drove the entire way far above the speed limit, as if making good time would fix anything.

When I walked into the house, I was surprised to find it empty except for Tiffany. She sat at the kitchen table drinking coffee and reading the *Los Angeles Times*.

"Where is everyone?" I asked.

"Dad's at work. Mom went out. She said she couldn't stand to look at you when you got home," she said without looking up.

"Yeah, I'm in big trouble this time," I said weakly. She didn't respond.

"Wait, you're not going to give me a hard time!" I said, suddenly shocked.

"You stayed out all night? You couldn't have seen him and just come home?" she said.

"Oh my God! What's the big deal! I was just tired! It's a long drive. I lived at Stanford the whole summer by myself last year! I'm leaving for college in a month! I can sleep anywhere I want then!" I shouted.

"Exactly. You can sleep anywhere you want *then*. For the rest of your life. You didn't have to rub it in their faces now. We all knew you weren't coming home when you left and you lied and said you were. Come on. You want people to treat you like an adult, then act like one."

I stared mouth agape at this stranger at the kitchen table. Then I had to laugh.

"Are you seriously lecturing me about being responsible and respectful?" I said.

She looked up at me. "You just shouldn't have done it, and you know it."

I turned on my heel and left the room. I went upstairs and combed my hair into a ponytail and put on my Islands uniform.

When I got back in my car to drive to work, all I could think was, please don't let this level-headed girl posing as my sister disappear. I don't mind being the bad apple. Please let it be her turn to shine, to feel good, to be happy in her own skin.

A week later when she drove off, I repeated my prayer silently to myself. Let this be her time. But God wasn't listening.

CHAPTER FOURTEEN

"**A**bsolutely *not*. Let me get this straight. You want to spend the summer living with your boyfriend a million miles away in Washington, D.C., doing some unpaid job instead of going on auditions, and I'm footing the bill for the whole thing? Ha! You've got a lot of nerve!"

And with that, the phone went dead. Mom had always been the queen of slamming down the phone. She loved to end a conversation that way. The sound of the handset crashing into the cradle a split second before a dial tone replaced her screaming voice. It was the perfect exclamation mark to whatever dramatic speech she'd just finished.

Years ago, the proliferation of the cordless phone had robbed her of one of her dearest forms of expression. Now when she wanted to let someone know that their response didn't matter, she could only tell them by punching a button and then slamming the phone down on the nearest counter, the second act devoid of its most important witness.

I looked out the window of my dorm room and sighed. Eliot

House was a hulking limestone dorm on the bank of the Charles River. My third-floor room overlooked JFK Boulevard, where packs of athletes in practice uniforms carrying lacrosse sticks or rowing bags streamed from Harvard Yard over the Charles River to the practice fields just beyond the stone bridge. I watched them and was willing to bet that their parents would applaud their industry and gumption.

My mom's response wasn't unexpected. Still, I'd hoped. The unpaid job she'd spat at was a prestigious internship with NBC News in D.C. that I'd landed after months of letters and phone calls and begging. I'd be working on the *Today* show and I'd get to go to the White House and sit with the press corps in the West Wing. But to Mom, the job was in the wrong industry and the wrong zip code.

The year before, I'd waltzed into the career counseling office at Harvard with no clue about what I wanted to do with my summer break. Every smart, aggressive freshman was sniffing around for a jump on something or other. Half of them were gearing up to be consultants, which didn't make sense to me. We knew next to nothing about nothing, so how could we possibly tell a company how to do its business better? Still there seemed to be three tracks at Harvard: Wall Street consulting or investment banking, law school, or medical school. Those options seemed too dreary for someone like me who had already had a career with a lot more sparkle.

Then I'd found a lone scrap of paper with a description of a job that had never occurred to me: KTTV—News Intern. KTTV was the local Fox News affiliate in downtown Los Angeles. "Reports to the Assignment Manager, generating story ideas and assisting the assignment desk." I didn't know how to come up with a news story or what an assignment desk was, but the job sounded a whole lot better than making copies in a law office.

I called, wrote, and interviewed and eventually the golden yet unpaid position was mine. I came home every day exhausted with a migraine from the frantic yelling and racing to the top of each newscast. I was hooked. News was everything entertainment television wasn't: unscripted, unrehearsed, no safety net. Get in front of the camera and use the brain God gave you or risk being utterly exposed in your underpants.

That's not to say my actual duties as an intern were far above making copies in a law office. But I'd seen my future and then made a map to get there. That involved more internships with more connections who would vouch for me and get me through the next door, until I could make a tape, pedal the reel around tiny markets, and finally get on the air.

Now, my mom's reaction to the *Today* show internship was a roadblock. I sulked for a while before giving up and heading downstairs to meet my boyfriend, Zach, in the dining hall for the very end of lunch before the dining hall closed to prep for dinner.

Zach was tall and preppy with dark hair and high cheekbones that always made me wonder if his Arizona roots had reached out and intertwined with those of some Native Americans. He'd beaten me to the dining hall, made his way through the line, and was already seated at one end of a long table in the oversized wood-paneled room.

"Sorry I'm late. Talking to my mom. What's for lunch?" I said, looking at his tray.

"Chickwich. The one meal they can't screw up. You better hurry if you want one. I saw bricks of lasagna waiting in the wings for dinner so this may be the last good meal of the day," he said, rubbing his palms together over his plate.

I walked to the food line in the great hall and grabbed a red, battered tray off the stack. A thousand meals had traveled on the tray, scratching the surface into its own unique pattern. The line inched forward twisting and turning into the heart of the kitchen, where a pillowy Slavic woman greeted us each day from behind the sneeze guard.

"Hi, honey. What do you want for lunch?" she asked, sounding almost like an aunt or a grandmother so warm and sincere I almost believed I could tell her I wanted a rack of lamb and she'd turn around and produce one.

"I'll take a chickwich, thanks," I said.

"Just about the last one," she said smiling.

She picked up a breaded chicken patty from a bed of lettuce using flat metal tongs and dropped it onto a bun she'd pulled from a bag that said "institutional use only," which made me think I was eating prison food.

I returned to Zach's table and sat down across from him. He'd already eaten one chickwich and was focused on the second. Unlike most rumpled college boys, Zach was neat as a pin. His shirt was pressed, cuffs folded back so they wouldn't catch the honey mustard.

He covered his mouth with his hand so he could talk and eat at the same time without being rude.

"So what did your mom say?"

"'No,' basically. I told her how great the internship is, that I know a bunch of people here who tried to get jobs like it, and struck out entirely. I explained that I've been working and begging and calling and writing and planning for months. All that didn't matter," I said, looking down at my tray and shaking my head.

"Well, she wants you to come home," he said matter-of-factly. He was cute, but not particularly helpful.

"No shit, Sherlock. But I don't want to go home." I frowned. "I want to go see another city. I've lived in L.A. and Boston. I want to try out D.C."

"So just come with me. You're twenty years old!" he said easily.

Zach only had his mom. She was relentlessly and untiringly proud of every single thing he did. They'd been alone since his parents had split up when he was little, so he'd developed a solid sense of self-reliance that I admired. He always worked, and he always had a plan. I was a planner myself, but next to Zach, I felt like a slouch.

"I can't just go without her signing off on it," I grumbled.

"Why not?" he pressed.

"I don't have enough money."

Mom had me and she knew it.

Zach shook his head and grimaced as if he were saying, "I told you so." He worked as many hours as he could muster at Harvard Law School in Alan Dershowitz's office. Dershowitz was a famous appeals lawyer who made his name as much in the media as the courtroom. Zach was smart enough to score a job that paid, had cachet, and got him closer to getting into Harvard Law.

He was pretty pleased with himself.

"If you had a job this semester . . . ," he nagged.

"I know. I know! Advanced micro and calculus were sort of kicking my ass. I barely made it through my classes."

It was true. I'd decided to major in economics and found my calculus skills weren't quite up to the task. I was struggling to get through the more technical parts of my major and since all my professors graded on a curve, I had to climb over half my rabid classmates just to get a B. It was much harder slogging than I was used to.

"I can pay for stuff," Zach offered, softening his rebuke.

"Well, maybe there's still time for me to work it out," I said.

I spent the afternoon in my dorm room calling around campus looking for work. My choices for employment were bleak so deep into the semester. I could clean dorm rooms or do food prep in a hairnet in the dining halls. Both were humbling and barely compensated. All the better-paying, more dignified jobs had been snapped up months earlier.

My roommate, Debbie, walked in and plunked herself down on my bed. Her blonde bowl cut framed her face with a blunt edge except where the strands mixed with the humidity in the air and feathered around her ears. She brushed her bangs back, and her bare forehead made her wide blue eyes appear even larger above her freckled cheeks.

"What are you doing?" she asked.

"Looking for a way to make money," I replied.

She crossed her jeans-clad legs and tugged at the bottom of her pale T-shirt. Debbie's low-maintenance style clashed with my penchant for make-up and trendy clothes and made us seem like an odd couple. But we'd been fast friends from the day she walked into my freshman dorm. I'd never cried or complained about a problem she couldn't walk her way through, and vice versa.

"What do you need cash for?" she asked.

"I want to take that internship in D.C. for the summer and go with Zach. He's working for the public defender's office. But it's not paid and my parents want me to come home so they aren't going to give me money to do it."

"Can you use the *Little House* money or whatever?" she asked, going to the obvious solution.

"Not really. It's complicated," I lied. "The only thing I can find on short notice is working in the dining hall, or dorm crew."

She flinched at the last suggestion. Harvard sent financial aid students around the dorms with buckets and toilet bowl brushes cleaning other students' filth. The task was revolting and demeaning. You might knock on someone's door to clean their toilet and then sit next to them an hour later in art history. I always thought there had to be an easier way to earn money. Now I wondered if they were just poor planners like myself.

"Kitchen has to be better than dorm crew. Anything would be," she said with a shudder. "How bad could it be?"

The next day I descended into the bowels of Eliot House to find out. It turned out the kitchen that churned out three meals a day for us also served our next-door neighbors at Kirkland House. The steaming, belching food factory buried deep underground connected both houses by tunnels that reached out like two long arms to the dining halls above.

Sounds of metal utensils clashing and thick local accents mixed with the stifling damp air and swirled around me as I walked through the tunnel toward the manager's office. This zone was off-limits to students, making the trek through the tunnel feel like a journey to the other side.

"You the new kid?" asked a stout man from behind a desk, looking up from piles of paperwork as I walked through the door. I wondered how he could read anything given the smudges on his wire-rimmed glasses.

He spun his chair around and opened a big drawer behind him. After rummaging through piles of checked fabric, he eventually produced a well-worn pair of pants. He threw them on the desk and then rose to his feet before opening another drawer higher up on the cabinet. From there he pulled a white short-sleeved shirt that was frayed around the collar.

"Everyone wears a uniform. You can have these but you have to bring them back. You can wear what you have on to train today, but wear the uniform tomorrow."

He stood up and squeezed past me with a grunt, motioning for me to follow him. The three hairs that still remained on top of his head fluttered as we moved down the hall, and I wished that someone, somewhere would open a window.

Eventually we arrived at the kitchen. I don't know what I

expected. Certainly not Wolfgang Puck given what the finished product tasted like. But my suspicion about the prisonlike quality of our meals seemed to be immediately confirmed.

Half a dozen women and one lone guy stood at prep stations around the room, quietly chopping, mixing, and sorting. In the center of the room, an island of burners held pots big enough to boil naughty children one by one. Blue flames licked the bottom of the pots as white foam bubbled to the surface. On the far side, a wall of ovens radiated heat and cooked the room. A sharp scent of antiseptic cleaning fluid overpowered anything that might smell like food.

I looked at the people working quietly and recognized one woman's decidedly Irish, pale face from behind the counter upstairs. I'd seen her schlep heavy metal trays through the door at the back of the dining hall countless times and only casually wondered where they came from. Now I knew.

"Bess, I've got a pair of hands here to help you," the manager barked and with that he marched back toward his office.

A squat woman with gray hair pulled back into a tight bun waved me over. The creases around her eyes turned up as she smiled.

"Want to staht with choppin'?" she asked.

"Sure," I said.

Bess set me up at a chopping board with a sharp, gleaming cleaver. Then she built a giant, tumbling mountain of washed whole vegetables to one side of my board before disappearing into a closet near the door where we'd entered. She reemerged with a freshly washed but still stained apron and handed it to me. I slipped the strap over my head and tied the long waist straps around my middle and got started.

Over the next few hours, I diligently deconstructed the hill of potatoes and carrots, chopping and slicing until my wrist hurt. At first the task was satisfying, dicing the hard vegetables into symmetrical shapes, but the pleasure of creating organized little orange and beige piles soon wore into tedium.

Eventually I'd worked through everything Bess had given me, and she let me go.

"Come back tomorrow if you want. Hank has plenty of shifts. If you want," she said.

"I'll be back," I said, wiping the perspiration from my forehead.

"You guys usually don't last too many shifts. Get a nice job in the library." She smiled, showing me her yellowed teeth.

I nodded and took off my apron, retreating to where I'd left my folded uniform for the following day's shift. As I trudged back through the tunnel, I calculated what I'd earned for my exhaustion. At this rate, I'd have to work a dozen shifts just to pay one month's rent, not to mention any other expenses. It was hopeless.

Later that night I sat with Debbie in the dining hall in the middle of a long table, staring at the carrots and potatoes that filled out the evening's stew. I wondered if I'd chopped the carrots on my plate. I had a whole new appreciation for the food we had denigrated at every meal.

Some of our neighbors from down the hall sat with us at the table.

"You know, she chopped those vegetables," Debbie said, pointing at me with her knife. She'd been impressed with my gumption, but I was less thrilled to volunteer to my classmates that I was so hard up for money.

"You what?" Caitlin said. She tossed her dark, shiny hair behind her shoulder, eyes wide with disbelief.

"She spent the afternoon working in the kitchen. Apparently we have no idea what goes into these meals," Debbie said.

"I don't want to know," Caitlin said with obvious disdain. She looked directly at me. "Why on earth would you do that?"

I'd tried to blend in since I got to Harvard, sharing almost nothing about my family. Mom had been loud and braggy the two or three times she, Dad, and Marilyn had come to visit. But so many of the kids at Harvard had real money, old money; they were at ease with the cash that seemed to flow endlessly from their pockets. I knew any airs Mom put on were mortifyingly transparent.

Since the vast majority of students lived on campus for their entire undergrad stay, sleeping in dorm-issued beds, your clothes and bed linens were the only indications of where you'd come from. That and what you shared about yourself. I felt like my story was so tangled and complicated that the less I offered, the better. Of course everyone knew I'd grown up on television, and *Little House* was still in reruns on a local Boston station every single day. But beyond that, I just kept my mouth shut.

"Oh, my mom doesn't want me living in D.C. this summer so she's going to try to starve me home," I said casually.

"My mom would never let me work in the kitchen, serving other students. It's demeaning," Caitlin sniffed.

I could see the hair on the back of Debbie's neck stand up. "What's demeaning about working? Do you think you're better than the people that work in the dining hall to make the food you're eating right now?"

"Well, yes. I think our parents sent us here so we wouldn't have to chop vegetables and wash dishes. And my mom wants me to focus on studying and getting A's. I'm not sure working in the dining hall is the best use of my time at this school. There are a million things we could be learning . . . libraries, museums, clubs, classes. We only have so much time here. I don't think it makes sense to spend it cutting up food," she argued.

Her dark eyes shone against her pale skin. Enough of her red lipstick remained to give her the appearance of Snow White. I wondered if there was a poison apple handy.

"Well, I got a summer job that's going to help me get the job I want after graduation. Whatever I have to do to get to D.C. this summer is worth it, I guess," I said evenly.

I didn't want to encourage the debate. There was so much more to the story I had no intention of explaining. No one at Harvard needed to know how crazy and controlling my mom was, or how she'd relentlessly drained and mismanaged our finances without anyone stopping her or even challenging her.

So instead of inviting more questions, I just stood up from the table and carried my tray to the conveyor belt where we dumped them when we were done with a meal. I'd always pictured the napkin-littered trays falling into a black hole once they got beyond the end of the rubber runway. Now I knew there was a lone worker at the other end where the belt snaked behind the wall, pulling them off one by one and wiping them down.

After a week of cramming in shifts inside the underground labyrinth of kitchens, I had cleared next to nothing. But when I told Mom what I was doing, her combined shock and horror led her to rethink her hard-line position.

"You don't have to be so dramatic. Obviously I will help you," she said with exasperation.

It certainly hadn't been obvious to me.

"What's your sister doing this summer?" Debbie asked as we walked across campus to class a week later. Spring had taken hold on campus, and cherry blossoms exploded in pale pink and then fell to the ground in front of us, staining our path like wet tissue paper.

I hadn't thought about Tiffany's plans. The summer we'd spent together almost two years ago when she'd returned from

Europe was the last time we'd felt close to each other, much as I had feared at the time. She'd melted back into the Berkeley scene and disappeared from my life, as if that wonderful summer had been a figment of my imagination.

I'd tried to connect with her on the phone but the distance was too great. There was always something going on in the background on both of our ends, or awkward silences. When I'd been home the previous summer, she'd only come home once, and she'd brought her boyfriend and her best friend, Molly, so there hadn't been an opportunity to even try to revive the connection that had been so precious and just as fragile as I'd feared.

Debbie had a sister she was close to, and their bond always made me envious. I didn't know why Tiffany and I couldn't be best friends like that, since we'd also been together since birth and shared the same tumultuous history.

When we were little Tiffany had been the one I relied on to dig us out of trouble. I remembered our earliest days of riding horses together. When I was about six years old, Mom would let us spend half of the day on Saturday riding ponies at a local Western stable in the Valley. It was long before we started riding more seriously out of Fairfield. She'd drop us off with some cash for food and then pay to rent each of us the pony of our choice for three hours.

I always chose Windy, an old gray and white mare with a long white mane that had yellowed over time. Her coat was shaggy, but she was gentle and predictable and I wasn't terribly brave. Tiffany loved Trixie, a beautiful bay with a glossy black mane and tail who had been named for her ornery and defiant personality. Trixie was always available to rent on Saturdays because no one wanted to pay for the challenge she presented.

Mom's rule was that we weren't allowed to ride the horses off the property onto any of the neighboring trails. So we did her one better. We'd ride the ponies down the sidewalk of the busiest street to 7-Eleven to buy candy. Mom wouldn't allow us to have candy in the house, so our only chance to stock up was via pony when we were left alone. We both knew we'd be skinned alive if our routine was discovered, but the lure of unmonitored sugar was too great.

One Saturday when we were inside 7-Eleven emptying the shelves, the ponies rubbed off their bridles and escaped. We returned to the parking lot where we'd tied them to a chain link fence and found only their bridles hanging limply to the ground.

My stomach dropped and I instantly began to sob. Arms full of the candy that had caused so much trouble, I turned to Tiffany and wailed.

"They're going to send us to jail for losing Windy and Trixie!" I cried.

Tiffany rolled her eyes. "No, they aren't. You're six. I'm ten. We can't go to jail," she shot back, her voice tight with fear.

"Then Mom will kill us!" I cried.

"Just shut up! Let me think! What should we do?" she asked herself, since I wasn't helping.

Tiffany took the candy out of my hands and threw the bags in the trash, ditching the evidence of our disobedience. Then she grabbed my hand and dragged me as we ran back to the barn. Along the way we looked for signs of the horses and found nothing.

When we got back to the front gate of the stable, Linda, the owner, was standing by with a wry smile on her face.

"Lose something?" she asked. Her round stomach and breasts tested the limits of her navy blue T-shirt, which barely covered the top of her jeans. Her face was tanned and well worn by the sun, and her dusty brown hair fell to her shoulders in long straight ropes that made me think of the lead lines we used to tie up the horses.

I couldn't talk for all the tears that were streaming down my face. Tiffany bit her lip as Linda gestured to the two errant ponies, now feeding greedily on the grass near the front of the barn.

The horses, smart as they were, had broken free and just trotted home for food, leaving the two us to get home on foot. I'd fallen apart, but Tiffany had held it together, the way I thought she always would.

"I'm not sure what my sister's doing," I said to Debbie as we arrived at class. "She's starting law school in the fall at the University of San Diego. I think she's just packing up her home in Berkeley and getting set up in San Diego."

"So you'll see her when you go home?" Debbie asked.

"Yeah, I'm sure."

But I wasn't sure at all.

When summer arrived, Mom let me write a check from her account for part of the rent for my apartment in Washington, D.C., but she'd taken a pound of flesh in exchange for her generosity. I'd listened endlessly to what I should be doing differently, how much I was costing her, what shows other kids I knew growing up in Hollywood were currently working on.

"Shannen's got another series! Boy, she just keeps on working," she zinged.

"Yep," I said flatly, digging my fingernails into my arm.

Before I left Harvard for the summer internship, I'd lined up not one, but two jobs for the fall. I'd be working as a paid intern for the *MacNeil/Lehrer NewsHour* on PBS. The show's economic correspondent worked from a studio in Cambridge, so I could ride my bike to his office four days a week and do anything his team needed, which eventually included going out and doing interviews on my own with a crew.

I also got hired to work on a tech support team at Harvard

Business School. The job was a little like being a flight attendant, going up to the graduate students' rooms and helping them get familiar with the Internet, which was just making its debut. I also showed them how to use new applications to open their case studies online. The office where I stood ready by the phone had a free soda machine, and I could do my homework while I waited for calls for help. Eventually, I managed the whole tech team for twenty-five bucks an hour.

For the next two years, I never worked less than forty hours a week so I wouldn't get caught short again. The *Today* show internship turned out to be everything I'd hoped, a glimpse into a rarefied world I might be able to join after graduation if I worked hard enough and stockpiled cash to cover being paid very little, if at all, to start. I hoarded every nickel possible and scraped together fifteen thousand dollars by the time I graduated, so that I could afford to take an entry-level job as a producer cutting tape and running a teleprompter for a local television station in Maine right out of school. I'd driven all over New England to get the job, but the position only paid minimum wage, something my scrounging and saving had afforded me the luxury of keeping to myself. Still, even at $6.10 per hour, I was on my way.

CHAPTER FIFTEEN

We walked off the plane at LAX and into the terminal. It was almost ten at night and the airport was empty except for an Indian woman, nearly asleep, standing behind the register in Hudson News.

Wray walked next to me a stride faster, slowing occasionally so I could catch up. He was so tall, he easily outpaced me, but I was dragging my feet, dreading what lay ahead.

Wray and I had been dating for about eight months. He'd been my next-door neighbor at Harvard in Eliot House, the huge, Oxford-style dorm shaped like an imposing stone hexagon. He and a handful of messy, clever guys like him lived on the other side of the fire door in my dorm room, stacking pizza boxes in the hall and generally entertaining my roommates and me at any hour. I'd hit on him a fair bit during my sophomore year, but he didn't seem to notice. I even went to watch him play on the varsity volleyball team because I liked the way he looked in his shorts. He had sandy brown hair and big blue eyes, but more than that an irrepressible charisma that got him elected president of everything on campus.

I didn't see him after he left Harvard until a year after I graduated, when my best friend, Nicole, invited me down to New York from Manchester, New Hampshire, where I was struggling with my first on-air news reporting job. Turns out news was nothing like acting, though I think I'd been hired on the premise that experience in one would help with the other.

Nicole was working as a first-year analyst for an investment bank, pulling all-nighters at her desk analyzing every detail of a potential corporate buyout, only to then stay out until dawn the next night to soak up the New York nightlife. She was the most glamorous brain I'd ever met.

"Come on down for the weekend," Nicole said, explaining that her boyfriend had a bunch of cute friends. "We'll go out, you'll have fun. You've got nothing better to do in Manch-Vegas."

I'd only been working in New Hampshire for a month, and I didn't know anyone who lived in the state, so I had nothing to do on the weekend except shop at the state's only Gap. I threw a weekend bag in my car and drove four hours down the interstate to crash on Nicole's couch for the weekend.

I joined the party already in progress at a place called the Bubble Lounge down in Tribeca. I talked the oversized bouncer into letting me jump the line by explaining that my group was already inside.

When I got through the door, I was immediately deafened by the pounding music. I scanned the crowd and saw Nicole near the bar waving her right hand at me, her other hand combing through her long blonde hair. She was the picture of hip New York fashion, in knee-high black boots and a shiny blue top that simultaneously set off her eyes and hugged every curve of her perfect body. Not surprisingly, a team of guys swarmed around her. It took me less than thirty seconds to realize the team was, in fact, my old next-door neighbors from Harvard.

I talked to Nicole for a few minutes, and tried to tell her these were not new, cute guys, but rather my hapless, essentially unchanged college neighbors. She laughed it off and handed me a shot of tequila.

After a few minutes, Wray worked his way over and introduced himself. He didn't even recognize me. I thought about getting in my car and driving back to my apartment three states away, but I was too tired, and I'd just had a shot of tequila. So I let him buy me a drink and talk endlessly while I barely responded.

I had to remind him that he'd already met me, and in fact, lived next to me for almost a year. I knew I looked different with the newscaster makeover the new station had given me, complete with the classic anchor bob, but I didn't think I looked *that* different.

"I can't believe you don't recognize me. I'm twenty-two, not forty. It's not like it's been a decade since we were in school together," I said, annoyed.

"Well, I've been out for more than three years. Wait! You had a whole bunch of roommates . . . Debbie and Sue and Alex. I remember Greg hitting on Alex. God, he never got anywhere with that. And you were dating some guy the whole entire time. Some guy from Kirkland House right? What was his name?" he said.

I didn't help him. "So what do you do now?" I asked, changing the subject.

"I work for a private equity fund. We buy companies and do things to make them run better and then sell them," he said, his deep blue eyes looking pleased with this statement.

"Do things like . . . laying people off?" I said.

I'd been indoctrinated into the value of economic efficiency, so I wasn't judging him, but I thought it couldn't hurt to give him a hard time.

"You buy companies and then chop them up into little pieces and sell them bit by bit?" I continued.

"I wish! Those are the easy deals. The low-hanging fruit. Most of those deals have been done already and there aren't many dinosaurs like that lying around waiting to be worked out," he said grinning. It was going to take more than that to get his goat.

"This feels like *Pretty Woman*," I said.

"Why, are you not really a reporter?" he smiled.

"No. I mean, yes, I am. I'm saying that you sound like Richard Gere trying to dismantle that shipping company or whatever."

"Yeah. Though it's not clear what that guy did. I guess he was sort of in private equity or just some guy with family money buying stuff to amuse himself. I don't have family money. I have to get up early in the morning and go to work every day," he said, taking a step closer. "So you're a news reporter in New Hampshire. Like in print? Or on TV?"

"On TV. I work for the ABC station in Manchester. It's local news. I was a producer right out of school for the local NBC in Maine. In fact, I was the only person in my class who thought it was a good idea to move to Maine after graduation," I said, and he laughed.

"What made you go into news? Didn't you act growing up? My roommate, Greg, is an actor here in New York." He gestured to his friend, whom I had recognized right when I came in.

"I was in acting my whole life growing up. And I went off to Harvard to kind of see if I could live without it. Turns out I could," I said.

I wasn't sure why I was telling him so much. Maybe it was the drink, maybe I was just tired. He was a good audience, though, so I had a hard time stopping.

"I interned at the Fox station in L.A. after my freshman year and news was immediately addicting. It was such a rush to see everyone race to airtime. And there's no safety net. It's totally unlike entertainment. There's barely a script, there's no rehearsal, no support. You're responsible for coming up with everything you say. Live or die, it's all on you. It's exhilarating. I love it. But it's stressful too."

He'd moved even closer while I was talking so he could touch my wrist resting on the bar. His finger sent a chill up my arm, raising an army of goose bumps. I had tried to be annoyed by him, but he was melting my resistance.

He charmed and entertained and cajoled me for hours, totally ignoring his friends and everyone else. He was happy and unconcerned in a way I had never been.

"Your eyes are yellow," he said, now completely in my personal space.

"Yes, I know." I looked down, uncomfortable with the way he looked through them.

"They are really pretty. I'm not sure I noticed that when you lived next door," he said with a smile.

"No, you were too busy hanging out with your friends at the Fox Club," I teased.

"Well, we were seniors by the time you came along. I was the president of the club. I had a duty to hang out there," he said.

"You know I came by to hit on you, at the Fox, and in your room," I admitted. "I even went to watch you play volleyball."

"I'm pretty sure you came by to hit on Greg."

"No," I said. "That was my cover. I talked to him, but I was after you."

"Well, I think I would have noticed if you were hitting on me. You may have been too subtle. Or I was just an idiot. My fault, I'm sure. It's not like there was an abundance of pretty girls at Harvard," he said.

"Is that why you were always busing in girls from Wellesley?" I teased.

A few drinks later, the arm he'd had on the bar was now wrapped around my waist. He leaned in and kissed me, right in the middle of the crowd. The room full of people blurred into the background. I had no idea where any of our friends had gone, and I hadn't thought to look for them for a while.

The rest of the weekend, I tried to put my finger on his energy, dissect it and understand it. Instead I got wrapped up in its freedom and carried away.

For months, I looked for signs that his charisma was a façade, a magic trick, but couldn't find any. Now that our casual dating had turned serious, I'd brought him home to L.A. to see if he could survive a weekend with my family. The odds were less than even. But I had landed a job near New York and we were planning on moving in together, so the collision of Wray and my family became inevitable.

"My family is crazy," I warned him for the tenth time as we got into the rental car and started to exit the airport. He laughed, which made me think he didn't understand the gravity of the situation.

He was going to spend forty-eight hours among the crazies in their natural habitat. He'd see how they resembled electrons rapidly orbiting around each other, invisibly bound to some center while also fighting to get away. It was enough to make me vomit.

Just to complicate the family dynamic further, Tiffany had

moved back home with Mom and Dad. She had made her way through Berkeley, and had even scraped through the University of San Diego Law School. But she'd barely cleared the second hurdle. She didn't have the focus or the stamina for law school, ending up at the bottom of her class with no sign of a job on the horizon. Now she was at home studying for the bar. I hoped that with a vocation, she'd have something solid to keep her centered and supported. But she was off to a rough start now that she was back home, not working, essentially not doing anything except going on the occasional job interview and taking a bar review course. She hung around the house and bickered with Mom much of the time. None of the friends she'd made in school lived in the area. Her life at the moment sounded lonely and direc-tionless to me.

Wray adjusted the rearview mirror and cleared his throat, amused by my discomfort. He put his hand on my leg, as if to tell me I was worrying for nothing.

"You've met *my* family. Now *they* are totally crazy," he said, removing his hand to chew on his cuticle.

"No," I said. "Everyone says their family is crazy. Mine actually is. It's a clinical thing. We could be studied on an aca-demic level. It's not like annoying or quirky. It's real crazy-crazy."

He turned quickly to look directly at me in the passenger seat as we sped down the highway, his blondish brown hair rum-pled from the six-hour plane ride. He smiled in a way that made me smile involuntarily.

"Stop worrying. It's going to be fun."

I loved his misguided optimism.

It took about an hour to navigate the 405 Freeway, merge to the 101, and make our way all the way out to Westlake Boulevard, where Mom and Dad now lived.

The Northridge earthquake of the mid-'90s cracked the foundation of the house I grew up in, and forced the city to declare the structure uninhabitable. Mom and Dad were at home and asleep when the earthquake struck. Though books and pictures and everything else that wasn't nailed in place had fallen and shattered as the ground rolled and rumbled, there was plenty of time for them to get outside without getting hurt.

When the shaking stopped, Allstate forked over a sizable settlement and in turn, Mom got one of the things she'd always wanted, a brand-new house in a gated and guarded community, Lake Sherwood, out in Westlake Village.

When I left for college, I'd assumed they'd stay in our house forever, that the place would remain a museum to my childhood. Even as the walls showed the dings and scratches of time, it seemed like nothing would actually pry my parents loose from that house, no matter how much Mom mused about renovating or moving. They'd have to come up with a plan and execute it as a team, which meant coming together and taking action. That was unthinkable, with so many chiefs and not a single indian. My family was incapable of working together as a productive group.

Ultimately, I wasn't far off. It took a natural disaster to dislodge them, and nothing less.

We got off at Westlake Village Blvd. and drove through the town center out to the rolling grasslands and farmlands of Hidden Valley. At the edges of two pastures sat a brick guard gate. Through the dark night, I could make out an escaped cow that stood on the mowed lawn to the right of the guardhouse, eating a late-night snack.

"Hello, folks, who are you here to see?" the potbellied guard asked, leaning toward the car from inside the guardhouse. He didn't bother to get to his feet.

"Is that cow here to greet us?" I asked.

"No," he laughed. "She's an escapee from the down the

street. I called the guy she belongs to. He's coming down with a trailer to get her. It's not the first time she's come down here. She prefers this tender stuff, I guess," he said, gesturing to the neatly trimmed lawn. This new neighborhood was nothing if not idyllic, I thought.

"We're going to the Francis residence," Wray said, and with that the guard pushed a button and the imposing wrought iron gates swung open.

We drove our small rental sedan through the towering gates and followed Stafford Road past a slew of enormous homes illuminated by streetlights, then wound around a golf course down the oak-lined street.

"It's right there, on the right. Pull in there," I said, pointing to a more modest home across the street from the course.

Wray pulled into the driveway, and my heart started to pound. I really adored him, and I felt fairly certain the people inside the house were going to ruin this for me.

We got out and headed for the door, leaving our luggage in the trunk. I walked a step behind Wray on the brick path, my boot heels echoing in the silence of the evening air.

When we arrived at the front door, I pushed it open and led Wray inside. A soft, rose-colored light bathed the inside of the house, bouncing off the shiny pine floors like candlelight. Mom had cornered the market on antique pine armoires that stretched up to the ceiling. She had filled almost every room with at least one if not two pieces. Overstuffed armchairs dwarfed adjoining antique pine side tables, draped with Pierre Deux fabrics, every available surface covered with porcelain knickknacks, minute Tiffany Limoges boxes, and picture frames.

We walked past the dining room, where the table was set for dinner, cluttered with country French linens and colorful dishes and silverware, the ceiling painted like a night sky. Candles shaped like food filled in the spots between dishes in the center of the oval table. The house was decorated within an inch of its life.

"Wray, good to see you," Mom said in a formal tone, sweeping in from the kitchen. Her voice was stilted and unnatural. I could tell she was nervous about having him there.

My eyes drifted across the tabletops covered with tchotchkes, marveling at all that had appeared since the last time I'd visited. Every surface held a dozen items, each intricate and unquestionably beautiful, but presented in such abundance that it was difficult to appreciate any particular one. I couldn't imagine the time and energy Mom had spent accumulating these trinkets and assembling the scene before us.

Dad came out from the living room, where he had been sitting in a hunter green wingback chair, watching C-SPAN. The House was voting on another piece of pork barrel legislation, and he was watching the tally, as if something tangible were at stake outside this room.

Wray dwarfed my parents, in size and presence. I considered the possibility of just going back to New York in the morning if we survived the night.

"Where's Tiff?" I asked.

"Upstairs. She'll be down in a second. I told her you were on your way," Mom said, looking Wray over.

I wondered which Tiffany would emerge from upstairs. I hoped for the steady, eye-rolling big sister who had returned refreshed and clearheaded from a semester backpacking around in Europe. But it had been three or four years since I'd seen that version. I'd grown to expect the nervous person I'd seen last Christmas, who hit the wine a little too hard. She'd be fine one minute, then a switch would flip somewhere in her brain, and she seemed to want to crawl out of her skin. Most of the time I blamed her edginess on Mom, but now it seemed like more and more things made her uncomfortable. It was hard to pinpoint and understand since I only saw her occasionally.

Last Christmas had been the first time my family had met Wray. I was reporting for a local station in Rhode Island, and as the newest hire, I had to work the whole holiday on the air. Mom, Dad, Tiffany, and Marilyn had flown out to offer their support. But then when the time for Christmas dinner rolled around, Mom got angry about something someone had said, though no one knew what it was because she locked herself in her hotel room, and refused to come to the holiday meal at my apartment. Wray had flown back from his family's home in Florida to meet my family, and that's what he came up against.

"Wait, your mom flew all the way here, and now she's boy-cotting the dinner?" he asked, laughing in disbelief. "And you don't even know why?"

Tiffany, Dad, and I shrugged in unison. We had no idea, but we did know we were enjoying the meal, and Marilyn was stuck with Mom. She was only really punishing herself and Marilyn, it seemed.

I noticed Tiffany drank more than her share of wine dur-ing dinner though, and the rest of the trip, especially when Mom was actually around, she was anxious and on edge, quiet and constantly tugging her hair. It wasn't good. She was spend-ing too much time cooped up with Mom. She needed to start her own life.

"Come into the kitchen. Can I make you something to eat?" Mom said now, as if that was a normal thing for her to do. "I've got steaks I could broil."

She gestured to the Viking range that I was sure she had no idea how to operate. Dad and I exchanged knowing looks.

"I can grill them," Dad said, walking to the Sub-Zero and opening it, rescuing her.

Tiffany walked down the stairs and into the room, crossing to me first and giving me an awkward hug. Her face looked tired. She had no makeup on, and her skin looked red and bumpy, her eyes strained. The stress of living in the house with Mom and having nowhere to go during the day was getting to her.

"How was your flight, Miss?" she asked. Her voice sounded like a little girl's, high and soft.

"Long," Wray offered, jumping into the conversation. "And there was no movie."

Dad cooked steaks on the grill outside the kitchen door, and Wray kept the conversation going through the preparation and all the way to the end of dinner. He could chat with himself if need be. It was a great skill. Tiffany piped in occasionally, shifting uncomfortably in her chair, pulling on strands of her hair.

At one point when we'd eaten most of the food, the conversation turned to politics. Fueled by a few drinks now, Tiffany moved in to defend Bill Clinton.

"He's doing a good job. He'll probably have a budget surplus next year in spite of your terror over his spending. His only problem is he can't keep his dick in his pants," she said.

Mom blanched at the off-color comment and Dad grimaced, but Tiffany looked delightfully guilty, like a child acting out for attention. Unsure of her target and not liking the unpredictability of the situation, I stood up from the table and started clearing the plates. Wray shot me a look like I was the one being rude. I just wanted the dinner to end so we could go to bed and get the day over with.

Wray followed my lead eventually and insisted on doing the dishes, taking the plates that each of us handed to him and scraping the last bits of food into the garbage disposal before rinsing them off and loading them into the dishwasher.

He chatted happily with Mom while he worked. She'd found an audience who hadn't heard all her stories about the house, decorating, and my acting career. She embellished details and drew out the dramatic moments, and he laughed at the punch lines and frowned at the appropriate pauses. Mom was in heaven.

Tiffany and Dad retired to the living room to watch *Law & Order*, and Wray and I yawned and stretched before heading upstairs. We were still on New York time, which gave us an excuse to exit early.

We peeled off into the room that was designated as mine, although I'd never technically lived in this new house. The room had plush off-white carpet and a marble bathroom all its own, with a deep tub and an elegant polished vanity. The furniture in this room was far more sparse, and looked like a collection of leftovers or things that hadn't worked elsewhere in the house.

I kept thinking it would have been nice to grow up in this room. There was less pressure and more beauty. It was hard to believe an earthquake had instigated such an upgrade. Our lives were apparently worth so much more once a disaster had destroyed the foundation.

A queen bed stood against the wall. I didn't love the idea of sleeping in the same bed with my boyfriend in my parents' house, even though we'd just moved in together in New York. But the idea of sending him to another room seemed weird too. The sleeping arrangements just added to the awkwardness of the whole visit. Wray read my mind and put his arms around me.

"Seriously, you need to relax. Your parents are great. I have no idea why you are so worked up, but you're freaking out for nothing. Breathe," he said.

* * *

The next day I wandered down in my sweats alone while Wray was still snoring. Mom had gotten up early to make banana bread from a mix and brew coffee. I loved the happy-homemaker façade. I'd practically starved to death foraging for food in our house while growing up and now she was putting on a show for Wray as if she were Martha Stewart. She even quoted Martha for good measure.

"You never want to cool bread too quickly, Martha says," she remarked to no one in particular. I looked over at Tiffany, who rolled her eyes dramatically. Dad chuckled.

"What? What's funny? What are you all laughing at?" Mom asked.

I heard the shower running upstairs. A short while later, Wray emerged totally ready for the day, pressed and shaven. We all stared at him, having barely ingested coffee.

"How did everyone sleep?" he chirped. No one responded.

Mom sliced him some banana bread and he made a show of breathing in the aroma.

We sat around for at least an hour, watching television and discussing different plans for the day. Most of the action was going to center on a football game on television and another opportunity to grill. Dad planned to go for a long walk, which was his exercise ritual, though I knew Wray would not consider anything less than an hour–long run a decent workout. He had more energy than my entire family put together.

Wray and I volunteered to go to the grocery store to get food to graze on during the game and meat for the grill. Mom scribbled down items she wanted on a list. Tiffany mentioned some exotic vegetables that would make a good side dish. She'd taken up cooking now that she was living at home, mostly to escape into the vacuum that was the normally empty kitchen.

"Okay, so we'll do the shopping," Wray announced. "Let me go upstairs and grab the keys to the rental car. I'll be right back."

I followed him upstairs to get my purse and change into clothes suitable for a run to a grocery store. When we returned downstairs, the place had cleared out. We walked out the front door without locking it and got in the car.

"Your family is great. Your sister is a little off," Wray ventured. "But I'd be like that too if I had to move back in with my parents."

"Yeah. I don't know," I said.

"She's studying for the bar?" he asked.

"In theory. I don't know how much studying she's doing. She said she was going to take the Kaplan course. But I thought that's why you go to law school, basically to study for the bar," I said.

"Right," Wray said, following the winding lane around the golf course. We went through the gatehouse and out onto the main road.

"Turn right here. There's a Bristol Farms back next to the exit from the freeway," I said. "I was hoping that Tiffany would get a normal office job and her own apartment, and just start her life, sort of. Mom always says Tiffany wants to keep hiding in school. That's why she went to law school. So she wouldn't have to face life. She took almost six years to graduate from Berkeley, well, just over five, I guess. And then spent three more years in law school. She took a break in the middle. She's been milking it for a long time. She's never had anything like a nine-to-five, five-day-a-week job. I think it would do her a lot of good. Even if she was just like a paralegal or something. Turn here," I said, pointing to the light at the intersection.

"How old is she now?" he asked.

"Twenty-seven," I said.

"Well, normally you apply for jobs as you're graduating, right? So did she do that? How did she not sort of lock something down before she left San Diego," Wray asked, turning on Westlake Boulevard with the highway now in sight.

"I don't know. I think her grades were pretty terrible. When I went down there for graduation, she seemed like she was sort of holding on by a thread. In college she'd made a pack of friends, but I didn't meet anyone really at law school that she seemed to hang out with except her boyfriend, who was a jerk, a real angry loud type. Her apartment was a disaster and when we went out to dinner, she spoke sort of frantically and didn't always make sense. The whole vibe was not good. I couldn't figure out what was going on, but it was not normal."

And it seemed to me that she was drinking a lot but I didn't say this to Wray. I noticed that Mom would snap at her and nag when she drank now, but her complaints didn't get any traction with Tiffany or Dad, since Tiffany wasn't driving and she wasn't so drunk she was knocking over the furniture or anything. Plus she and Dad were drinking from the same bottle, so clearly he didn't think there was anything wrong with it. Since I had been away from the group and now stepped back in, it was easier for me to see her casual drinking was escalating.

We pulled into the parking lot of Bristol Farms, and right into a spot in the front row next to the bay of shopping carts.

When I got out of the passenger side, I saw them. Tiffany and Dad getting out of one car, Mom closing the door of another, one row away.

"Didn't we all agree that you and I would do the shopping?" Wray asked, befuddled, pointing to my dad and sister.

"Yep. And look," I said, "there's Mom, too. In a third car."

"Wow," Wray said.

"No one trusts anyone else in this family to do anything, even shop for lunch."

CHAPTER SIXTEEN

"We should just elope," I said to Wray, still admiring the ring he'd given me. He'd taken me to the top of the Empire State Building and surprised me with a beautiful square diamond. I said yes immediately. Now the sun bounced off my new ring like a disco ball.

I was on a cell phone, sitting in a news van with my news crew, waiting for the search-and-rescue team to find a downed Cessna. We'd been on high alert deep in the Connecticut woods for four hours, and it had gotten old.

"If I had a dime for every private plane crash I've covered in New England, we could pay for this wedding ourselves. Why do people fly in these two-seaters? They fall out of the sky like rocks. And I'll be damned if they don't find the thing the moment we decide to go for dinner," I said into the phone. The photographer up front grunted in agreement at every sentence.

"Come on. It's gonna be great! It's a huge party with all our friends," Wray said.

"You have no idea what you are in for," I said, knowing he was comfortably seated at his desk at his office near the Flatiron Building in Manhattan, while I was crouched in a van in the woods, rummaging through my purse for a granola bar.

"Sure our moms have gotten a little nutty with the details but it's going to be beautiful," Wray assured me.

My call waiting beeped in. It was Mom.

"Okay, it's my mom again. With yet another detail I'm sure. She's spending so much money. I don't know how they can afford this. I'm sure my dad has no idea how much she's spending."

"Doesn't he ask her?" Wray said.

"No, I'm sure not. Communication isn't their forte," I replied.

"Well, why don't you tell her we don't need so many elaborate details and frills?" Wray said, always trying to solve the problem.

"Yes. I have said that and it's like talking to a wall. She tells me that I didn't have any trouble spending a fortune on my dress."

"I'll pay for that. If I can also pick out what's under it," Wray said.

I ignored him. "I have less understanding of their finances than ever."

Beep.

"Shit. I have to take her call or she won't leave me alone. Bye."

"How many times a day does she call you?" he said, as I cut him off.

"Hi, Mom," I said into the phone.

"*There* you are," she said, completely annoyed.

"Yes, Mom. I'm working. I'm in the woods . . ."

"Well, don't get a tick bite. That would ruin the wedding. Especially if it was on someplace that showed," she said.

"What's going on?" I pressed, not wanting to make the call last any longer than necessary.

"We have to decide if the chairs should be wrapped in pale pink chiffon fabric or apricot. The fabric makes a gorgeous bow on the back. Not too big," she said.

Beep.

More call waiting. This time it was Dana from the assignment desk. She was the assignment manager for the station, but also a close friend who was in the wedding, and she'd suffered through the details as much as I had. Besides Wray, she was the main person keeping me sane through this process, the only one who understood I was juggling this job and Mom the Wedding Planner. I thought about conferencing her into the fabric vote since I didn't care.

"Do we need to wrap the chairs?" I asked. "How much is that?"

"It's a fortune, but it's necessary," Mom said.

Beep.

"Necessary? Mom, I'm working. I have to answer that," I said, realizing that Dana could be calling about something other than my pending nuptials.

"Pink or apricot?"

"Hold on," I said, clicking over to Dana. "What's up? My mom is driving me bananas."

"They found the plane! Where are you? I just heard it on the scanner! Are you sitting in the truck? Get out of the truck, grab Brian, and run!" Dana yelled.

I hung up on both calls and threw the van door open. Brian's boots beat me to the dusty path in front of us and I chased him in the direction of the barking dogs. He had his camera up on his shoulder, rolling tape as he ran. I pulled the stick micro-phone out of my pocket and flipped it upside down to switch it on from the base.

We caught up to the search party and other TV crews in time to see them pry open the plane door. Brian widened his stance to steady himself as he shot the state trooper climbing onto the plane's wing. The trooper dipped his shaved head inside the cabin as two searchers held the door back.

"Let's get him out!" he shouted with his head still inside. Two rescue workers climbed inside the cabin and struggled to free the pilot, who was apparently still breathing.

My phone rang again. It was Mom.

"I cannot talk," I shouted into the receiver. "I don't care what color the chairs are. Pick one. Or we can stand. I have to go. They're prying this pilot from the plane."

And with that I snapped the clamshell shut and turned it off.

Two weeks later Wray and I boarded a much larger plane to L.A, loaded down with everything we'd need for the wedding and the honeymoon. I'd spent the previous day, Monday, standing on a train platform in New Haven, where a mother and her four sons had been struck and killed trying to cross the tracks in the mid-dle of the night. The tragedy had led every local newscast. Like most reporters, I'd become immune to death and destruction. I was used to seeing mangled cars containing bloody bodies right up close. Plus you start to notice how often a bad decision had set off a deadly chain of events. But this was too much. When we arrived, the children's shoes were still lying on the tracks. The scene rocked even the most seasoned reporters among us. It was not an auspicious start to the week that would end with my wedding.

"When's Dana coming?" Wray asked as we boarded United's flight to L.A.

"Thursday. Which seems like a year from now." I was banking on Dana to be my life jacket during this storm and keep me laughing. She always had the perfect quip or sarcastic remark to remind me that my mom's nitpicking and crazy making was not life or death. It was like traveling with your own stand-up comic. I knew that when Mom fumed about some imaginary insult from a friend or family member or obsessed about the centerpieces, Dana would have the perfect joke about how our marriage hinged on the number of roses on each table.

Wray tried to soothe my nerves, but he didn't take them that seriously. He was relentlessly positive about the rest of the wedding week. He thought he could smooth over any bumps in the road. I wasn't sure he understood that smoothing over landmines didn't stop them from exploding. Still my worrying wasn't helping and I'd been snappy with him all evening, barking at him all the way to the taxi that we were leaving for the airport too late. I didn't want to start our future life together this way.

"I'm really happy to be getting married. It's not that. I'm just a little stressed about how this wedding is going to turn out. Bringing all these different worlds together seems like we're courting disaster. My friends, your friends, your family, and my family . . ."

Initially, I'd been most concerned about Mom, who could be offended by the change of a stoplight. I'd seen her return a dish of food at a restaurant just to spite a waiter. She'd stopped talking to each of her sisters for years at a time over simple disagreements, like whose turn it was to pick up the check. Already, she'd channeled a little hostility my future mother-in-law's way for no reason, dismissing or denigrating any of her ideas for the wedding weekend. Wray's mom had even chosen a gray dress for the ceremony so she wouldn't upstage anyone, but when she'd called to tell Mom about her dress, Mom was put out by the intrusion. It was irrational. I just wanted her to play nice this one time.

But I was actually most concerned about my sister, who didn't even come to my bachelorette weekend in New York, when all my bridesmaids and close friends came to the city for a final weekend of staying out all night bar-hopping without boyfriends or husbands.

"It's so far, and I don't really know your friends. You don't want me to come. I'm too old for you guys anyway!" she'd protested.

I'd told her that wasn't true. But in my heart, I was relieved. She'd gone from being a party girl to a recluse in my parents' house. All she had left was a few friends from Berkeley that she didn't see much. She'd had a few jobs working in legal offices in the past year, but couldn't hold on to them, telling us her job had been eliminated, or she didn't like her boss. There was always a reason the job didn't last. She didn't go out with friends anymore. She hadn't even wanted to go out with me and Wray the last time we visited. My parents had gone from concerned to frustrated to helpless.

Now I was flying in for this all-consuming wedding. Her little sister was getting married. I felt guilty about the position I was putting her in, how I'm sure my wedding made her feel, that I was leapfrogging her one last time, getting married first. And at the same time I felt resentful. I wished she could just share my joy, and I could share hers. That's what sisters were supposed to do. But I had no idea how to help her make some joy of her own. She was stuck, and even worse, sinking.

When we arrived in Westlake Village, Wray took me to my parents' house and abandoned me after a quick hello to my family.

He checked into a nearby hotel with his family, where most of our guests would be staying too. The plan was for us to stay apart until the actual wedding. This was a horrible plan. I should have paid more attention when this scheme was being hatched.

The next two days were a series of gatherings where the wedding planner and my mom broke down the smallest decision into excruciating detail. Wray mostly hung out by the hotel pool and played golf with his groomsmen, while I got entangled in things I'd never notice on the wedding schedule, like who was going to tie two hundred bows on the programs I didn't think we really needed anyway. Then when the programs disappeared, Mom blamed Wray's side, none of whom had been within a hundred feet of them.

"Every time I enter a room, there's a bunch of women crying," Wray joked during one of the rare moments when I saw him. We were having lunch at Jack's, a little café in Westlake Village Center.

"I'm dreading the rehearsal dinner tonight," I said, taking a bite of salad. I had a hard time eating when I was stressed, and now most of the clothes I'd bought for the wedding week and honeymoon were hanging off me loosely. It was such a cliché to shrink before your own wedding, but I couldn't help it.

"It's going to be great. It's a fish fry!" Wray said.

"Your mom realizes this is Southern California right? No one eats anything fried here. It's like a sin. Even if it is fried, no restaurant would even admit it. It's the kiss of death. They call it blackened or pan seared or pan-anything-but-fried."

"Well, that's more for us. She's making everyone who came from Florida feel at home," he said, always on his family's side no matter what.

"Whatever. It's sort of the least of my problems at this point. I gotta go back. I have another dress fitting." I kissed him and bolted.

*   *   *

That night a hundred guests for the rehearsal dinner crowded into the courtyard of Lake Sherwood Country Club, just a few yards from where the wedding would take place the following day. A strong breeze swept through the clusters of couples as they stood in between the dining tables and chatted. Ladies more accustomed to Florida's humid climate shivered in their short dresses as their dates held on to fluttering cocktail napkins. Waiters adjusted the temperature on the portable heaters they'd scattered through the party, even though it was nearly June.

Towering palms filled the center of each table, with delicate hanging votives dangling from the branches and twinkling in the night air. When a breeze struck, a tall arrangement here and there would topple over, causing a waiter to leap into action before the peach tablecloths caught fire.

In the middle of a group of guests, Wray's mom, Martha, stood wearing cocktail pants and a tight camisole that showed off her slender build. Every strand of her cropped blonde hair was teased and softly sprayed into place. Her southern accent rose above the crowd as she greeted her friends. She was exactly the type of well-meaning, attractive, social woman Mom hated.

"Wow, Wray's mom is so fit," said Nicole, my chic friend from New York who had reintroduced me to Wray at the Bubble Lounge in New York. She was a perfect physical specimen herself.

"You should have seen her on the bike trip we took through the Loire Valley. She and Wray left the rest of us in the dust," I said.

"That's a nightmare," Nicole said with a laugh.

A handful of waiters were busy setting out a buffet of traditional southern fish fry, consisting of small juicy chunks of flaky white grouper lightly battered, with tartar sauce and cheese grits on the side.

I stood with a few friends from high school and saw Tiffany hanging as close to Dad as a preschooler reluctant to be dropped off at a new school. She spoke to no one. I headed over to talk to her.

"Hey, I love that dress," I said, as she pulled on the black knit hem.

"I got it with Mom at Nordstrom's." Her eyes only met mine for a second.

"Did you say hi to Dana, my friend from work? Have you met her yet? She's so great," I offered. I'd asked Dana to try to look out for Tiffany, but I didn't see her now. Dana was disarming and funny, and the perfect person to put Tiffany at ease and try to include her.

"Did you know Wray's family is doing a song? They are like standing up and singing. Can they sing?" Tiffany asked.

"Well, his sister can," I said.

"Yep. It's supposed to be a surprise but I saw them rehearsing. With props."

"Shut up!" I gasped. She nodded slowly.

Before I could get more details, a tall, slender waitress with a neat blonde ponytail moved through the crowd letting everyone know the buffet had opened. Half the guests moved in, while the locals hung back, unsure of the cuisine.

I ushered Tiffany over to the line and took a plate.

"Is that Cream of Wheat?" my college roommate, Debbie, asked me as I stepped next to her in line.

"It's cheese grits," Wray said from behind me with a smile. "It's delicious."

Nicole was at the front of the line. A Texan, she had no aversion to Southern fare.

My bridesmaids and I settled at a table to the side, talking and eating, as my parents came and joined us. Waiters filled and refilled the wine glasses around the table. Mom smiled and talked to Dana, who'd been my salvation, occupying and appeasing

Mom all day, while Dad tried to get Tiffany to come out of her shell and join in the conversation.

I put a bite of fish in my mouth and suddenly noticed Wray's sister, Ali, his aunt, Pam, and his mom, all standing up in front of the crowd, wearing theatrical Sunday hats as if they were going to the Mother's Day Parade on Fifth Avenue. Wray's two little cousins, who were just five and eight, stood in front of them.

"Going to the chapel and they're gonna get married," they began to sing out of the clear blue. Nicole looked at me as if the people belting out the song before us had lost their minds.

In spite of their enthusiastic efforts, they were wildly off-key. They'd made up lyrics that explained how Wray and I had met, but it was impossible to hear the words as they all sang on top of each other. They must have reached the end because they stopped singing, and after a pause, the crowd started clapping.

Mom stood up and walked to the back of my chair with a rueful smile. "You would *kill* me if we stood up and embarrassed you like that," she said, leaning over to speak in my ear. "Good luck with that."

She was right. I would have been furious with them. But it was hardly the time to point it out.

"Please, just stay here with me," I begged Wray as he deposited me in the room that was supposed to be mine but had nothing of mine in it. I'd fled the rehearsal dinner shortly after dessert.

"No, sweetie. I can't do that. I have a million people waiting for me." He smiled, itching to get back out the door.

I tried to kiss him. "Please, don't leave me here. I don't know what I'm going to do. Tomorrow is going to be a disaster. There are so many people and personalities to manage, I'm not sure how I'm going to keep everyone together for the whole day.

Tiffany can't relax and Mom is going to insult someone beyond repair. I can feel it. It's going to be a disaster." I sighed.

"Stop saying things like that. It's going to be wonderful! You are starting to hurt my feelings with all this," he said.

"You know that's not what I mean. I just wish we'd planned a beach wedding somewhere, with no dress, and no programs, and no chairs with bows. Just here's the beach where we are getting married, come if you can, don't wear shoes, we'll have a big party afterward with lots of margaritas. No big deal. We would have planned it. Very little fanfare. It would have been perfect. It would have been *my* wedding."

"You're tired. You're stressed. Our families are making you crazy. Have a drink. Take some Advil. Go to bed. What can I get you?" he said.

I went inside the walk-in closet and changed out of my dress and into a chemise while we were talking. Then I walked out and pulled him to me and kissed him, thinking I could use some feminine wiles to keep him there.

"No. Not tonight. Tomorrow. Not here. Not now. Go to bed. Or come out with us," he suggested.

"No. The last thing I need is to stay out all night drinking. I'll be hungover and splotchy tomorrow."

"Okay . . . ," he agreed.

And with that, he disappeared.

In the morning I got up and went down to the kitchen to find Deborah, the wedding planner, waiting with coffee already made.

"Good morning! It's the bride," she said with way too much energy. I wanted to turn down her volume but I didn't see the knob.

The doorbell rang, and Wray's little sister, Ali, wandered in. It wasn't even nine, and she'd agreed to be the hair and makeup artists' first victim. Asking her to show up early was Mom's subtle way of hazing Wray's family. Ali looked like she hadn't slept.

"My mom dropped me off in the driveway. I'm sorry, she's still in her workout clothes. She didn't want to come in."

The wedding planner handed her a cup of coffee, which she took politely and then set in the middle of the coffee table without sipping.

"Do you want something in it?" I asked.

"No. Thanks. I'd rather have a Diet Coke," she answered. Then she dove into the couch and hid her head under a stiff decorative pillow.

Ali was a senior at Florida State, a sorority sister, and an all-around good sport. She'd been nothing but welcoming to me, even as I joined a family where she'd always been the unchallenged princess and the only girl. Now she was trying to power through an intense hangover to get ready, ridiculously early, for a full day of wedding formalities. She was a superstar. I stopped myself short of making any comparisons to my own sister.

"I will go check and see if they're ready to start your makeup," I said, walking up the stairs. When I got to the top, Tiffany was standing on the landing.

"Who's here?" she asked. Her long hair was pulled back into a ponytail. The remnants of last night's black eyeliner had bled into dark circles under eyes; her skin looked red and irritated.

"Ali just got here. What are you doing?" I said.

She pulled a small bottle of Kahlua out of the pocket of her robe.

"Look! I got this for our coffee. For while we're getting ready," she said with a sly smile.

"Seriously? It's like nine o'clock in the morning. Not even," I said. I flashed back to the bathroom at Magic Mountain.

"But this day is going to be absolute torture," she said.

"It doesn't have to be," I said.

"Exactly," she said, putting the bottle in her pocket and going back inside her room.

Tiffany stayed lost in her room for most of the day, while my other bridesmaids arrived and changed into plush, monogrammed robes. Together we reveled in the ceremony of getting our faces painted and our hair curled and pinned into place, tendril by tendril. We sipped tea and gossiped, as my friends politely ignored my sister's glaring absence.

Even though they were too gracious to say anything, I felt ashamed that my own sister, my maid of honor, didn't want to celebrate my wedding day with me the same way my girlfriends did. Friends representing every stage of my life had flown in and agreed to wear dresses they'd never choose for themselves or wear again, all for me. But the one person who'd been there from birth couldn't bring herself to lock arms with me and just be at my side. It hurt.

By the time we were ready to leave for the ceremony, the sky was still gray after drizzling that morning, which had sent Mom and Deborah into a tailspin. We were walking down a red velvet aisle, outside on a terrace, with no protection from the elements. We'd banked on the fact that it almost never rains in Southern California. The entire time I was in high school, rain never fell on a school day.

"Are you ready?" Mom said, walking into the bathroom. "You look so beautiful. I know you are going to be so happy."

"Thanks, Mom. Where's Tiffany?" I asked.

"She was just torturing me about that dress. She looks

beautiful, but she doesn't think so. She'd be happier if she were thinner. Your friends are gorgeous; that's hard for her," she said with a sigh.

"I know. I wish . . ." My voice broke off. I didn't want to get emotional yet; I knew it was going to be an emotional day. And I didn't want to say aloud that I just wished she would be normal for one day. Calm and relaxed in her skin. Or even able to just set aside her anxiety for one day to focus on something or someone else.

"Just let it go for now. It's your day. I love you. Now let's go," Mom said, for once the voice of reason.

When we pulled up in front of the Lake Sherwood Country Club, the cloud cover hung low, casting a foggy haze over the fairway that rolled up to the back door. I could see the edge of the terrace, where busboys were crouched down, mopping up the moisture that had collected on the stone deck. They moved back and forth quickly with small white towels, drying and polishing the limestone.

Clusters of pink and off-white lilies, hydrangeas, and roses greeted us at the door as we got out of the car and approached the main part of the club. Dana walked next to me, holding the train of my gown to make sure the thick white silk didn't pick up any dirt.

We stepped through the doorway where Deborah greeted us and ushered us into a back room, so none of the gathering guests would catch a glimpse of the dress.

"Perfect!" she said. "The dress fits like a glove."

I'd picked a two-piece wedding dress, a straight skirt, and jeweled corset that laced up the back, passing up the traditional wedding-cake-shaped gown with a full skirt and way too much fabric. I carried the long veil that I would put on right before I went down the aisle.

Deborah led us to a room right off the terrace where I was to wait with my bridesmaids for the ceremony to start. I could hear Wray in the next room, laughing loudly with his friends, having a great time. They were horsing around while we were sweating the last-minute details, like whether one of us needed more powder or lip gloss, or if there were enough chairs for the number of guests who turned out.

Eventually the time came for the girls to head down the aisle ahead of me. They went out one by one, holding small bouquets and smiling nervously. Tiffany was last. She'd been the last to arrive in the waiting room, brow furrowed and frowning.

"Are you ready?" I asked her. She was supposed to walk out ahead of me. When I looked in her face, I saw that her eyes were brimming with tears.

"What's wrong?" I asked, starting to panic. She didn't respond.

Deborah came over and tapped her arm to let her know it was her turn.

"Are you ready?" Deborah asked. Tiffany shook her head no, but then stepped across the threshold anyway.

I had been focusing on holding it together myself, but now Tiffany was a dam ready to burst, the last thing I needed.

"This is it, baby," my dad said, looping his arm through mine. "I love you so much."

When we emerged through the doorway, 176 heads swiveled to see us. I looked over the crowd and saw the faces of my life as I walked slowly down the aisle, arm in arm with Dad, trying not to trip on the carpet of the hem of my dress, smiling and nodding at guests here and there.

Wray stood to the right of the altar, so handsome in his black tuxedo, beaming with happiness, the Prince Charming at the end of any fairy tale. All his groomsmen surrounded him in black-tie glory. My eyes swept over my bridesmaids, each prettier than the one before, smiling, pink lip gloss freshly applied, hair cascading.

Then I saw Tiffany's face at the end of the line, flooded with tears that poured down her cheeks, landing on her steel gray dress in dark pools just below her neck. She stood there, crying as if someone had died, right next to a grand, graceful arch of greenery and flowers that buzzed with dozens of hummingbirds.

Wray and I spent two blissful weeks in Bali and then Hawaii, totally isolated from the world. A wave of relief washed over me as soon as we put distance between ourselves and the hysteria of the wedding, our families, our friends, everyone we knew in the world. I didn't worry about anything except getting a sunburn.

Wray was the polar opposite of my family. He had such carefree joy. Even when he saw a problem, he just solved it instead of assigning blame and making it worse, like my family always had. If we were late for dinner, he didn't get angry about who'd gotten ready too slowly. He just called the restaurant or sweet-talked the hostess to get us seated a little later.

"No need to panic," he'd tease with a smile. I didn't know how I'd gotten so lucky. He made happiness easy.

We'd been back in the country for twenty-four hours before I could bring myself to call my parents' house and break the spell. I got Dad.

"Well, I have something to tell you," he said. "Your sister is in rehab."

I didn't know what to say. I couldn't figure out what was

more startling, the news or the fact that my parents were acknowledging that Tiffany had a problem and they were doing something about it.

"Well. Wow," I said finally.

Looking back at the wedding, Tiffany's mood had shifted after the ceremony. She'd ditched her bridesmaid's dress and changed into a black number of her own choosing before the wait staff had even finished serving cocktails, a move no other bridesmaid in the modern era had ever had the nerve to pull.

I walked into the main dining room and saw her standing with my dad in a floor-length black halter-neck gown. I did a double take. I'm sure all of my bridesmaids would have preferred another dress over the one my mom had chosen for them, if only to avoid being dressed like quadruplets, but they wouldn't have dared to change. Only Tiffany would blow off protocol so blatantly.

Frankly, I didn't care about the dress. I wanted her to feel comfortable. But this new twist in her behavior was just another shock on top of her already jaw-dropping conduct during the ceremony.

"You changed," I said slowly.

"Yeah, isn't this cute?" she said with a smile, the flood of tears at the altar now long forgotten. "I just feel so much better in this dress. The one Mom made us all wear was awful."

I just nodded without really responding. The bridesmaids' dresses were pretty, long gray gowns without too much detail. The skirts might have been too full, tighter would have looked better, but overall they were nothing like so many of the over-the-top frilly prom styles I'd seen.

As the sister of the bride, Tiffany should have been the best sport, the most cooperative, not the most unmanageable. You'd never guess she was the maid of honor.

"Your sister *changed*?" my college roommate Debbie said, as she came up beside me. Debbie had been particularly under-standing about the bridesmaid dress, given that her usual wardrobe was urban hiking wear. Her biggest fashion decision was usually whether to wear her L.L.Bean or the Patagonia fleece. But she hadn't complained, even about the makeup, which she usually barely wore.

"I didn't know that was an option," she continued.

"It really wasn't," I said.

Over the next few hours, I never saw Tiffany without a drink in her hand. She bounced up and down wildly on the dance floor, arms flailing, shoes long gone. An hour in, she pulled her hair up into a sloppy ponytail, throwing any wedding deco-rum out the window. She was partying like it was New Year's Eve.

"Well, your sister seems to be having a wonderful time now," one of Wray's mom's friends commented primly. She was a slender tee-totaler with a neatly coiffed bouffant and a tight, perfectly tailored turquoise dress. Her dark eyes danced beneath her plucked brows as she observed Tiffany's behavior.

"It was so sweet the way she just sobbed when you were at the altar, her little sister getting married ahead of her. What a sweet and sensitive girl she is," she continued.

I didn't respond. Her comments felt like a dig. But I couldn't be sure, so I let it go.

Tiffany went from painfully withdrawn to sobbing to euphoric in the course of the night. Her moods, and the impact she was making on the other guests, were exhausting to track.

By the end of the night I was just done.

"So how did that happen?" I asked Dad, my thoughts returning to rehab.

"Well, it turns out, she didn't exactly leave her job at Wal-ters and Flemming of her own accord. They caught her drinking during the day at work. She admitted it to me a few days before the wedding but I didn't want to make a big deal out of it while you were here. And I talked to her buddy Molly, who admitted that they drank and dabbled in a little of everything at Cal, but said she too was really worried that Tiffany never sort of settled down. She seemed stalled. Maybe she needs to kick the booze to jump-start her life."

"I hope alcohol is the problem," I said.

"Why? You think it's drugs?" he asked.

I realized that I had felt unsure of Tiffany's moods for a long time. Her behavior wasn't so easily explained by substances. "No. I just don't know if removing the alcohol eliminates the problem, or just unmasks it," I said. "I'd love to think alcohol was the reason she behaved like a jerk at the wedding, but I just don't know."

I called a few days later and got Mom.

"So you heard about Tiffany?" she said. Her tone oozed irritation.

"Yeah. It's good news. A fresh start," I said, immediately wanting to be positive.

"Do you have any idea what rehab costs? It's gonna be like ten thousand dollars. And you know, they don't even guarantee it works on the first try! They almost guarantee it *won't* work. I'm going to kill her if she comes out and throws it all away drinking again," Mom said.

"I don't think anyone ever just does it once, and presto! they're fixed," I said, trying to manage her expectations.

"Well, we don't have the money to do this again. Do you?" she said.

"No. That's a pretty big percentage of my reporter's salary."

"And now the wedding bills are all piling up! And she adds

this to it. At least I'm done paying for you. Once we pay for the wedding, that's it."

I hadn't called to talk about money. So I tried to change the subject.

"How's everything else going? What's new with you?" I asked.

"Nothing. Have you heard more from everyone about how beautiful the wedding was?" she solicited.

"Yes, all my friends thought it was the most beautiful wedding ever," I replied. Never mind that most of them weren't married and we didn't have that much experience to draw on.

"Like who? What did they say? I want details. I worked so hard, I want to hear every word . . ."

I could tell we were going to have a lot of conversations like this over the next few months.

Tiffany emerged from rehab a month later. I had to call home a number of times to actually get her.

"Hey," I said when I finally caught up with her.

"Hey. So. How's married life?" she said in an even tone.

"Good. How about you?" I asked. I wanted to tell her I was proud of her, but that seemed condescending coming from a little sister.

"Good. It was nice to get away from Mom for a month," she joked.

"I'm sure. But I'm serious. How are you really feeling?"

"Good and awful. It sucks. I don't know," she said.

"I'm sorry. But you are doing the right thing," I tried. "I'm sure it sucks. But I think you're really brave and tough. Hey, if we survived Mom, we can survive anything, right?"

* * *

Tiffany and Dad focused on getting healthy, working out, and eating right. They shopped at the grocery store together and tried to occupy her time and mind with better living.

But then I heard from Dad that she and Mom were at each other's throats again, with Mom harping on Tiffany about getting a job. Mom was right, it would make her feel better to get some validation in the real world, but she had a spotty track record, which made it hard to land a job. Tiffany admitted finally that she'd been fired more than once for drinking at work or coming back from lunch inebriated.

Only a few months later Mom called me to say she'd found a liquor bottle in the back of Tiffany's car. So she'd taken her car away, as if Tiffany were an errant teenager. Dad decided to stop drinking and ban alcohol from the house, but that didn't work either. Mom discovered more bottles under the sink, and Tiffany went back to rehab.

Dad thought he could spend all his time watching her, but Mom started to wonder if her behavior was out of their control. For once, I worried that Mom was right.

CHAPTER SEVENTEEN

Two months after we returned from our honeymoon, Wray landed a new private equity job at a growing fund outside San Francisco. I had had no intention of moving back to California, ever. But he felt like this was an offer he couldn't pass up. And my contract with the local CBS station in Connecticut was about to expire, so the stars seemed to be aligning for the move.

There were plenty of reporting jobs in San Francisco. And I rationalized that the Bay Area wasn't L.A. Moving back west rattled my nerves, but I'd always believed San Francisco was the most magical city in the country. The fog cast a fairy-tale haze over the ornate Victorian homes stacked like stairs up the steep winding streets, the trolley cars rattling along tracks in front of them.

We rented an apartment on Telegraph Hill, in the shadow of Coit Tower, the solid concrete tribute to Art Deco that looms high on the hill overlooking Fisherman's Wharf. We had an unobstructed view of the icy, deep blue waters that surround Alcatraz, and the red metal and wire engineering feat that is the Golden Gate Bridge.

Our apartment took up the entire top floor of the building. It had a roof deck and skylights that let in the barking of the sea lions below as their calls cut through the crisp morning air.

It was serenity, a postcard-perfect San Francisco home.

So my family drove up for a visit.

"We're almost there. Tell me again where you are," Dad said into the phone.

"We're at the very end of Chestnut Street, right under Coit Tower. Chestnut dead-ends on our block into a hill. There's a staircase that takes you down to the wharf, but if you find yourself down by the wharf in the car, you're on the wrong part of Chestnut," I said.

"Turn here! Are we going back over the bridge?" Mom snapped at Dad in the background.

"Just follow the house numbers, we're 321. You can park on the street in front of the building or on the left side of the driveway. Or the sidewalk. Everyone parks on the sidewalk here," I said, adjusting the shutters.

"Okay. See you in a second," he said, fumbling with the phone.

I adjusted the blue and white throw pillows on the couch one more time and sat down. I wasn't sure I was strong enough to face the whole team at once. I wondered how long the tornado that was my family would swirl through town before moving on. They never set a firm departure date for any visit, especially when they drove. They loved to fly by the seats of their pants.

I could handle each family member individually and find an activity that would pass the time pain-free. Dad wanted to walk around leisurely and look at the city. He'd lived in San Francisco as a bachelor and thought it was the greatest city on earth. He reveled in walking tours of his old haunts. He'd listed half a dozen places he wanted to go back to, and to me, that sounded like a blast.

Mom liked to go out for coffee and cake, or drive around looking at houses, stopping at a store here and there. Marilyn was along for the ride as well. During half my life, Mom and Marilyn had been inseparable. The other half, they hadn't been speaking because Mom had flown into one of a hundred unpredictable huffs and cut her sister out of our lives on a whim. She'd call Marilyn six months later, as if nothing had happened, and Marilyn would just quietly take her back. Dad told me they were in another joined-at-the-hip phase. I knew that could inadvertently divide the group into teams.

I realized I didn't know what Tiffany liked to do anymore. She was in a sober phase, but I had warned Dad that cutting alcohol out of her life was probably only the first step in the rehab process. Once that problem had been dealt with, I suspected the real work would need to begin. Some deeper unhappiness or instability kept pushing her to self-medicate.

Mom, Dad, Tiffany and Marilyn stumbled into the apartment, refugees from the long car ride.

"It took us six and a half hours, because Mom and Marilyn insisted on stopping at that cattle ranch for lunch," Dad muttered after crossing the threshold. He walked directly to the window and stared out into the endless blue waters. "Wow! That's some view."

He smiled with his hands stuffed in the pockets of his Levi's, K-Swiss sneakers white as ever, blue and white button-down shirt pressed but untucked after the long journey.

Tiffany schlepped up next. She had a harder time getting up the stairs, breathing heavily once she entered. She ran her hand nervously through the top of her hair, which was longer than ever.

Mom and Marilyn lagged behind her by a mile, entering like bookends in black slacks and cardigan sweaters, sunglasses pushed up on top of their heads. Marilyn was carrying her trademark black leather shoulder bag, stuffed to the gills with everything you would possibly need if you thought you might never go home again.

"I'm sorry it's so many stairs. But look! It's worth it," I made a sweeping gesture toward the 180-degree view, like Vanna White.

"Have a seat on the couch. Do you guys want some water?" I asked.

Tiffany and Mom collapsed on the couch. Marilyn took the armchair facing the windows.

"This is quite a place, Miss Melissa," Marilyn said.

"God, I'm carsick. Between your father's driving and the streets," Mom complained.

"Dad's driving is fine," Tiffany said.

Dad stood at the window, lost in the view.

"Where's my boyfriend, Wray?" Mom said.

"He's at work. I was able to get the day off. But he'll join us for dinner. I hope. You never know with this job," I said.

"Your furniture looks nice here. Is this all from New York? What's new?" Marilyn asked.

I explained that the big, floor-to-ceiling mirror hanging behind the dining table came from a little frame shop on Union Street. I was describing the vintage shop so it took a few moments for me to realize that Tiffany wasn't playing around.

Her arm had shot up to her chest at an angle, her fingers extended, rigid as steel. Her face froze in a pained expression, her mouth caught in a frown, as she slid off the couch and convulsed.

I watched, paralyzed, as Mom screamed for Dad to help, and Dad moved quickly to Tiffany's side on the floor.

After several long seconds, the convulsions just stopped, and she quieted. Her eyelids fluttered as if she were waking from a spell, but she wasn't getting up from the floor.

"Stay there! Just lie there. Can you hear me?" Dad said, trying to sound calm. "Call 9-1-1!"

He hovered over Tiffany on the floor. Mom panted with fear, as Marilyn began to cry. I scrambled to my phone and dialed.

We hardly moved, all of us gathered around Tiffany in stunned silence. Tears rolled down her cheeks but she lay quietly on floor.

The paramedics arrived within minutes. I heard the sirens outside the window and ran down the four flights to show them where to go.

"Over here, up the stairs!" I shouted, before darting back up the stairs ahead of the two muscle-bound men in blue uniforms. They charged up the stairs, carrying either end of a gurney.

When we reached the top, I led them into the living room.

"What happened?" the paramedic in front asked.

"She had a seizure," Dad responded.

I had no idea what name to put to the terrifying event I'd just witnessed. But my father did.

"Do you take any medication?" the paramedic asked Tiffany.

"No," Dad answered.

The paramedics didn't look at him, wanting to hear from my sister. "Can you hear me?" one paramedic said to her.

"Yes," she responded softly, tears still running down the side of her face.

I ran into the guest bedroom near the living room and got a small pillow, which the second paramedic took from my hands.

"Do you feel like I can lift your head a little? This will make you more comfortable." She mumbled assent as he slipped the pillow under her head.

"Are you on any medications?" the first paramedic asked again.

"No," she said.

"Have you been drinking any alcohol?" he asked.

"No," she said.

"Any illegal drugs?" he continued.

"No," she said.

"Are you prone to seizures?" he asked.

"No. This happened once before though," Dad said.

They checked her vital signs and eventually helped her move up to the couch. Mom and I stepped back, hovering but trying to give them more space to work. Dad stayed by Tiffany's side.

The paramedics checked her vital signs, asked more questions, and found nothing alarming. Eventually they offered to take her to the hospital for observation, but Tiffany declined, since the trauma seemed to have passed.

The paramedics gathered their equipment. I followed them to the door to show them out.

"Thank you," I said.

"This is pretty normal for someone who is detoxing. She said she's been in rehab recently. Just keep a close eye on her. Take it slow," the first paramedic advised.

I closed the door behind them, heaving a sigh of relief. I looked over at Tiffany, who still looked shaky but was sitting up. What might have started out as a run-of-the-mill rebellion for Tiffany had now done real physical damage.

"So this happened before?" I asked Dad as we walked out onto the roof deck.

Tiffany had gone into the guest bedroom to lie down. Mom was watching television in the living room with Marilyn. They were whispering to each other and shaking their heads. Dad and I had decided to go up on the roof deck so Dad could smoke.

There was no railing around the perimeter of the deck,

which made me feel like the slightest breeze could push me over the edge to my death. From where we stood, we had a staggering 360-degree view of one of the most gorgeous scenes in America, from the swarms of tourists buzzing through the shops of Fisherman's Wharf straight in front of us, to the Golden Gate Bridge slicing through the clouds to the northwest, to the high-priced homes that perched in judgment atop Russian Hill behind us.

Dad took a drag from his cigarette as his eyes slowly moved across the landscape.

"God, I think I could live up on this roof. It's so peaceful," he said wistfully.

I felt for him. I knew it cut through his heart to watch Tiffany struggle like this. He saw himself as a man who could solve problems, though he tended to wait until the house had almost burned to the ground before he went looking for a bucket.

"This happened in rehab at New House, in Ventura. They called and told us afterward. They said it was pretty normal when your body is used to a steady diet of alcohol and you suddenly stop drinking. She's got other problems too. With her pancreas. She's done a lot of damage to her body," he said, taking another drag.

This news was a lot to take in. I knew plenty of people who seemed to drink gallons of vodka or liquor or whatever and lived long lives. How could my sister have done such serious damage to her body when she was barely thirty? Even if she had, I still wondered if the real problem was in her head, not her body. I felt like the older she got, the more volatile her moods had become.

"But have they looked at anything else?" I asked.

"What do you mean? Besides her pancreas?" he said.

"No. I mean . . . I was looking at stuff online, and on WebMD. Do you think she's bipolar?" I ventured.

"What does that mean?" he asked, flicking the ashes of his cigarette away from me, where they fluttered through the air before landing on the rooftop, blending in with the tarpaper beyond the edge of the deck.

I had been thinking about this since Tiffany had gone into rehab, and wondered how to bring it up with either of my parents.

"Well, it means she has sort of pronounced highs and lows. Lots of energy, and then none," I explained.

"That's the alcohol," Dad said.

"I don't think so. I mean, I thought about that. But when I think about the way she acts, the way she's *always* acted. Really happy, or really agitated, like wired, frantic. Then other times, so depressed. Totally drained."

"That doesn't sound like Tiffany," he said quickly.

"Seriously?" I replied. I took a breath and eased back before continuing. "Didn't you tell me she got up in the middle of the night? You heard all these pots and pans crashing because she was cleaning out the kitchen and cooking all this food at like three in the morning? Turned the entire place upside down? One night, not too long before the wedding," I said. "Doesn't it seem like she goes from jumping out of her skin to lifelessly depressed?"

"I don't know. Most of her problems have to do with Mom riding her all the time. If Mom could lay off, Tiffany could relax. I could relax. Hell, you escaped. Ran away." He laughed.

I smiled, accepting the jab.

"I think I need to get her away from Mom," he said, staring off into the distance.

"Yes, Mom makes it worse for sure. They are like oil and water. But I'm not sure Mom's the root of the problem. I think Tiffany needs therapy and medication to beat a chemical imbalance. I'm talking about the kind of thing that's genetic. Chemical. It's no one's fault. If you started there, she might still have a chance at a normal life."

"I'm not sure your theory is right . . ." He protested.

"Neither am I. Obviously. You're right. I'm playing amateur therapist because I read too much. So ask a professional. I'm sure there are tests or evaluations that can help."

He didn't respond.

"What if a medication could do half the work for her? How great would that be?" I pressed.

He raised his eyebrows and nodded, dragging on the cigarette until it was all but gone. Then he flicked it over the edge of the roof and thrust both his hands into the pockets of his windbreaker.

"There's more going on though," he said. "I didn't want to tell you because I didn't want to worry you. You had so much on your plate with you and Wray pulling up stakes and moving out west. And it's hard to really talk on the phone," he said, meeting my eye for a second and then returning his eyes to the water line.

"We're broke," he said shaking his head. "Mom spent everything. On the house, on the furniture, on silly pillows and fancy dishes, stupid fucking tchotchkes, on the wedding . . . on whatever!" He rolled his eyes and shrugged his shoulders in disbelief.

"I'm making money," he continued, "but I had no idea of the size of the bills she was racking up. I mean, it's a mountain. Now there are medical bills for Tiffany piling up on top of everything." He paused, letting it sink in.

I had heard him talk like this a few times while I was growing up, but he was always ready with a solution.

"I don't see any way to get ahead of it. We can't use the house as a piggy bank like we did when this happened before, refinancing and taking equity out to pay the bills. The math on that doesn't work now because the new house is worth too damn much, and we already owe a lot. Even if we qualify for another loan, we can't make a bigger payment," he explained.

"So what's the answer? What does that mean?" I asked. My mind was racing to a solution, and I could only see one.

"We have to sell the house, cash out. Pay off the loan, pay off the other debt, downsize. Take what's left, find another place to live, and live within our means. For once!" he said, nostrils flaring.

"It's hard to imagine Mom doing that," I said, rubbing my forehead and temples.

The news of my parents' financial straits coupled with Tiffany's seizure was too much crisis for me to handle in one day. A migraine was blooming quickly and I could see the spots starting to form in my line of vision.

"Ha! What do you think Mom said?" Dad asked scornfully. "It's my fault. I'm not working hard enough, I should be making more money. Tiffany should be working. Everyone but her, right? Have you ever noticed that Mom has never had a job in your lifetime?" he cracked.

"Yes, in fact, I have noticed that. She always said she would scrub floors to take care of us if need be, but I don't think I ever saw her clean a floor, or much of anything else, the whole time I was growing up. She'd call the housekeeper," I replied with a laugh.

Dad laughed too, welcoming a break in the continuing flow of bad news. "Right, well, to be fair, she drove you to all those auditions. Sat on the set and taught you your lines. She's not qualified to do anything now. She didn't go to college. Who would hire her?"

"So she can't work as a receptionist at a doctor's office? She can't work in retail? She can't work at Nordstrom's? She can't file at some office? I don't buy it," I said.

He shrugged.

"I've worked my whole entire life," I drilled on. "From day one. In commercials, at restaurants. I worked in the kitchen at my dorm when she said she wouldn't give me money so I could be a summer intern for the *Today* show. I was tech support for Harvard Business School for three years to save money so I could afford to take a crappy job producing local news after graduation. I have never *not* worked. In my whole, entire life."

Dad nodded, fishing for another cigarette.

I wasn't done. "Everyone can work. It's liberating. If you are willing to work hard, there's a restaurant, there's a store. It may not be the job you want or the wage you want . . ."

I was angry now. My rage at the stew of helplessness and inaction that saturated our family bubbled to the surface as our problems finally came to a boil.

"Well, she can't earn enough doing anything to make a difference, or to pay the mortgage, or to make a dent in the debt," he resolved.

I wanted to say that if Mom were working, she wouldn't be spending, and she might feel better about herself and not dig so deep into me and now Tiffany, but we were heading into the weeds now, and settling nothing.

So I stopped.

And we both just looked quietly into the abyss.

My family returned to L.A. after only a few days. Tiffany was spent and exhausted and wanted to get back to her own bed.

I settled in to a new reporting job in San Francisco. An Internet company hired me to report on tech and financial news for their website. It was the height of the dot-com craze, and everyone at the company was under thirty and sure they'd be able to retire on their options within a few years. Some of the older employees who'd been in news for a while saw the stock as a gift from Jesus and quickly cashed out.

At the same time, Wray worked from before dawn until late into the night trying to manage a portfolio of assets. I didn't see that much of him.

I had a hard time getting Tiffany to come to the phone when I called my family, but I talked to Mom and Dad separately every few days and their account of current events varied wildly. The only common theme was the descent into chaos.

"Hey, how are you guys," I asked Mom. I'd called from my desk during lunch. I thought I'd get the day's update out of the way while I ate a sandwich.

"I guess we're selling the house. We got an offer that was way too low," she moaned.

"What do you mean too low?" I asked.

"Well, it was barely above the asking price," she said dismissively, but not without a hint of pride. Another phenomenon of the dot-com economy: offers that exceeded the asking price.

"Above the ask? That sounds good to me. How much?"

"It's almost double what we paid! Once again, I've made a brilliant real estate investment for this family, and I made us a lot of money," she said with a sigh.

I didn't point out the fact that she'd pre-spent that profit on porcelain knickknacks.

"That's great. Are you going to accept it?" I asked.

"Then where will we go?" she said.

"You have to find another place. Downsize," I said.

"Oh, that's easy for you to say. You're married to Wray. I'm married to your father," she sniped.

"I don't know what to tell you," I said, disgusted by her self-pity over a situation of her own making.

"If I sell this, and take the profit, it's just gone. We pay our bills, then what? Soon we'll have nothing left," she said, blurting out the obvious. "We should hang on to the house and watch it go up further. Or buy another house and do it again."

"But I think it's going to be a challenge to make the payments going forward, right?" I pointed out.

"That's your father's job," she said.

"Why don't you manage kids? You've always been great at show business," I suggested. "You could make some real money. I never understood why you didn't do that."

"Because I only ever wanted to make *you* a star. Both of you. I don't want to do that for some stranger. Share that magic with someone outside the family," she said.

That was her standard answer, whenever this idea had been suggested.

"I don't know what else to tell you. You can buy something smaller and make it beautiful. You already have all the stuff," I said.

She didn't respond.

"How's Tiffany?" I continued.

"Hopeless," she said.

"Come on. How is she feeling? Is she around? Can I talk to her?" I asked.

"She's not here. She's polluted her body with God knows what all these years. Everything she could get her hands on, I guess. My baby. She was such a beautiful little girl. What happened? The doctor says her pancreas is shot. They are going to try some medications. She never feels well." She trailed off. "She's at the doctor with your father now."

"You didn't go with them?" I asked.

"No. I don't feel well either. I'm losing my house," she said. Click.

A few days later, I called home and got Dad.

"Hey," I said when he answered.

"Hi, baby. How are you?" he said.

"Pretty good. How are you guys? How's Tiffany?" I asked.

"She's not so good. She spent last night in the hospital. She's home now resting. She was in a lot of pain, so we took her to Dr. Lewis and they admitted her for some tests. I didn't want to call you late and worry you. I know you and Wray have a lot going on."

My stomach sank. "Is it . . . more serious?"

"Well, they don't know. You always say doctors have no idea what they're doing, and I hate to think you're right," he said.

"I know a lot of people from school who are close to being doctors now. They're great people, but even they admit there's a lot of room for error, and different ways of interpreting the same data," I warned.

"They are going to try some new medications, but she's having trouble digesting food. I hope it's all temporary but I'm not totally sure about that," he said. I could hear the edge of despair in his voice. "The doctors also put her on Lithium. They agree with you. She's bipolar."

"Maybe that will help," I said. I was worried it was too late.

"What about the house? Mom said you got a great offer?" I asked, hoping to boost his spirits.

"We did. And we went back and forth again. He came up even higher," he said.

"Well, you know Wray's mom is the best broker in Florida.

She always says you should make a deal with the first guy, because that's always the best offer."

"We are going to. But he wants to close pretty quickly. I have no idea where we will go. Your mom is out looking at bigger mansions, like we're moving up. She's unbelievable," he said.

"Is she being nicer to Tiffany?" I asked.

"No. She's still picking on her. Criticizing her hair or her skin or whatever. It's cruel. I tell her to lay off, but you know Mom," he said.

"Yes, I do."

"I wish she could just have some compassion. But Tiffany baits her. I can't worry about Mom's insanity right now . . . I need to worry about Tiffany's health first. Get the house sold, get us on solid ground, help Tiffany," he said, sounding overwhelmed.

They sold the house after a healthy period of holding out that only raised the price further, and then set a closing date for mid-May.

I was planning Wray's thirtieth birthday party at the time, and his family was coming into town. I was a little worried about mixing Mom with them. Apparently, she'd mailed back a Christmas gift that Martha had sent her, a large hand-painted ceramic bowl. I'd seen it in the store in Florida and it was lovely. Martha had sent it to Mom with a Christmas card, and Mom had rejected it, firing it right back to Florida without explanation. Martha didn't tell me. I'm sure she guessed that I would be mortified by Mom's behavior, and she didn't want to embarrass me. Wray told me after the fact. And I had nothing to say. I'm sure if I had asked, Mom would have cited an imagined slight she was responding to. I could feel the feud of a lifetime taking shape. I loved Wray's family. They could turn any family gathering into a free-for-all party. They could laugh until we were all doubled over and crying, even at a funeral. And they loved each other.

I could tell Mom was going to try to ruin this for me. Wray's family had been gracious at every turn, and she'd made every effort to insult them. They were a threat to her control. She called them loud, just loudly enough for them to hear. She said she didn't believe that Martha was as nice as she seemed, and if she wasn't as conniving as Mom suspected, then she wasn't very clever. Mom's insults and paranoia made my head spin.

I did not relish the idea of bringing them together again.

The closing of the sale of my parents' house took place a day before the party.

"Are you guys coming up?" I asked Mom on the phone.

"Well, your aunt and I are. I don't know about your father and your sister," Mom said.

"What do you mean?" I said.

"I packed up the house, but we still don't have anywhere to go," she said.

"But you close in like two days, right?" I asked, not believing what I was hearing.

"Noon. The day after tomorrow I guess," she said, like it was no big deal.

"You know that at noon, you hand over the key and don't go back inside, right?" I wondered if anyone had explained this to her.

"I know what it means," she shot back, annoyed.

"But what are you going to do with all your stuff?" I asked.

"The moving company said they would hold it in storage until we know what we're doing," she said, as if that were normal.

"But where are you going to sleep?" I said, cutting to the obvious question.

"I don't know. I can always stay with Marilyn. Or you, right?" she said.

My mouth fell open at the other end of the line.

"What about Dad and Tiffany?" I asked, deflecting the question.

"They are such good buddies, always leaving me out and making fun of me, they can do whatever they want," she said.

I just assumed they'd all to go to Marilyn's condo, or a hotel together, but neither was a long-term solution.

On the day of the party, Mom called to say she was driving up with Marilyn. The party was at an Italian restaurant and bar in Russian Hill that Wray and I loved. We had about fifty friends coming. I had been running around town all day, finishing the final details, like favors and balloons. I was exhausted.

"So where do you live now?" I asked Mom, jokingly.

"I'm staying with Marilyn, but your sister and father are staying at a hotel," she huffed.

"Seriously?" I said, surprised they weren't all staying in the same place.

"Ask them. I don't know what they're doing and they aren't decent enough to tell me. After all these years, they just pulled away from the house and laughed," she said.

"Really?" I said. I wasn't sure what to think.

"Yes, that's the thanks you get. At least I have my sister," she said.

I got off the phone and called Dad. I didn't have time for this, but I wanted to know what was going on.

"Did you guys really move into a hotel and leave Mom high and dry?" I asked Dad when he finally answered.

"No, of course not. We had appointments to look at some

temporary rentals. We told her where they were and she turned her nose up at them, and said she was going to Marilyn's. There isn't room for all of us at Marilyn's really, especially with Tiffany's cat, so Tiffany and I checked into a motel. We're going to look at three places today. Why, what did she say?"

"Basically that you left her high and dry," I replied.

"Whatever," he said, sounding disgusted. "I don't have time for this. We're living out of suitcases in a motel because we sold our home and still don't have a plan for where we're going to live. This is totally insane!"

"Are you coming up here for Wray's birthday party?" I asked.

"When is it?" he asked.

"Tonight," I said, going over the list of RSVPs in front of me.

"I'm sorry, honey. We'd love to be there. But we're so overwhelmed with finding a place to live, and Tiffany isn't that strong right now. I thought the trip would be too much for her, and I thought I told you that, but we'll drive up in a few weeks. Tell Wray we love him, and happy birthday," he said.

Mom held court in the corner of Wray's party, talking to some of our friends but largely ignoring Martha and the rest of his family. When dinner was served she sat at a table with Marilyn, and many of my girlfriends made their way over to her to say hello and make her feel welcomed. I was grateful to them, and grateful for the fact Mom didn't appear insane to the naked eye.

The celebration stretched into the night, long after Mom and Marilyn went back to their hotel. In the morning, she called from a bed and breakfast on Union Street.

"Melissa, I want you to come down and see this place. It's so cute. Union Street Inn. Marilyn, what's the street number?" she asked with her hand over the phone.

I was still in bed and nursing a pretty severe hangover. The last thing I wanted to do was get up and drive to the place where she was staying.

"Mom, I'm still sleeping, can I call you later?" I said.

"Well, why don't you just throw on some clothes and come down. I want you and Wray to see it," she insisted.

"Why Wray? He's definitely sleeping," I said, poking him next to me in the bed. He grabbed an extra pillow and covered his face with it.

"Because the broker is on her way. I think it would be a great investment for you two," she said pointedly.

Almost asleep, I had my eyes closed, but with that, they flew wide open.

"A what?"

"Investment. You know I'm good at real estate. Look how much money I made on the Sherwood house. Look how much money I made on the Northridge house. You buy this bed and breakfast, Marilyn and I will move up here and run it for you. Then we'll all sell it for a profit," she said.

I thought she might be kidding, but in my bones, I knew she wasn't.

"Oh my God. I do not need to buy a hotel. We're trying to buy a house to live in," I said.

"This is only one point three million. You don't have to put much down these days. Not even ten percent."

"How could a hotel on Union Street be that cheap? Not that we could afford one in addition to a house, but that doesn't sound like much for a hotel," I asked.

"There's only one guest room," she said.

I hung up.

Within a week, Dad and Tiffany found a house to rent. They looked all around Westlake at a few small ranch-style homes with yards in various tracts that sprang up in the '80s and '90s, as well as a few condos in meticulously designed developments, before settling on what they described as a nice, modest three-bedroom with a fruit and vegetable garden in the back.

The one-story wood-frame house with a brown shingle roof lacked the grandeur of Lake Sherwood, but the quiet neighborhood and hilltop view were peaceful. When I saw the ad for the rental online, the photo looked like a home where Dad and Tiffany could relax.

It also looked like a home that would repel Mom on sight.

"So is Mom going to live there?" I asked Dad when he told me the lease was signed.

"I have no idea. I called her every time we were going to look at something. She never showed. She never called. We tried to include her. She's certainly welcome, but at this point, it's pretty peaceful without her."

They drove up to San Francisco to visit Wray and me for the few days until their lease kicked in. I took the day off from work, and I met up with Dad and Tiffany at an outdoor restaurant called Sam's on the other side of the Golden Gate Bridge.

Sam's was famous for mouth-watering cheeseburgers and enormous seagulls that swooped down from the sky like ancient pterodactyls with their enormous claws threatening to snatch unguarded food, and perhaps a few small children while they were at it. The menacing birds and whipping winds made eating on the deck at Sam's an adrenaline-fueled adventure.

"So she wanted me to buy her a bed and breakfast, so that she could move up here with me and run it," I said between bites, knowing this particular audience would feast on the madness of my predicament.

"Wow, if you run a bed and breakfast, don't you have to

make breakfast?" Tiffany asked. "Isn't she allergic to making breakfast? I know she doesn't know how to work a stove."

"There are so many questions." I laughed.

"People would expect food. How would that work?" Tiffany said, on a roll. "Who would do the laundry?"

"Maybe Marilyn?" I offered.

"So she's taking all the things she didn't do for us growing up, and turning that ball of wax into a career? Those would be some disappointed and confused guests," she joked.

Dad stopped laughing and set his burger down, risking an airborne attack. He suddenly looked serious. "She wanted you to put up the down payment?" he asked, wiping his mouth.

"In theory, yes. I guess. I didn't get that far. She definitely wanted me and Wray to invest, whatever that means."

"Did she mention she took all the money?" he said, looking hard into my eyes.

"What?" I asked, sure that I hadn't heard him correctly.

"Did she mention, when she was asking you to buy her a hotel, that she took every dollar from the sale of the house?" he said.

In spite of everything I knew Mom had ever done, I was floored by this accusation. All of a sudden, this conversation wasn't funny anymore.

"No," I said.

Tiffany just nodded her head. "That's exactly what she did," Tiffany said. "Can you believe it? I told Dad to call the cops."

"She took all the money?" I asked, shocked by Tiffany's harsh words and feeling certain that they were exaggerating to make the story more entertaining to top mine.

"The mortgage company sent us a check for what was left after the mortgage was paid off and everyone else got what they were supposed to get. She deposited that check in our joint account, and closed it, taking the entire balance and stashing it somewhere else in her name alone," he said.

Even for Mom, this was off the reservation. I could imagine her, looking at the check for the sale of the house, hands shaking, deciding she couldn't possibly share it, convinced it was hers.

Tiffany shook her head. I kept looking from my sister to my father, waiting for one of them to say this was a joke.

"Wasn't the check made out to both of you?" I asked my father. Now none of us was eating.

"It's been cashed. I called the title company. She forged my name. She's broken the law," he said.

That was sort of the least of it, I thought.

"How do you know she's just not managing it like always? Or buying another house? Or maybe it's a scheme she's cooked up to not pay taxes. It's not like she's running off with it to Mexico," I tried.

They looked at each other.

"I mean," I tried to collect my thoughts. "Do you think she plans to cut you out and run off or something? Why?"

"And she wrote a huge check to herself from my corporate account, and forged my name to that, and cashed that too, draining the company's operating cash. Why would she do that if she wasn't planning on not seeing me, or us, again?"

I looked from Dad to Tiffany, and back to Dad, soaking in what they were telling me, but still not absorbing the magnitude of Mom's pure, unfiltered greed. There was no denying this was her idea of a divorce settlement. Either that or the ultimate bank job.

"That's definitely illegal," I said.

"When I went down to the bank and pointed out that they'd honored a forged check from my corporate account and had broken about fifty laws, they reversed the transaction, putting *that* money back, at least. But I don't know where she put the balance of our joint accounts."

"What did she say when you confronted her?" I asked. "Did she think you'd just let her steal everything and live down the street at Marilyn's?"

"She screamed into the phone some nonsense about every wrong I've ever heaped upon her, not addressing the situation at all, saying she wanted a divorce, and then suddenly hung up, slamming down the phone."

"Yes, I've been on the other end of some of those conversations. When did this happen?" I asked.

"The day of Wray's party, *before* she came up to see you."

Wray was at work still, and I wasn't sure how I was going to tell him any of this. I was mortified to be related to someone who would steal from her own family.

We'd made a plan that morning to grill chicken kabobs on the roof when Wray got home, so once Tiffany, Dad, and I got back to my apartment from Sam's, I invited Tiffany to go to the store with me, angling for a few moments alone with her.

We walked down the staircase to the garage on the first floor of our building. Now painfully thin, Tiffany moved down each step gingerly. She seemed drained of energy. I'd noticed at lunch that she didn't have much of an appetite. All of the fight seemed to have gone out of her.

When we got into my silver-blue Saab, she sighed.

I drove slowly down Chestnut Street. "I can't believe it," I said to her now that we were alone.

"I know," she responded. "It confirms what we always thought about Mom stealing and hoarding any dime that came in. But you still don't want to believe your own mom could do this."

"Yeah. We're related to her. It's so embarrassing. I don't know how I'm going to tell Wray," I said.

"On the other hand, as long as she has the money, she's going to stay far away so she doesn't have to give any back," she said.

"But Dad can't just let her keep it. There are bills to pay," I said.

"He says he can make more money. I don't know what he's going to do," Tiffany said, pulling down the mirror on the visor and playing with her hair.

"How are you feeling?" I asked.

"Okay. Well, not really. I can't eat anything. Anything with fat in it makes me feel sick. I spend a lot of time with doctors," she said, her voice thin.

"I'm sorry. I love you. I wish there was something I could do," I said. She didn't respond. "At least Mom isn't bugging you. Maybe you and Dad can live alone in peace for a while," I offered.

"Yeah, that's a plus. But . . ."

She got quiet, and when I looked over at her at the stoplight, I saw a tear tumble down her face and land in her lap. She was half the size she'd always been. She looked like a little girl.

"You know, I was lying in the hospital last time and in the middle of the night I was just in so much pain. And . . . so scared." She paused, and took a gulp of air, trying to steady herself.

The car behind me honked, and I waved my hand out the window, signaling for him to go around us.

I put my hand on top of hers as my own eyes filled with tears that spilled over.

"All I could think was, it would be so nice to have a mom," Tiffany whispered.

* * *

I waited until Dad and Tiffany left San Francisco to confront Mom myself.

I had walked home from work early, wanting to be alone in the apartment to make the call. I'd thought all night about what I wanted to say to Mom, my anger and outrage festering and feeding on itself.

I sat on my couch and looked out the oversized windows at another stunningly beautiful day in San Francisco. Blue and white sailboats crisscrossed the bay in the distance, as groups of people walked back and forth on the water's edge, looking so carefree.

I dialed the number.

I had built up such a head of rage, my hands shook as I pushed the digits, forcing me to grip the phone to hold it steady.

"Hello?" she said.

"I know you took the money," I said.

"What money?" she said plainly.

"*All* the money," I replied steadily. "From the house. From the company account. I know everything. And then you came up here and pretended that you hadn't done anything."

"Your father's a liar! They both are. They laughed at me. They were going off without me, they were going to leave me with nothing, in the street, after all I've done for this family! I've given my life to this family, to you! To them! Your father would be nothing without me! An engineer. And your sister! A drunk! Your father too!"

"Enough!" I shouted.

She was quiet for a moment.

I gasped for air. "Everything is gone. It's in the past. I will forgive it all, forget it all, anything that's ever happened. It's gone. We can never mention it if you like." My voice was shaking. I knew exactly what I wanted to say, and I didn't want her to miss a word.

"But you *cannot* have a relationship with me, at all, going forward, if you don't return the money. You have to treat all three of us like adults, with decency, from this day forward."

"What are you talking about?" she spat.

"You cannot throw them away, throw Tiffany away like trash, your daughter who is sick, who is scared, and needs you, has always needed you. You are her mom. You cannot throw her away like she's worthless, and have a relationship with me. Or Wray, or my children in the future. I won't do it."

She was silent.

"All the craziness. It ends with me. I swear it, once and for all. One way or the other. It's your choice *how* it ends. *But it ends with me.*"

She slammed down the phone.

And I never heard from her again.

CHAPTER EIGHTEEN

It had been a terrible week. The Internet company where I'd spent the last two years was teeing us up for massive layoffs. I called it the curse of an opulent new building. Anytime a company builds a flashy new headquarters, they inevitably jump the shark and have to downsize.

But now I was worried that the impending layoff was a sign. Maybe it was time to move back to New York. The dot-com bubble had burst, soaking my prospects for another job in the area.

It was the Fourth of July, and Wray and I hadn't bothered to stay out long enough to see the conclusion of the fireworks. Our worries weighed too heavily on us for our spirits to be lifted by patriotic celebration. After looking for more than a year, Wray and I had bought a sweet jewel box of a house on the waterfront in the marina at the foot of the Golden Gate Bridge. I unlocked the door and assessed the living room, worried that we had decorated too hastily.

Wray closed the door behind us and fell onto the couch. As

I slid off my jacket and removed my phone from my pocket, I noticed I'd missed a call.

It was my dad. I dialed his phone.

"Melissa . . . ," he said into the phone. He usually answered with what we called his radio voice, a rich, warm baritone that would have been perfect for broadcasting. But this time his voice was paper-thin.

"I have something really terrible to tell you."

He was crying. I think I'd only seen him cry twice—when his father died and when Tiffany was flown by medevac to Holy Cross Hospital after the truck accident in high school.

"Tiffany is dead. She's dead," he cried.

I slid down the wall of my cheery yellow kitchen, crumpling into a heap on the pine floor, not knowing I was replicating her final motion.

"What do you mean?" I asked.

"I just found her in the corner of the bathroom. Against the wall. In her bathrobe. I thought she was taking a shower. But instead, she was dead. In the corner," he sobbed.

"Oh, no," I cried.

Seeing me on the floor, Wray rushed over to lift me up.

"You have to come. Right now," Dad said, choking.

The phone clicked and I just shook my head, staring blankly in front of me but saying nothing.

"What?" Wray said fifty times.

"She's dead."

A tsunami of grief washed over me, and as it receded, I realized a lifetime of worry had ended. Just like that.

I got in the blue Saab with Wray and we drove through the night to Westlake. As we got closer, I felt more and more panicked. I was terrified of the scene we were going to find. I had no idea who he had called, or if he'd even moved Tiffany's body. I didn't want to ask.

Wray drove but neither of us spoke, except for the few times Wray kept saying he was so sorry.

We pulled into the driveway of the small, one-story home they'd been renting. It was only the second time I'd been there. I swallowed so I wouldn't throw up.

I knocked on the solid brown door, and my father answered, still hunched over and weeping, hours and hours later. Tears and snot poured down his face, but he didn't wipe any of it away. It was as if he didn't even notice his own disarray.

He wrapped his arms around me and clutched me, crushing my bones with his grief, soaking my hair and my shirt with his tears.

Then he grabbed my hand, his whole arm trembling violently, and pulled me through the doorway.

"Here. Come back here," he said, dragging me through the narrow hallway that led to the back of the house. We took a left into the master bedroom and walked toward the bathroom.

I shut my eyes, terrified to see my sister's lifeless body.

"There!" he said, pointing and shaking.

But when I opened my eyes, all I saw was Tiffany's bathrobe on the floor. The white, monogrammed bathrobe, the one Mom had had made for my wedding, lay in a heap in the corner.

"Right there," he said, as if Tiffany were still there. "That's where I found her. She was already gone."

I wasn't sure why I had to stand there and look, or what I was supposed to see. My eyes drifted from the worn robe to the twisted trail of shampoo and conditioner on the floor of the shower. There must have been a dozen or more bottles, standing up or spilling over. That was Tiffany. She couldn't leave the grocery store without spending fifteen minutes in the beauty aisle, sniffing shampoo. Now that jumble was left, but the paramedics had taken my sister away, saying there was nothing more they could do. She was gone.

In my mind, I heard Tiffany say, "I'm so scared . . . it would be so nice to have a mom." And as I stood there and looked at her tattered robe on the tile floor, I closed the door on my mother forever.

She'd never called, never returned the money, never opened her heart to the daughter who needed her.

There was nothing to forgive. And nothing to salvage. Our bond was just wiped away. Gone.

Tiffany had spent that one semester in college, backpacking around Europe, and had come home the sister I had always wanted. Calm, clear, sharp. Full of life and at ease with it at the same time. I had blown off friends and boys to be with her. I thought maybe during the sabbatical from college she'd left the crazy life she'd created at Berkeley and the weight of Mom's boundless disapproval in a Eurail car, hopping off the train before it could catch up to her and crush her.

I remembered that day on the beach, racing down to the water as the bottoms of our feet burned, jumping into the waves as the surf sprayed our clothes. Our only worries: how dark we could make our tans, and if we should try to beat the beach traffic home. That day, she was the person I knew had the capacity to be happy.

It was the best summer of my life, and I will always save the memory of it in a quiet corner of my heart.

When Tiffany drove back to college that fall, I mourned. I wanted to hang on to that new sister for dear life, and not let her out of my sight, fearful that I had imagined her, that she had been a dream, a mirage. I worried that she'd disappear and I'd never know if she'd really ever existed.

I was right to be afraid. I never saw that girl again.

I told my dad that I would take care of telling Mom. It had been more than a year since I had given her the choice of coming back to help Tiffany or losing us forever, and she had chosen to throw all of us away. Thirteen months of silence.

I wrote her a letter and sent it to Marilyn's house, since I wasn't even sure where Mom was living, I informed her that her oldest daughter was dead, and the window of opportunity with me was now closed forever. She'd made her choice, and now she'd have to live with it. Her chance to make things right on this earth was gone.

This cycle of madness, this pain—it ends with me.

EPILOGUE

I held my first son after his birth, and I could not believe how much I loved him, and at the same time, how much of a stranger he was. I wanted to breathe him in, consume him, devour him. Where did this person I could not get enough of come from?

I had spent my life making sure that I didn't drown. Sometimes swimming strongly, sometimes barely staying afloat. But I did not do enough to keep Tiffany's head above water. Not nearly enough. Or she'd be here now. That's my pain to carry forever.

I have never been able to save anyone but myself. I've never been able to bank on anyone but myself. So who was this person tied to me now? This little boy?

I knew who he was. The person I'd drown to save.

I would happily give my life for his, and not even consider it a sacrifice. It would be my *pleasure*, my love for him is so great.

I have whispered in his ear a thousand times that he is the smartest boy in the world. He is my most precious treasure. And

I know I love him above myself, as I was not ultimately loved by my own mother. As neither my sister nor I was loved.

The endlessness of my love for my son was matched only by the enormity of the love I later felt for his little brother when he arrived. Those boys make it impossible for me to understand my mother.

I haven't figured out what I am going to tell my children about any of this. I don't know how to tell them where my mother is, or why they will never see her. Or what happened to my sister—their aunt they will never meet.

My dad is an important and loving part of our lives. My sons cherish him and chant to him on the phone when he is not visiting.

"Hi, Grandpa!" they shout.

He pretends to scare them through the phone, "Boo!"

They scream and run laughing, a game they love when he is here. He is the only thing they know of my family before Wray.

My older son asked me if Martha, Wray's mom, is my mom too. I could see the wheels turning in his head.

I simply said, "No."

He couldn't quite figure out what to ask next. But he'll be back.

With the rest of the world as well, I have become a master of not answering questions. The skill is subtle. I do not lie.

"Does your family still live in California?" someone asks.

"Yes," I reply.

"Are they coming for the holidays?" they ask.

"Not this year," I respond.

"Do you have any siblings?" they ask.

"It's just me," I say obliquely.

If you tell someone you had a sister, but she died, they are mortified that they've pulled the scab off an old wound. The truth kills the conversation. If you tell someone you have no idea where your mom is, where she lives, if she's alive, and you haven't seen her for more than a decade, they blanch. It is so abnormal, it begs an avalanche of uncomfortable questions that even friends are too shocked to ask.

My non-answers are not lies, but, of course, they aren't the whole truth either.

The truth is that my Dad and I grieve the loss of my sister, and that pain will never go away. It just dulls very slowly over time. We cried over her ashes, just the two of us without a formal funeral, and there was nothing more to do but say goodbye.

Dad told me that Mom came by his house shortly after she received my letter. She sped up his driveway in the Porsche she'd bought, though Dad couldn't discern exactly what she wanted. She just stood on his front porch, yelling and crying, angry and hysterical, screaming that her most treasured daughter was dead.

Dad said she'd had the unflinching nerve to claim that the daughter she'd deprived of love, the daughter from whom she'd hoarded and stolen money when that girl was actually dying and needed her the most, was her princess, her favorite child. The girl she'd hardly bothered to nurture as she grew up had turned into a woman she heartlessly let wither and die without a mom.

"My baby," she'd called her, weeping.

Dad said he told her there was nothing left for her there. Tiffany was gone. And then she sped off as quickly as she'd appeared.

Poof.

To this day, he hasn't heard from her again.

They never formally divorced, she never gave back a dime. She's just gone.

A few months after Tiffany's death, I was offered the job I'd always wanted, reporting for a financial news network in New York. The job at CNBC was exactly what I'd been aiming for since college.

There wasn't a doubt in my mind that I wanted to physically move away from all the pain. Put a continent between myself and all that had cast a long shadow over my life.

My mom had held a power over me, over all of us, for a long time. I was a hostage to her moods, her violence, her praise, her favor, all doled out in random doses and with confusing inconsistency, which had been designed to control me, training me to crave her attention like a starving dog.

I thought when I anchored shows on CNBC four years later, visibly pregnant with my son, Thompson, or three years after that, with my son, Greyson, she would be compelled to act. When I read the news on the *Today* show or stood on the promenade at the close of the program, in Rockefeller Center, holding my older son as he waved into the camera and grabbed my microphone to speak to millions of viewers, I wondered if she would be watching somewhere and wouldn't be able to stop herself from reaching out.

But I've heard nothing.

Make no mistake, I'm relieved by that. I used to live in fear that she'd show up at my door. Just the thought of one of her loud, angry, manic scenes playing out in my home or my office would make my muscles tense. I told myself that if she ever knocked, I simply wouldn't open the door. I'd stay calm and say almost nothing. I'd tell her the truth through the intercom or through the window: There is nothing left. Go away.

Now I've grown confident in the silence that I won't have to explain myself again. I won't have to tell her that I've seen so many other women, especially in news and on television and in other driven careers, who can physically weather a hurricane or climb over a hundred other women gunning for their jobs, and do it with ease. But those same heroines are instantly reduced to tears, cut down in their path, by a few hard words from the controlling moms who gave them strength in the first place.

"You look fat in that dress," one such mom offered a fellow anchor over the phone after a newscast, quietly crushing her.

When I see those moms and daughters, I feel relieved that I've escaped. And I wonder if a different approach to mothering my sister would have stopped the descent into tragedy before it accelerated beyond recovery.

Having my own children has shown me that they are each different from the other. Like my mom, I have two very different kids. Ask my younger son, Greyson, a question, he shouts out an answer immediately. Sometimes right, sometimes wrong.

"What sound does O make?" I ask him, reading from a book.

"Ooooooo," he sings, not yet two years old, but his big blue eyes and wide smile are already brimming with confidence. He'll try anything, unafraid of a mistake.

But it took time for me to realize that when my older son, Thompson, refuses to participate, he's not defying me, or testing my will. He's telling me something else.

"Which one in the top row," I said, pointing at a workbook, "goes with something in the bottom row?" I was trying to help him with a type of question I knew he'd be asked at preschool soon. I'd learned firsthand how valuable it was to be the first one to know the answer to a teacher's query, even at four years old.

But his eyes wouldn't touch the page.

"Thompson?" I asked. My son, usually the mayor of any room, gregarious and friendly like any handsome politician courting votes, this time pretended not to hear me. He wouldn't look my way.

"I don't want to," he said turning his back to me.

"You can do it," I said softly. "You are the smartest boy in the world. You *know* that. Look at these things in the top row. An airplane! You love those," I said, tempting him.

"Look! It's flying through the sky. An airplane and what's that?" I asked, pointing to the object next to it.

Silence.

"Hmmm. Looks like something we take to the park to scoop sand," I said.

"A shovel," he said, turning to me now, still pretending not to care.

"For the sandbox! Remember last week, we played in the sandbox in Central Park. That was fun. Now look at the bottom row," I said.

His eyes slid down the page and he came and stood next to me.

"A train, and a flower. You ride in a plane. Is there anything you *ride in* down there," I said, pointing back to the train and the flower.

"Train! Airplane and train go together!" he said, now suddenly pleased with himself and sitting next to me. A few examples later, he was holding the book and asking *me* the questions with authority.

When the time came, he aced the exercise at school, confident that he could do it.

It took failed attempts at forcing him to do things for me to realize that if he doesn't believe he can do it, he won't try. Unlike his brother, who may not know the answer but will bark out a guess without hesitation.

"I won't, really means, I don't think I can," a wise teacher told me around this time. I didn't believe her at first. Why would he put pressure on himself to succeed at things he hadn't even been taught to do yet? How could he be so hard on himself? He was brilliant! Was that my fault? Did I expect too much?

"Don't see him as not trying, or defying you. Hear him telling you 'I don't think I can,'" she said.

She was right.

It's just one small example of how differently my sons are hard–wired. They were just born that way. From the start. Different children. And Wray and I have had to adjust the way we nurture and teach them to bring out the best in each of them. We had to figure it out along the way.

The once–size–fits–all, hardline approach: pushing children as hard as you can and demanding the very best doesn't fit them all, as it didn't fit Tiffany and me. A fire-breathing dragon of a mom may produce a champion, or she might burn her child to death.

Still the biggest lesson my boys have taught me is also the hardest.

"What do you want to see first, boys?" Wray asks, pushing Greyson's stroller through the entrance to the American Museum of Natural History. At five and nearly two years old, the boys make the "Dinosaur Museum," as they call it, a regular outing in New York City.

"Brancasaurus! And T. rex!" shouts Greyson, his unruly corkscrew curls bouncing with excitement. He has his father's hearty laugh, wide toothy smile, and shining blue eyes, every bit the classic Gerber baby.

"Are those your favorite dinosaurs, little one?" Thompson asks his younger brother, always the caretaker, from the moment he jumps into Greyson's crib each morning. They greet the new day together, laughing and chatting. He bends down and gives his brother a kiss on the cheek before patting his head. They are thick as thieves, though they look nothing alike. Thompson's short dark hair and olive skin set off his ruby lips and blue eyes, which have flecks of my yellow in the iris. He's movie star gorgeous already.

"And stegosaurus!" Greyson shouts, straining mightily against the belts in his stroller.

"Mama," Thompson starts, right pointer finger raised straight up in the air for emphasis, "T. rex is a theropod. You can tell by his feet. And he's a carnivore, which means he eats meat, like Greyson."

"*Roar!*" Greyson yells on cue. Then he puts his feet on the floor and stands up, now wearing his lightweight travel stroller like a backpack. He looks like Godzilla.

"Whoa. You are getting strong," Wray says, unclipping him and laughing. "Let's go, boys!"

Thompson turns back to me, glowing. "Mom, can we go see the Creatures of Light next? They have alien stingers!"

"Whatever you want, my sweet."

"I love you, Mommy," he says, before running after his father and brother.

The texture and color of my love for all three of them has proven to me that I can love, even though I was not ultimately loved myself. It doesn't matter what's come before if I can let go and try to do better. That truth was an awakening. My own family is a new beginning.

ACKNOWLEDGMENTS

I would like to thank Publishing Director Georgina Levitt and everyone at Weinstein Books, especially Editorial Director Amanda Murray; this work is a direct product of her tireless cheerleading, coaching, advice, and support. Thank you as well to Judy Hottensen for being among the first to see potential in this project, and to editor Maggie Crawford for contributing her energy and wisdom.

I'd also like to thank my agent, Mel Berger, who convinced me to climb this mountain and provided all the tools along the way to get to the top. A special thanks to Roger Ailes and my Fox colleagues for understanding what this project means to me and getting behind it.

I feel lucky to have my husband's family in my life; they blindly supported this effort, having no idea what I might say about them. They are the kindest people I have ever known.

I'm eternally grateful to my dad, Anton Francis, who has been next to me on every step of this journey, through joy and despair, never leaving my side, always believing, and my sister, Tiffany, whom I will always love and never for a minute forget.

I can never adequately thank my beloved sons, Greyson and Thompson, for filling every day of my life with laughter, love, joy, and meaning. You are both gifts from God.

And most of all, I thank my husband, Wray, who is my everything.